3RD EDITION

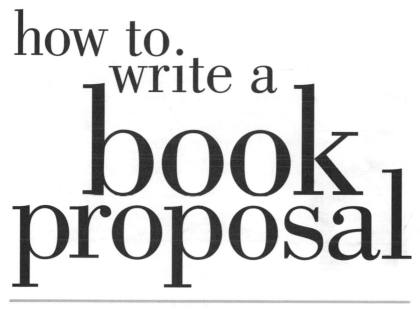

how to. write a book proposal

michael larsen

WRITER'S DIGEST BOOKS
CINCINNATI, OHIO
WWW.WRITERSDIGEST.COM

For Elizabeth,
who learned the hard way about the perils of accepting a very
short proposal with no outline or sample chapter.

Visit our Web site at www.writersdigest.com for information on more resources
for writers.

To receive a free weekly e-mail newsletter delivering tips and updates about writing
and about Writer's Digest products, register directly at our Web site at http://
newsletters.fwpublications.com.

08   07   06   05   5   4   3

Library of Congress Cataloging-in-Publication Data

Larsen, Michael
   How to write a book proposal / by Michael Larsen.—3rd ed.
      p.   cm.
   Includes index.
   ISBN 1-58297-251-6 (alk. paper)
      1. Book proposals. I. Title.

PN161.L37   2003
808′.02—dc22   2003060212
                                                          CIP

Edited by Kelly Nickell and Michelle Ruberg
Designed by Clare Finney and Angela Wilcox
Cover by Brian Roeth
Production coordinated by Robin Richie

Proposal of *Reading Water*, by Rebecca Lawton, copyright © 2003 by Rebecca Lawton.
Used with permission.

About the Author

Born and educated in New York, Michael Larsen worked in promotion for three major publishers: William Morrow, Bantam, and Pyramid (which was later absorbed into Berkley). He and his wife, Elizabeth Pomada, moved to San Francisco in 1970.

They started Michael Larsen/Elizabeth Pomada Literary Agents, Northern California's oldest literary agency, in 1972. Since then, the agency has sold books, mostly by new writers, to more than a hundred publishers. Both principals are members of the Association of Authors' Representatives.

The agency represents book-length fiction and nonfiction for adults. Michael handles most of the agency's nonfiction, while Elizabeth represents novelists, narrative nonfiction, and books directed to women.

Mike is the author of *Literary Agents: What They Do, How They Do It and How to Find and Work With the Right One For You*, a selection of the Writer's Digest Book Club and Quality Paperback Book Club. With Jay Conrad Levinson, author of *Guerrilla Marketing*, and Rick Frishman, president of Planned Television Arts, he is the co-author of *Guerrilla Marketing for Writers: 100 Weapons for Selling Your Work*.

He also wrote *The Worry Bead Book: A Guide to the World's Oldest and Simplest Way to Beat Stress*, and *How to Write With a Collaborator* with Hal Zina Bennett.

In 1972, Michael and Elizabeth created *California Publicity Outlets*, which is now a book titled *Metro California Media*. They also coauthored the six books in the Painted Ladies series:

Painted Ladies: San Francisco's Resplendent Victorians
Daughters of Painted Laides: America's Resplendent Victorians, which *Publishers Weekly* selected as one of the best books of 1987
The Painted Ladies Guide to Victorian California
How to Create Your Own Painted Lady: A Comprehensive Guide to Beautifying Your Victorian Home
The Painted Ladies Revisited: San Francisco's Resplendent Victorians Inside and Out
America's Painted Ladies: The Ultimate Celebration of Our Victorians

Mike has reviewed books for the *San Francisco Chronicle*, and his articles have appeared in the *San Francisco Examiner, Writer's Digest, Publishers Weekly*, and Writer's Digest's *Guide to Literary Agents*.

Michael and Elizabeth give talks on writing, agenting, proposals, publishing, and guerrilla marketing for writer's groups and conferences. They also present talks and seminars on "How to Make Yourself Irresistible to Any Agent or Publisher" based on the last part of Michael's book on agents.

If you have completed a novel and tried it out on your professional networks to make sure it's 100 percent, Elizabeth will be glad to see the first ten pages followed by a two-page synopsis. If you have had a novel published in the past, please send the whole manuscript and a synopsis for your new book.

Please include a self-addressed, stamped envelope with all correspondence, and allow two weeks for a response to a letter and six to eight weeks for a reading.

For a free brochure about the agency, please send a stamped, self-addressed #10 envelope to 1029 Jones Street, San Francisco, California 94109.

The agency can also be reached at 415-673-0939, 10-5 PST, Monday through Friday, and at larsenpoma@aol.com or www.larsen-pom ada.com.

With Wendy Nelder, former president of the San Francisco Board of Supervisors, Michael and Elizabeth have founded the San Francisco Writers Conference, www.sfwc.biz, which takes place on President's Day weekend in February.

Contents

Fourteen Reasons for This New Edition

The most important reason for the new edition of this book is that it is a bread-and-butter book that I have to keep at a state-of-the-art level so my partner, Elizabeth Pomada, and I can use it with our clients. It's far easier to sell nonfiction than fiction, so we sell more nonfiction books, many by first-time authors. Our livelihood depends on the effectiveness of this book. It enables our clients to help us help them. Over the last thirty-one years, we've sold books to more than one hundred publishers because our writers keep proving that this book works.

By following the book, our writers enable us to sell their work to the shrinking number of multimedia, multinational New York conglomerates that dominate trade publishing and to a handful of medium-sized independent houses, most of which are in New York. As prisoners of the literary-industrial complex, this is the only way we can make a living.

Judging from the letters and reviews we've received over the last eighteen years, the book has helped many writers. If you have a salable idea and you prove that you can write it, this book can help you launch your career. Once you've sold one book, you can go from book to book and advance to advance.

What's New?

To help make the book industrial strength, I added these features:

1. Four new annotated sample proposals, that, like most of the other examples this book uses, are about books that we have sold.

2. Seven new ways to test-market your book.
3. How to write a five- to ten-page mini-proposal that can speed up the process of getting an agent and a publisher.
4. A checklist to ensure that your proposal has everything it needs.
5. More lists and shorter chapters to make the book faster and easier to read and consult.
6. A list of nine options for getting your book published.
7. A greatly simplified promotion plan that makes more sense for new writers.
8. The word (*Optional*) appears before most of the parts of the Overview so you can skip them if they don't apply to your book.
9. Four new ways to find an agent and how an agent can help you.
10. Two new parts of the Overview, a Mission Statement, and the Author's Platform, all of which will assist you in setting up your promotion plan.
11. A chart of the publishing process.
12. A list of subsidiary rights.
13. Eleven reasons to write your manuscript before you write your proposal.
14. Golden Rules, which convey the essence of the goals for the parts of your proposal.

Two additional time-savers: The book now recommends for most books writing only one sample chapter instead of two. And, if you plan to write your book before selling it, you can use a two-page synopsis instead of a full outline.

I will update the book and add sample proposals on our Web site (www.larsen-pomada.com) so you won't have to wait until the next edition for them.

Once you know what you will need to write your proposal, you can start compiling information for your proposal.

Agents and editors recommend the book, and I'm very proud of that. I continue to believe that it's the fastest, easiest way for you to get the best agent, editor, publisher, and deal for your work. I also believe that if you start with the right idea, your first book will be the foundation of a long, successful career.

If you have questions, please call or write. Part of what sustained me through this arduous revision was letters from writers who sold their books because of this one. I hope that you'll soon be one of those writers and help me make the next edition even more helpful to writers.

Writing and Selling an Irresistible Proposal

If there is a book that you want to read and it hasn't been written yet, then you must write it.

—Nobel prize-winning author Toni Morrison

Want a million dollars to write a book?

The subject? You can pick one later.

Does this sound like a fantasy? It happened to Robert Woodward, co-author of *All the President's Men*. The catch: It happened *after* his fourth consecutive book hit the top of the best-seller list.

You can't count on enjoying the spectacular career that Robert Woodward has earned, but writing a successful book can transform your life. Now is an amazing time to be a writer. You are blessed with more ways to get your books written and published and more ways to promote and profit from them than ever before. And technology makes researching, writing, promoting your book, building networks, and finding an agent and publisher easier and faster than ever.

Getting Paid to Write Your Book

In *The Insider's Guide to Getting Published*, John Boswell notes that "today fully 90 percent of all nonfiction books sold to trade publishers are acquired on the basis of a proposal alone." If you have an idea for a book that will interest enough people and you can prove to a publisher that you can research, organize, and write a book about it, you can get published. But this requires a fundamental shift in your thinking from being an artist to being a merchant, from being a writer with something to say to being an author with something to sell. You have to sell your proposal to an agent or editor by making it irresistible *before* you mail it. The fate of your proposal is sealed with the envelope you mail it in.

An "In the Bleachers" cartoon by Steve Moore shows a jockey sitting at the starting gate saying to himself:

> Why am I dressed like this? Who are all these people? What am I doing on a horse? Where *am* I?

The caption says:

> Seconds before the start of the race, Filipe suffers a mental lapse commonly known among jockeys as "rider's block."

Jockeys may have a problem, but writers shouldn't. The world is awash with ideas. The challenge in this bottomless sea of possibilities is for you to raise a sunken treasure—to find the best idea for you to write about now, based on the following criteria:

- your passion for it
- your ability to write about it
- your ability to promote it
- its commercial potential
- its series potential

Finding the right focus for your book—neither too broad nor too narrow—is essential. As one wag put it, "You shouldn't start vast projects with half-vast ideas."

Four Steps to Take When You Have an Idea

A *New Yorker* cartoon by Mick Stevens shows Adam and Eve sitting together under a tree in Eden, and Adam is saying, "I can't help thinking that there's a book in this."

Someone once said, "Getting an idea should be like sitting on a pin; it should make you jump up and do something." The moment you have an idea that excites you, take these four steps immediately:

1. Test the idea on your writing, speaking, and field networks. (Chapter twenty-two discusses the value of networks.)

2. Check the competition. (Appendix D gives sources for tracking down competitive books.)

3. Read all about it. The more you learn, the more you earn. Make yourself an expert on your subject by reading the most important competitive books and browsing through the others. For any kind of book you want to write, models abound. Successful books that deal

with your subject but won't compete with your work help sell your book by proving there's a market for books on the subject. One of the publishers of such books may buy yours.

4. Write your proposal ASAP. Ideas are in the air because the raw material for them is in the media. When a subject is hot, publishers are deluged with proposals about it. They also mine their backlists for books on the subject. If your book is about a breaking news story or a hot subject, you must write your proposal quickly without sacrificing quality and sell it before another writer beats you to it or interest in the subject wanes.

However, if time and money are not crucial to the writing and success of your book, consider these two suggestions:
- Write your manuscript before you write your proposal. (Chapter eighteen lists twelve advantages to writing your manuscript first.)
- Guarantee your book's success by test-marketing it. (Chapter twenty-three describes how to test-market your book.)

The Parts of an Irresistible Proposal
Nothing is particularly hard if you divide it into small jobs.

—Henry Ford

Some writers find it easier to write a book than a proposal. For others, writing the proposal is the most creative part of producing a book. Why? Because you have the freedom to plan the book in the way that excites you most without:
- bearing the responsibility for writing it
- changing your vision to suit your publisher's needs
- being pressured by the deadline that comes with a contract

Even one of the following ten hot buttons can excite editors enough to buy your book:
- Your idea
- Your title
- Your writing
- Your credentials
- Your book's timing
- Your ability to promote your book
- The size of the markets for your book
- Your book's subsidiary-rights potential
- Your book's potential for bulk sales to businesses
- Your book's potential as a series of books that sell each other

Your job: Push as many hot buttons as you can.

English author Somerset Maugham once said, "There are three rules for writing a novel. Unfortunately, no one knows what they are." Fortunately, I can be more helpful about writing a proposal. A nonfiction book can be a how-to book, a biography, a memoir, a humor book, a history, a reference book, a gift book, or an illustrated book.

As competitive books prove, there is not just one way to write a proposal any more than there is just one way to write a book. My approach has evolved over the last three decades, and it continues to evolve as what editors need to see changes. I don't want to waste a second of your time, my time, or the time of the writers we work for, so this book lays out the fastest, easiest way I know for you to produce a rejection-proof proposal and obtain the best editor, publisher, and deal for your book.

Most proposals range from thirty to fifty pages. Your proposal will have three parts in a logical sequence, each of which has a goal. Your goal is to impress agents and editors enough with each part of your proposal to convince them to go on to the next. The following sections provide an overview of the three parts of a proposal.

The Introduction

Your introduction should prove that you have a marketable, practical idea and that you are the right person to write about it and promote it. The introduction has three parts: the "Overview," "Resources Needed to Complete the Book," and "About the Author." They give you the opportunity to provide as much ammunition about you and your book as you can muster.

Overview

The overview consists of thirteen parts, ten of which are optional:

Your subject hook: This is the most exciting, compelling thing that you can write in as few words as possible that justifies the existence of your book. Use a quote, event, fact, trend, anecdote, statistic, idea, or joke. For example, your subject hook could be an anecdote about someone using your advice to solve a problem followed by a statistic about the number of people with the problem.

Your book hook: This includes your title, your selling handle, and the length of your book:

- Your title: The titles for most books have to tell and sell. Make sure yours says what your book is and gives browsers an irresistible reason to buy it.

- Your selling handle: This is a sentence that ideally says, "[Your book's title] will be the first book to . . . " You can also use Hollywood shorthand by comparing your book to one or two successful books: "[Your book's title] is *Seabiscuit* meets *What to Expect When You're Expecting.*"
- The length of your book (and number of illustrations, if it will have them): Provide a page or word count for your manuscript that you determine by outlining your book and estimating the length of your chapters and back matter.

(Optional) **Your book's special features:** This includes humor, structure, anecdotes, checklists, exercises, sidebars, the tone and style of your book, and anything you will do to give the text visual appeal. Use competitive books as models.

(Optional) **A foreword by a well-known authority:** Find someone who will give your book credibility and salability in fifty states two years from now to write a foreword. If getting a foreword isn't possible, write: "The author will contact [names of potential authorities] for a foreword."

(Optional) **Answers to technical or legal questions:** If your book's on a specialized subject, name the expert who has reviewed it. If your book may present legal problems, name the intellectual property attorney who has reviewed it.

(Optional) **Your back matter:** Check competitive books to see if your book needs an appendix, a glossary, a resource directory, a bibliography, or footnotes.

(Optional) **Markets for your book:** List the groups of people who will buy your book and the channels through which it can be sold, starting with the largest ones.

(Optional) **Your book's subsidiary-rights possibilities:** Start with the most commercial category, whether it's movie rights, foreign rights, book club rights, or even merchandising rights (for products like T-shirts), which usually require a book to be a best-seller before manufacturers will be interested.

(Optional) **Spin-offs:** If your book can be a series or lend itself to sequels, mention up to five of them in descending order of their commercial appeal.

(Optional) **A mission statement:** If you feel a sense of mission about writing and promoting your book, describe it in one first-person paragraph.

(Optional) **Your platform:** In descending order of impressiveness, list what you are doing to promote your work and yourself.

(**Optional**) **Your promotion plan:** List in descending order of importance what you will do to promote your book when and after it's published. If you're writing a reference book or a gift book, you may not need a promotion plan. Also, small and medium-sized houses outside of New York don't need the promotional ammunition big publishers do. At the beginning of your career, or if your idea or your ability to promote your book isn't as strong as it needs to be to excite Big Apple publishers, you may find small and medium-sized publishers more receptive to your work.

(**Optional**) **Competitive and Complementary Books:** List books that will compete with and complement yours. Provide basic information on the half-dozen most important titles.

(Optional) Resources Needed to Complete the Book
Starting with the largest expense, list out-of-pocket expenses of five hundred dollars or more for a foreword, permissions, travel, or illustrations (not for office expenses). Use a round figure for how much each will cost and give the total. (You or your agent may decide not to include the dollar amounts when submitting your proposal, but you do have to know what they are because they affect the money you need to write your book as well as the negotiation of your contract.)

About the Author
Include everything that you want editors to know about you in descending order of relevance and importance that is not in your platform.

The Outline

Your outline is a paragraph to a page of prose outlining your chapters to prove that there's a book's worth of information in your idea and that you have devised the best structure for organizing it. Aim for about one line of outline for every page of text you guesstimate; for example, nineteen lines of outline for a nineteen-page chapter. To help make your outlines enjoyable to read, start each one with the strongest anecdote or slice of copy from each chapter, then outline it.

Sample Chapter

Include the one sample chapter that best shows how you will make your book as enjoyable to read as it is informative.

❖ ❖ ❖

In *Editors on Editing*, Jane von Mehren, editor in chief of Penguin Books, said, "The best proposals are those that elicit the fewest questions. Why? Because you've anticipated and answered them all."

This guide presents the parts of a proposal in the order that agents and editors will read them. You may write your proposal in any order you wish, then assemble the pieces. If you want to start with the easiest parts, try these: your bio, a mission statement, your platform, spin-offs, the markets for your book, back matter, and special features.

Let's go step-by-step through the process of creating a proposal that will get you the editor, publisher, and deal that you want for your book. We'll start with your first challenge: creating an enticing subject hook.

1 | Your Subject Hook

You've heard the saying: "To sell the steak, you've got to sell the sizzle." Your introduction is the sizzle in your proposal. If the introduction doesn't sell you and your idea, agents and editors won't check the bones—the outline of your book—or try the steak—your sample chapter.

The two fundamental questions your proposal must answer are:

Why this book?
Why you?

The first part of your proposal must convince readers that your book will have what it takes to succeed in an increasingly competitive marketplace. The introduction sets the standard for the tone, style, and quality of what follows. It provides thirteen pieces of information that must convince an editor that:

- You have a salable idea.
- You can write it.
- You can promote it.

Whether you are selling a proposal with a sample chapter, a complete manuscript, or a self-published or previously published book, you need an introduction.

When you go to a bookstore, how many pages do you give a book before you decide whether to buy it or stick it back on the shelf? Writers tell me that they need as little as one page to make a decision. If they like what they read enough to want to turn the page, they buy the book. If not, they keep on browsing. United Press International tells its journalists that if they hook readers with the first six words, then readers will read the first paragraph. If they read the first paragraph, they will read the first three paragraphs, and if they stay with the story through the first three paragraphs, they'll finish it.

The Crucial First Paragraphs of Your Introduction

Start halfway down page one, and type and center the word

Introduction

Then, in the first paragraph or two of your proposal, hook the editor to your subject with a quote, an event, an idea, a joke, a cartoon, or a statistic: the single most exciting thing that you can write about the subject that makes your book sound new, needed, and timely. A subject hook can also be a compelling anecdote, a statistic, or an anecdote that gives rise to a statistic.

For example, if you are writing a how-to book, consider starting with an anecdote about how someone used your technique to solve a problem or improve his life. Then provide a round, accurate figure for how many people need your book.

For a business how-to book, the anecdote might be about how the Wide Open Spaces Company in Wherever, Texas, used your technique and increased its sales by 100 percent in six months. Your next sentence can mention how many other companies can benefit from the same approach. You must convince editors that your subject warrants a book. Try to make your subject hook grab readers the way the lead paragraph in a magazine story does. If you're writing a memoir or another type of narrative book, start with the most exciting scene.

Example: Subject Hook for a How-To Book

Here is an excellent subject hook by Michelle Saadi, a client whose book was called *Claiming Your Share: How to Get Full Payment and Protect Your Rights After an Auto Accident*:

After driving for twenty-five years without an accident, John Smith had his car rear-ended as he stopped for a light. He suffered neck and back injuries and lost two months of work. Instead of paying Mr. Smith, the other driver's insurance company went to court, convinced the jury Smith had made a panic stop, and won the case. Although he lost $5,000 and was an innocent victim, Smith never recovered a cent from the accident.

According to figures from the National Safety Council and the Insurance Information Institute, John Smith represents the one out of every five drivers who have accidents each year. There are 149 million drivers in this country, and every year they have eighteen million accidents. Although most of these drivers carry insurance, many of the victims in these accidents, like Mr. Smith, recover nothing.

Hot Tip

People like to read about other people. That's why anecdotes are an effective way to get your points across. Use fictional techniques to make them short stories that pack a wallop by being as humorous, dramatic, inspirational, or startling as possible. Anecdotes humanize a book by presenting a slice of life that readers can relate to. They also make for more enjoyable, memorable reading than abstract ideas. As Jack Canfield says, "Facts tell, stories sell."

Example: Subject Hook for a Humor Book

For us to sell his self-published humor book, *101 Ways to Get Your Adult Children to Move Out (and Make Them Think It Was Their Idea)*, to Doubleday, Rich Melheim needed just the first part of a proposal. To hook editors to the subject, he used an anecdote that includes one of the "101 ways" and, at the same time, explains the genesis of the book:

A woman once came to the author for counseling. Her twenty-eight-year-old son and his new bride had just lost their jobs and moved back into her house. She didn't relish the idea of hosting their honeymoon at her dining room table each night when she came home from work. "It's not working. I love the kids, but I can't have them in my house," she told the author. "I'd just like to be able to walk around the place in my underwear again."

The author told her to start walking around the house in her underwear, and they'd be gone.

She did.

They left.

The book was born.

Eleven million "twenty-somethings" are infesting their parents' homes. Half of our adult children will return home at least once. The average stay is six months. Less than a quarter of them pay rent. About half of the "boomeranged" parents say they enjoy having their kids around the house.

The other half, while stumbling over dogs, cats, babies, and significant others who don't belong there, find themselves enduring varying degrees of frustration. *101 Ways* is for parents who believe the ends justify the means and are willing to be just bizarre enough to reclaim their homes before their adult children drive them out. The author believes that embracing a little insanity is preferable to having it thrust upon you.

You may not need a story if your statistics suggest a big enough potential market for your book. Just the numbers in Michelle Saadi's proposal—149 million drivers and 18 million accidents—prove that there's a large potential audience for a book on the subject. In Rich Melheim's book, eleven million indicates more than that number of anxious parents, and even more if you count stepparents.

Hot Tip

Avoid the words *I*, *we*, *us*, and *our* unless the book is about you. Editors are wary of authors who overuse the word *I* unless it's relevant to the book. Unless you or your experience are part of the book, write about the subject, not yourself. Also avoid the words *you* and *your* in your introduction and outline. The first two parts of the proposal are about the book. You're writing them for the editor, not the book buyer. If you want to address readers directly, as this sentence does, do it in your sample chapter and the opening anecdotes for your outline. The most effective way to sell your book is to stick to the subject and the book.

Let's say you want to write a book about a new way to stop smoking. Like average readers, editors are aware of the problem in a general way. You need to provide statistics on how many people smoke and the toll it takes in lives, health costs, and lost work time to convince editors that the subject merits another book.

Using round numbers and naming a reliable source lend credibility to your statement and to you as an authority on the subject. Dates, geography, money, size, the number of people, the growth of a trend—

use whatever data that will put the subject into context for an editor and prove that there will be wide national interest in the subject when your book comes out. Mention the number again in your section on markets.

Example: Subject Hook for a Memoir

Wild Child: Life With Jim Morrison is Linda Ashcroft's memoir about her relationship with the rock star (which we sold to Thunder's Mouth Press), so she wrote her subject hook in the first person. She uses an anecdote that conveys the nature of their relationship and how well she will write about it:

> On a sunny July day in 1967, Jim Morrison and I sat cross-legged in a Golden Gate Park gully waiting for the wind to raise our Chinese kites. Jim recalled a story about how when he was four or five, he and his family witnessed an accident in New Mexico in which a Navajo Indian was killed. This first glimpse of death shook Jim, who pleaded with his father to do something.
>
> As the family car drove slowly past the accident, Jim felt a blow against his chest. "I was never the same. I had this other presence in me. My inner music changed. My heartbeat was different. I could know things. Will things."
>
> With a single motion, Jim rose to his feet and began a dance drawn from Native American movements, but accompanied himself with a low, bluesy hum straight from the Delta. Only Jim could come so close to falling and right himself so gracefully.
>
> Soon, the wind rose. Jim grinned. At first, I was incredulous, but I was fifteen, and I believed Jim Morrison could call the wind. After we breathlessly reeled our kites in, Jim leaned down to me and whispered, "The wind comes up this time every afternoon. Sometimes, the magic is in the timing." Jim knew the same was true of the rocket he was riding that summer on the flames of "Light My Fire."
>
> No one else can write *Wild Child: My Friendship With Jim Morrison*, because I was the teenager for whom Jim wrote, "Not your mother's or your father's child, but our child." About the time of my sixteenth birthday, Jim climbed through my bedroom window in Stockton, California, to give me a white rose, a book of William Carlos Williams's poems, and the neatly

typed *Wild Child*. Jim was my real father, my big brother, and my first boyfriend. I was his child, his friend, his Natasha.

As Jim's confidant for four years, I hold the missing pieces to the puzzle that was Jim Morrison. In *Wild Child*, I will reveal his demons and his dreams. Jim was a brilliant, funny, reckless, and vulnerable young man who was haunted by a traumatic childhood. In Jim's own words, the book will explain for the first time the truth behind his estrangement from his family, and the meaning behind the imagery of his lyrics and poems.

❖ ❖ ❖

The last thing we find in making a book is to know what we must put first.

—Blaise Pascal

A common problem with subject hooks is that they are too long. Writers start discussing the subject and can't stop. Computers make it easy to add copy, but they don't tell us when to stop. One sentence, if it's compelling, may be all you need. Say as little as possible about the subject. The subject hook has to sell the subject; the rest of the overview sells the book and you. Your outline and writing samples will enable you to tell publishers what you want them to know about the subject.

2 | Your Title and Subtitle

In Search of Your Book's Most Powerful Sales Tool: Your Title

After you hook editors to your subject, the next challenge is to ensnare them with your book hook: a two-sentence paragraph containing three pieces of information.

In the first sentence, give the title and the selling handle for your book. Even though the full title is on the title page of your proposal, repeat it once more here. In the second sentence, indicate the number of pages your manuscript will have as well as the number of illustrations if you use them.

An example by Robert Stinnett whose book we sold to Free Press:

> *Day of Deceit: The Truth About FDR and Pearl Harbor* will be the first book to prove that FDR knew in advance about Pearl Harbor and approved it. The manuscript will be 564 pages with 43 illustrations.

The Two-Second Browse

You're in your favorite independent bookstore just after your book is published. You start walking the aisles delighted to find your book face up on the new nonfiction table in the front of the store. You pause to look at it and take in the books around it.

How long do you spend looking at the covers of other books? Two seconds each, if you are the average book buyer. And guess what? That's how long everyone who walks by the table will spend looking at your cover. Two seconds is less time than it took you to read the previous sentence.

Two seconds for the design, artwork, and the title. A large proportion of books have *tombstone covers*. Nobody could think of an image, symbol, or metaphor that could capture the essence of the book in a way that would help sell it, so words are all that browsers have to go on. Finding the perfect title for your book will be an "Aha!" experience. You will know it the moment you think of it or hear it. It will be love at first sound.

It's been said that most business books provide affirmation, not information, and that what it takes to be successful in business hasn't changed much. But authors keep coming up with fresh, timely ways of expressing their ideas in titles that make their books salable to new readers. This works for French cookbooks, too.

Ideally, your book should be new wine in a new bottle. It should contain new information that will face no competition and bear a title that separates it from other books. But if, as is true for most books, your book will not be the first one on the subject, then it's all the more essential that your "bottle" be new, that you conceptualize your book in a way that makes it irresistible. You need a title that justifies another book on the subject.

Assume that the editors at big houses who read your proposal are experts on the subject, have seen hundreds of proposals on the subject, and have bought some of them. They will know immediately how well your book will compete with others on the subject. The perfect title for your book will get them excited about it, in part because they know that your title will excite their editorial boards, publicists, sales reps, booksellers, and book buyers.

Titling on Both Sides of Your Brain

Creating the best title, and if necessary a subtitle, for your book involves using both sides of your brain, because the best titles appeal to the emotions as well as the mind. For the title, you need the right side of the brain. You need to draw on your creativity to synthesize your book's benefits in a short, simple, visual, and accurate title that paints a picture that creates an emotional response.

The left side of your brain faces the challenge of coming up with the shortest, simplest, clearest way of expressing what your book will do for your readers to justify their buying and reading it.

Two Ways to Find Good Titles

Here are two simple ways for finding titles:

1. The titles for serious reference works, biographies, or books proposing a scientific or political theory just have to tell, not sell. People buy them because they want the information, so you can simply name the information to create the title. As elsewhere, be guided by comparable books you admire. David McCullough didn't need anything fancier than *John Adams* to have a best-seller (not one of our books, alas, but a wonderful book that is a must-read for aspiring biographers and memoirists).

2. Your book may only need a title. Thanks to John Travolta, Karen Lustgarten's *The Complete Guide to Disco Dancing*—one of our books—didn't need a subtitle to hit the best-seller list. (The photo of her on the cover made its way onto a postage stamp commemorating the seventies. How's that for finding immortality?) Other books of ours that didn't require subtitles include:

- *Learn to Write Fiction From the Masters* by Barnaby Conrad
- *The Random House Webster's Quotationary* compiled by Leonard Roy Frank
- *Fun Places to Go With Children in Northern California* by Elizabeth Pomada, now in its ninth edition

Making Bullion Out of Bouillon Cubes: The Tell-and-Sell Factor

In *How to Drive the Competition Crazy*, Guy Kawasaki tells the story of how nobody at a private boy's school signed up for a course called "Home Economics for Boys," but the class filled up immediately when the school changed the name of the course to "Bachelor Living."

Your title must bridge the gap between what you're selling and what people are buying. The right title unites two realities: what your book says; and the most compelling way to conceptualize that body of information so it will include as many potential book buyers as possible and exclude as few as necessary. Author Susan Sontag once observed that, "The role of the writer is to make bouillon cubes out of chicken soup." If your book will be the essence of what you want to say, then your title will be the essence of that essence.

Titles for self-help books, books on popular culture—in fact, any book aimed at a mass audience—must have a high tell-and-sell factor. Together, your title and subtitle must tell, describe what your book is, and sell, motivate book buyers to pick it up off the shelf. Make your title as clear, concise, compelling, and commercial as your subject allows.

Hot Tip | The longer you make anything in your proposal—words, sentences, titles, paragraphs, chapters, anecdotes, and the book itself—the better it must be to justify its length.

Make your title a big red flag that screams, "Stop and pick me up! You can't live without me! I'm worth twice the price! Take me home now!" An effective how-to title incorporates the notions of a desirable activity or skill to be learned, a systematic approach to learning it, and if possible, a time within which the reader will acquire the skill:

- *French Made Simple*
- *30 Days to Building a Greater Vocabulary*
- *Total Fitness in 30 Minutes a Week*

Benefits that a book or chapter title might convey include speed, quality, economy, or a system or program of steps readers can take to bring about the change they seek. Using numbers, like in *10 Steps for Curing Health*, is a simple way to present a systematic approach and tell readers the structure of your book or chapter.

The following titles (which we sold) tell and sell and combine a catchy title and subtitle to convey each book's benefit:

- *Catch Your Dog Doing Something Right: How to Train Any Dog in Five Minutes a Day* by Krista Cantrell
- *How High Can You Bounce? The 9 Keys to Personal Resilience* by Roger Crawford, whose proposal is in Appendix E
- *The Royal Treatment: Taking Home the Secrets of the World's Greatest Spas* by Steve Capellini

Hot Tip | Try your title out on your networks to see how they respond to it. Don't offer agents or editors a string of titles to choose from; pick the best one. You can share the others after you place your proposal. Align your title and every word of your manuscript with your readers' needs, values, and fears. The more you help readers, the more they'll help you.

Generic Victorians

Shortly after we started our agency, I drove a cab for a while to make up for the royalties we hadn't started earning yet. Driving a taxi gave me the chance to see parts of San Francisco that we hadn't explored. It also enabled me to discover the beautifully painted Victorians that were sprouting up like flowers around the city.

I knew there was a book in them, so I took two sheets of slides and wrote a brief proposal for a book. It took a year and a half to sell. Local publishers said the color photos would make the book too costly to produce. New York editors said the book was too "regional," the kiss of death for a pitch to a New York publisher.

Finally, Cy Nelson, an editor of illustrated books, stopped in San Francisco on his way to visit his printer in Japan. After driving him around the city to see the houses, he became a believer and risked six thousand dollars on the first book.

When photographer Morley Baer and I were roaming around San Francisco shooting houses for the book, he suggested that we call it *Painted Ladies*. As soon as he said it, I laughed with delight. It was the perfect title. We knew we needed a subtitle, and *San Francisco's Victorians* was the logical choice, but we were stuck for the right adjective. Cy was right on target with the word *resplendent*.

The first book, published in 1978, started a national trend that led to five more books. The words *painted ladies*–now trademarked in all categories—have become generic for multicolored Victorians.

Hot Tip | If you luck into the title of a lifetime that has a word or phrase that you can use for your talks and for a series of books, trademark it and buy the domain name for your Web site ASAP.

If you can't think of an ideal title for your book, perhaps your agent or editor will, or maybe you will as you are writing the book. Your title may change in the course of writing and producing a book. If you're lucky, you will settle on a title that you, your editor, and the S&M (that's sales and marketing) crowd agree will create the strongest response on bookstore shelves.

Mystery novelist Raymond Chandler solved the mystery of what makes an effective title when he said, "A good title is the title of a successful book." If you come up with a good title for your book, you will be well on your way to solving the mystery of how to sell it.

Hot Tip

In between you and your book's place on bookstore shelves two years from now are nine gatekeepers who will have a say about the title for your book: you, your networks, your agent, your editor, your publisher's editorial board, your publisher's sales reps, the bookstore chains, the warehouse clubs, and discounters like Wal-Mart. If any one of them doesn't like the title, regardless of the previous responses to it, the title is toast.

Writers are less concerned about titles than they need to be and are usually too close to their work to create the best titles for their books. They may think that their publisher will change it anyway, but big publishers are working with too many books to pay enough attention to all of them. If they get stuck on a title, they choose the least objectionable one.

What percentage of published books have the best titles for them? My guess: fewer than 10 percent. Verify this for yourself on your bookshelves or in a bookstore.

The best insurance: Put your networks to work and do whatever it takes to come up with the best title for your book.

If you're planning a series of books, the title you choose must serve you well for the series. As I said before, you'll know it when you hear it; you'll get goose bumps. Finding the right title for your book challenges your publisher either to use it or find a better one.

Nineteen Questions to Answer
Before Deciding on Your Title

One New York editor said to us, "If the title is good enough, it doesn't matter what's in the book." *Everything Men Know About Women* proves her right. The book has sold more than 750,000 copies. How do I know that the title alone sold the book? Because it's 120 blank pages!

A *New Yorker* cartoon shows a man, his hand extended, introducing himself to a woman at a party, and he's saying to her: "Hi. I'm, I'm. . . . You'll have to forgive me. I'm terrible with names." Being terrible with names is not an option when it comes to naming your book.

When I worked at Bantam, the editors used to talk about a Little, Brown novel called *Five Days*. It didn't sell well, so when Bantam published the mass-market edition of the book, they changed the title to *Five Nights*. *Five Days* tells; *Five Nights* sells. This is a timeless example of what a title should be: evocative, intriguing, enticing, appealing more to the emotions than to the mind. This applies equally to the titles of your chapters.

At one of his writing seminars, veteran journalist Arky Gonzalez revealed the results of research to determine what article titles on a magazine cover would sell the most copies of the magazine. The two winners: "Proof Found of Personal Immortality" and "Pope's Daughter Found Murdered in Commie Love Nest."

What's in a name? Plenty! A symbol or metaphor that captures the essence of your book can crystallize the meaning and structure of the book for you, the agent, the editor, the sales reps, the booksellers, and the book buyers. Let your imagination run wild and have fun thinking about all the possibilities. The authors must have had fun coming up with these titles:

- *How to Pull Strings and Influence Puppets*
- *My Indecision Is Final*
- *Ventriloquism for the Complete Dummy*

Andrea Brown, an agent who specializes in children's books, finds that the right title is especially important for children's books. Humorous titles like *Cloudy With a Chance of Meatballs* or *The Cat Ate My Swimsuit* sell much better than straightforward titles.

You have to have a creative distance from your book and be a bit of a visionary or a poet to come up with a title that excites you. You need the distance that astronauts have when they behold Spaceship Earth. Here are nineteen questions to ask yourself to help you find the title for your book:

1. Does my title have an impact of an ad or article headline, compelling people to read the copy that follows? Using the word *free* helped Jay Conrad Levinson with *Guerrilla Marketing for Free: Dozens of No-Cost Tactics to Promote Your Business and Energize Your Profits*.

2. Does my title have three words that capture the essence of my book's promise? When one writer was stuck for a title, Oscar Dystel, then the president of Bantam, asked him, "What's the point of the book in three words, no more, no less?" The writer replied, "Quick weight loss," which became the heart of the title for the best-seller *The Doctor's Quick Weight Loss Diet*.

3. Does my title make use of a memorable image, symbol, or metaphor that captures the essence of my book in a way that can be the basis for my book's cover art, promotional materials, and future books? The title was one of the reasons *If Life Is a Game, These Are*

the Rules by Cherie Carter-Scott hit the top of the best-seller list. The subtitle—*Ten Rules for Being Human as Introduced in Chicken Soup for the Soul*—also helped, as did the hour Oprah joined her audience watching Cherie's presentation.

4. Does my title sell my solution? Don't sell a question; sell an answer. Don't sell a problem; sell a solution. Make your title positive and empowering. Convince book buyers that you're going to solve their problem. An example: *Edward Segal's Getting Your 15 Minutes of Fame and More! A Guide to Guaranteeing Your Business Success.*

5. For a how-to book: Is my title the prescription for the cure my book will provide? Readers want a how-to book to be a magic pill. They want to follow the directions and enjoy the benefit the title pre-scribes. Harold Lustig did this with his book: *4 Steps to Financial Security for Lesbian and Gay Couples.*

6. Does my title make the biggest promise that my book will fulfill? Here is a brilliant title by David J. Lieberman: *Get Anyone to Do Anything: Never Feel Powerless Again—With Psychological Secrets to Control and Influence Every Situation.*

7. Does my title broadcast my unique selling proposition (USP)? Create a USP that will make your book stand out from the competi-tion. This is particularly important for a book that will face a lot of competition, like *The Only Negotiating Book You Will Ever Need: 101 Tactics for Win-winning at Home and at Work*, by Peter Stark and Jane Flaherty, the proposal for which is on our Web site.

Hot Tip

When publishing people refer to a title, they only use one or two words, so do as they do: After you give the full title in your book hook, use a shorthand version of it in the rest of your proposal so editors won't have to keep reading the whole title.

Keep your title short and simple, six words or less, and add an explan-atory subtitle if you need to. *Jaws* did the job for Peter Benchley, but *Dry* gets my vote as the shortest title I've ever seen. (It's a memoir that involves alcohol and fishing.) You will also help book buyers who are researching books by subject if the first or second word of your title conveys the subject of the book. Ingram, the nation's largest wholesaler, gives only the first sixteen letters of a title in its computerized book list that booksellers use for ordering. That was a reason for calling my book about agents *Literary Agents.*

Then again, there's always *Everything You Ever Wanted to Know About Sex but Were Afraid to Ask* by David Rubin. Its thirteen words didn't keep it from becoming a best-seller.

8. Is the title of my book the same title as the talks that I will give about it? The same title for both creates synergy. Whether it's to hear you or read your book, you're asking for people's time, which is more valuable to them than their money. Your title must convince them that it will be time well spent.

9. Does my title use proprietary nomenclature, a way of capturing the essence of my book that makes it mine alone? Jay Conrad Levinson's name has become synonymous with Guerrilla Marketing, the brand he built.

10. Can I use a variation of my title for other books? The Guerrilla Marketing series, the Dummies books, and the Chicken Soup series prove that the right title helps create enduring brands.

11. Does my title broadcast my book's benefit so well that it creates an irresistible urge to buy my book? Another example by David J. Lieberman: *Never Be Lied to Again: How to Get the Truth in 5 Minutes or Less in Any Conversation or Situation.*

Hot Tip

In *Making the List: A Cultural History of the American Bestseller 1900–1999*, best-selling author and Simon & Schuster former editor in chief Michael Korda asks, "How different is the [best-seller list] today from what Americans were reading a hundred years ago? Not very. Celebrities, political history, self-help, and cookbooks brought Americans into bookstores then, as now, and what seems most new is usually just a gloss on the old." This should reassure you. What people need and want hasn't changed much, even if how they seek satisfaction has.

12. Does my title offer one or more of the golden oldies that people have always wanted and needed most: sex, love, food, health, laughter, pleasure, peace of mind, work, power, success, making money, and saving money? Also consider these trends that will create enduring interest in books about them:

- Aging baby boomers
- Growth and significance of technology and biotechnology
- Globalization of culture, commerce and statecraft
- East meeting West as authors draw on Asian traditions in lifestyle books about health, fitness, food, work, gardening, spirituality, and design

13. Does my title capture how my book will affect my readers? Will it inform them, enlighten them, entertain them, persuade them, inspire them, make them laugh, help them lead better lives, or any combina-

tion of these? Here's the something-for-everyone title for Francesca De Grandis's book: *Be a Goddess! A Guide to Celtic Spells and Wisdom for Self-Healing, Prosperity and Great Sex*. It was in its thirteenth printing as these words were written.

14. Does my title use wordplay to help make it memorable? Among the techniques you can use are:

- Rhyme: *Private Lives of Ministers' Wives* (by Liz Greenbacker and contributor Sherry Taylor)
- Rhythm: *If Life Is a Game, These Are the Rules* (by Cherie Carter-Scott)
- Alliteration: *Amazeing ART: Wonders of the Ancient World* (by Christopher Berg)
- Verbal and visual puns: *$ellmates: The Art of Living and Working Together*, one of my favorite ideas that needs a writer
- Wordplay—changing a letter or a word in a well-known phrase or using the opposite of one: *Tongue Fu! How to Deflect, Disarm and Defuse Any Verbal Conflict* (a great title by Sam Horn) or *Stuff Happens (And Then You Fix It): 9 Reality Rules to Steer Your Life Back in the Right Direction* (by John Alston, CPAE, and Lloyd Thaxton) and *Winning the Battle of the Exes: How to Make the Last Day of Your Divorce the First Day of a Lifelong Friendship*, another favorite idea that needs a writer
- Two contrasting or opposing phrases: *Men Are From Mars, Women Are From Venus* (by John Gray)
- Humorous titles, essential for books with humor: *I'm Not As Old As I Used to Be: Reclaiming Your Life in the Second Half* (by Frances Weaver) and *How Now Brown Sow: A Fat-Free Guide to Raising Pigs in Your Apartment*, an idea unlikely to find a writer

15. Does my title use words that sell?

- Words that sell products and services: *sex(y)*, *now*, *success*, *first*, *complete*, *how to*, *you*, *health*, *balance*, *transform*, *original*, *diet*, *weight loss*, *God*, *soul*, *spiritual*, *inspirational*, *overcome*
- Money words: *free*, *money(-making)*, *save*, *profit*, *risk-free*, *guarantee*, *income*, *tax-free*
- Superlatives: *biggest*, *largest*, *best*, *oldest*, *youngest*, *richest*, *most beautiful*, *most exciting*, *most complete*, *cheapest*
- Time words: *now*; *today*; a number followed by *seconds*, *minute(s)*, *hour(s)*, *day(s)*, *week(s)*, *month(s)*, *year(s)*; *speed*, *quick (-ly) (-er) (-est)*, *fast (-er) (-est)*, *instant(ly)*, *convenient*

- System words: a number followed by *secrets, steps, keys, ways*
- Crossover words: *at home and at work, in your personal and professional life, for parents and teachers*

16. Does my title promise an experience that will be funny, dramatic, inspirational, transforming, moving, amazing, or enlightening? *From Buchenwald to Carnegie Hall* is a Holocaust memoir that captures the essence of Marian Filar's remarkable story that Charles Patterson helped him tell.

17. Does my title make use of the title of a successful book? One tribute to a book's success is a parody of the book's title. Along with humorist Scott Friedman, I'm waiting for someone to write *The 7 Habits of Highly Effective Nuns.*

18. Does my title appeal to the needs, fears, and values of my potential readers? When one of our writers wanted to write a book called *The Health Food Hustlers,* I suggested that it would be more salable if he called it *The Insider's Guide to Health Foods,* which made the book a service instead of just an expose, and that was the title I used to sell the book.

19. Do I have a catchy subtitle that has nothing to do with the title? Two best-selling examples: Harvey Mackay's *Swim With the Sharks Without Being Eaten Alive: Outsell, Outmanage, Outmotivate, and Outnegotiate Your Competitors* and Richard Bolles's *What Color Is Your Parachute? A Practical Manual for Job-Hunters and Career Changers.*

❖ ❖ ❖

Any of these possibilities may spark the title for your book. Playing around with them will lead you to chapter titles, subheads, and phrases you can use in talks and articles. The titles of successful books, especially those in your subject area, will also inspire your creativity.

3 | Your Selling Handle and the Length of Your Book

Book hooks have two sentences. The first sentence gives your title and selling handle. The second gives the length of your book. After your title, you need a selling handle to finish the sentence. A sales rep once remarked in *Publishers Weekly*: "When we make our calls, we have on the average maybe fourteen seconds per book. . . . What we need is an expeditious, concise, sales-oriented handle that says a lot about [the book] in as few words as possible."

You just read a vital insight into the future of your book. You spend six months, twelve months, maybe longer, writing your book. Months later, sales reps call on bookstores and spend just fourteen seconds selling it! Then the store owner thinks about it for all of two seconds and either picks an order quantity 1, 2, 5, 10, or says "Skip." Orders for first books by unknown authors are usually at the low end of that scale, but that's where practically all writers start.

To get a number instead of a skip, reps need an effective one-line selling handle. Broadway producer David Belasco's warning to playwrights also applies to you: "If you can't write your idea on the back of my calling card, you don't have a clear idea." It's the high-concept idea of the log line, the one line of copy in *TV Guide* that must convince viewers to watch the show. Your selling handle will be a one-line statement of your primary literary goal for your book.

The book's handle may be its thematic or stylistic resemblance to one or two successful books or authors. Such comparisons give booksellers an immediate grasp of a book. The Hollywood version of a selling handle, what a screenwriter uses to pitch a movie idea, combines two successful movies: "It's gonna be colossal! It's *E.T.* meets *Jurassic Park*!"

The following examples can serve as selling handles because editors will immediately understand what you're selling, and you will both have a model on which to pin your literary and commercial hopes if you plan to write:

- a *Fast Food Nation* about fashion
- a *What to Expect When Your Pet Is Expecting* (not a bad idea, at least for an article)
- or a book in the high-energy, freewheeling style of Tom Wolfe

Establish Your Marketing Position

You can't just think about what you're selling; you must also think about what your potential readers are buying. Isolate what makes your book unique, what sets it apart from your competition. Then create a concise, memorable phrase that conveys your book's content and appeal.

You want to establish what in advertising is called your book's "marketing position." Since the best marketing position a product or service can have is to be the first of its kind, then write—if you can—that your book "will be the first book to . . . " If yours can't be the first book to do something, try to make it "the only book to . . . "

You don't have to use either of these approaches, but you do have to find a compelling phrase to explain why your book merits publication and why editors should read your proposal.

Hot Tip | Unless you have a complete manuscript draft or a self-published book, always use the word *will* when referring to your book, since it doesn't exist yet.

Your selling handle must broadcast the benefit readers will gain from your book. If you have trouble coming up with a strong title or selling handle, try this: List the book's substance and benefits in the form of phrases. Then see if you can abstract from them one enticing phrase that captures the essence of your book. Selling handles vary in length, but as everywhere else in your proposal, the fewer the words the better (fifteen at most).

Here is how some of our authors have created selling handles:

- For *Where the Chips May Fall: The Peril and Promise of the Semiconductor Revolution,* John Markoff and Lenny Siegel wrote that it "will be the first book which documents the social, economic, and ethical consequences of the explosive growth of the 'miracle chip.'" This example also illustrates how titles can change: The final title of this book was *The High Cost of High Tech: The Dark Side of the Chip.*

- Arthur Naiman wrote that his book, *Every Goy's Guide to Common Jewish Expressions,* was "the first humorous yet accurate, concise yet comprehensive handy pocket dictionary of the 450 Jewish words that crop up most frequently in books, conversations, comedy routines, movies, and jokes."

- In their proposal for *Home Before Morning: The Story of a Nurse in Vietnam,* Lynda Van Devanter and Christopher Morgan wrote that it "will be the first book to tell the story of a woman Vietnam veteran, the first book to shed light on this blind spot in our nation's vision."

- Of his book *The Mayor of Castro Street: The Life and Times of Harvey Milk,* Randy Shilts wrote that it "will chronicle the rise of both Milk and the gay movement he represented."

- In a proposal for an anthology edited by Lyn Reese, Jean Wilkinson, and Phyllis Sheen Koppelman and called *I'm on My Way Running: Women Speak on Coming of Age,* the handle was "a collection of writings in which women from different times and cultures reveal the joys and pains of coming of age."

- When he proposed *How to Speak Like a Pro,* Leon Fletcher wrote in his proposal that it "will present step-by-step, practical, platform-tested techniques and tips on how to plan and present effective speeches."

Hot Tip

Editors resist what seems self-serving. Let your idea, the supporting facts, and your writing make your case.

Why You?

Editors know that your proposal will have a bio, but seeing just a phrase that shows that you have the credentials to write your book will help give them the confidence to read on. If your job, knowledge, or experience will impress editors, use one of the following alternatives to begin your book hook:

"A sequel to the author's book, [title],"

"Based on the author's *x* years as a _____ ,"

"Based on *x* years of research,"

"Based on an article by the author [give the name of the publication, if impressive],"

"Based on *x* years as a teacher/professor of _____ [name the school or university if prestigious],"

"Based on *x* talks that the author has given to *y* people,"

Then give your title and selling handle.

If your introductory phrase, title, and selling handle are too long or don't read as well as you would like them to, add the "why-you" phrase as a sentence at the end of your selling handle: "The book will be based on . . . "

The more competition your book will face, the more important it is for your book hook to mention what your book will be the first to have. If you're writing a biography, a history, or an exposé, what your book will add to the record about your subject will determine the value of your book. So after your selling handle, list the new elements or features of your book in descending order of their news or commercial value.

Another way to show why your book will be different and better than the competition is to list, in descending order of importance, the benefits that readers will receive only from your book.

Example: A Selling Handle

Rick Crandall's subject and book hooks do an excellent job of proving the market and the timeliness of his self-published book, *Marketing Your Services: For People Who Hate to Sell*. In addition to making the point that almost 80 percent of the country's workers are in the service sector, he later pinpoints a vital source of sales: women. Rick's book hook—the first key listed below—works well, and his two other keys, as well as the two paragraphs that follow them, will also help the sales reps and his publicist:

> In a cover story this spring, *Fortune* magazine made a major change in the way they calculate their Fortune 500 list to take into account "a new economy, one much more driven by services." Tom Peters notes that 79 percent of people now work in

the service sector, and with corporate downsizing and growing entrepreneurship, the service sector will continue to expand.

Owners of service businesses have one major problem: They don't know how to market. The vast majority of them have no training in marketing. They fear rejection, and many of them feel that marketing is beneath their dignity.

Twenty years ago, "putting out a shingle" was enough to get business. Today, there's intense competition in every area. From professional services like accounting and law to trades like plumbing and construction, service providers need help.

Marketing Your Services: For People Who Hate to Sell provides three keys:

1. It is the first book to deal directly with service providers' resistance to the idea of selling their services.

2. It educates service providers who have had no training in marketing, and this is almost all of them.

3. Its marketing approach shows many ways to market that service providers can't object to, like providing better customer service, giving seminars, and writing newsletters. It does not base its marketing advice on how products are sold, which is what most books do.

The book shows service providers that there is more to marketing than selling and that they do not need to "hard sell." It gives them hundreds of examples and tools that they can use immediately in seven areas of marketing.

By the time you finish writing your proposal, you will have hooks at the beginning of your query letter, proposal, and outlines, and at the beginning and perhaps the end of your sample chapter.

Your first chapter has to hook readers to your book. In Roger Crawford's proposal in Appendix E, he has stories at the beginning and the end of his sample outline. They helped keep editors and readers turning the pages.

Once you have justified the existence of your book, editors will want to know that you have a clear vision of it. To prove that you do, tell them the length of your book.

The Length of Your Book

The second sentence of your book hook gives the length of your book:

"The manuscript will contain *x* pages, including *x* pages of back matter [if you will have back matter], *x* photographs, *x* line drawings,

x maps, and x charts [if you plan to include illustrations]." Don't count illustrations as manuscript pages. Unless you indicate otherwise, editors assume illustrations are in black and white. You will learn in chapter fifteen how to arrive at these numbers.

Nonfiction manuscripts generally run between 50,000 and 100,000 words (200 to 400 double-spaced, 250-word pages). But little gift books can be 32 pages; biographies, 1,000. Illustrated books may require less text. Follow your models, but make your manuscript not one word shorter or longer than it has to be.

The longer the manuscript, the higher the cover price, and price affects sales. Publishers shy away from projects that will be too expensive to produce or too expensive for consumers to buy. The length on which you and your editor agree will be in your contract. It's been said that no good book is ever too long, and no bad book is ever too short.

Hot Tip

Two trade-offs of short books:
- Because they will have lower cover prices, you will make less per book in royalties, which will affect the advance you receive based on potential royalties.
- Promotion budgets are usually based on projected sales. The shorter the book, and the lower the projected sales, the smaller the budget. Successful books in your field can help you decide how long to make your book.

By effectively communicating a convincing sense of herself as an authority in the field, Krista Cantrell showed a clear vision of her book and the need for it. Note how Krista implies the market for the book as she opens the proposal with a statistic that will startle editors. In the last sentence of her selling handle, she states the book's length.

In 1992, 12,600 dogs a day—4.6 million a year—were brought to humane societies across the country. The major reason: behavior problems. The owners could not find a source of information to help them solve their dogs' behavior problems.

Based on the author's twenty years of experience as a cognitive animal behaviorist, dog handler, and animal communicator, *Catch Your Dog Doing Something Right: How to Train Any Dog in Five Minutes a Day* will be the first book to demonstrate that when dogs are asked to think, problems disappear.

The manuscript will contain 257 pages, including 11 pages of back matter and 114 photos."

Hot Tip

When estimating the number of pages or the number of months it will take you to finish the manuscript (as you'll do later), don't give a range, such as 200 to 250 pages or six to nine months. Avoid the words *about*, *tentatively*, *estimated*, or *approximately*. Unless you have a finished manuscript, editors know you are guesstimating about time and length. Be specific, even though you can't be sure. This adds authority and credibility to your guesstimates.

The Importance of a Page Count

Your publisher will determine the number of pages in the printed book. What you control is the number of 250-word, double-spaced, typewritten pages on which you will write 25 lines with about 10 words on each 12-point, 60-character, 5-inch line. If you prefer, use a word count instead of a page count.

Providing editors with numbers:
- Gives them a sense of the length of your book.
- Helps them write their own proposals to buy books. To help justify the acquisition of a book, most editors have to complete a profit and loss statement or a proposal-to-publish form that includes the financial information the house needs to reach a decision.
- Shows that you've thought the project through and conveys the impression that you know what you're doing.

A finished manuscript is rarely the length guessed in a proposal. That's not as important as having a clear, realistic vision of your book that will make sense to editors. Once your book is sold to a publisher, you will be able to change it in any way you and your editor agree will improve the book.

One writer wanted to do a how-to book about writing. He had been sending potential clients a four-page how-to brochure. With new information he had gathered, he felt he could write fifteen pages of manuscript, enough for a chapter in a book he was working on.

When he revised the material, he had sixty pages of manuscript. He began working with an editor who sent suggestions. He followed them, and the manuscript grew to eighty-seven pages.

The editor then sent him nine single-spaced pages with changes. Unhappy but persistent, the writer trudged on but wound up with a

137-page manuscript. Then came the copyediting. What was the final result of what started out to be a chapter in a book? You're holding the third edition of it in your hands! The second edition was more than a hundred pages longer than the first, and this edition is more than sixty pages longer than that.

Selecting a Format for Your Book

If you want your book to be a standard-size hardcover or trade paperback or a mass-market book, you don't have to mention the format. If your book needs to be an unusual size, end the book hook by indicating how you envision it and explain why.

For example, if you are planning to use tax forms as illustrations, then an 8½″×11″ format will be best. Unless you think the format you want is imperative, present it in a way that suggests you're flexible enough to agree if the publisher thinks another format will be more economical or salable. Books larger than 8½″×11″ are expensive to produce and hard for booksellers to stock on standard shelves. Mentioning a successful competitive book in the format you want will help make your case.

One of the positive trends in the business is that publishers will produce a book in whatever format will sell the most copies, and then they will "repurpose" it in other formats if they think it will sell. A book might be a hardcover, then a mass-market paperback, and then a trade paperback. In addition to being published between covers, a book may go on to be published as an audiocassette, videocassette, CD, downloadable e-book, and whatever new formats technology makes possible. You are blessed with more ways to make money from your ideas than ever before.

❖ ❖ ❖

If you do an effective selling job with your subject hook and book hook, you will hook editors to the proposal, and they will keep reading. Up next: the special features your book may have that will make it a pleasure to read and use.

4 | Your Book's Special Features and Back Matter

The Golden Rule for Writing About Your Book's Special Features

Make your book as helpful, as visually appealing, and as pleasurable to read as you can.

The next part of your overview describes other important features your book will provide. Will the book be humorous, serious, or down-to-earth? Will it contain anecdotes? What kind of personality will it have? What themes will it develop?

If what you will illustrate is not already clear, explain it. Visual appeal is an essential element in selling the products and services people buy, so publishers want to avoid an endless chain of paragraphs, blocks of copy that aren't inviting to the eye.

Subheads are one way of breaking up copy; illustrations are another. Think about how to enhance your book's visual appeal. Sidebars, exercises, checklists, chapter summaries, copy in the margins, and boxed and screened information all are features that will add to your book's visual appeal and salability. Visual appeal is important in books intended for a wide audience, not serious books. Follow your models.

Quotations can also be used to break up text and enliven prose, but beware of "the term-paper effect." Including too many quotes can make your book read like a term paper or an annotated compilation of quotations instead of an original work.

Laughing to Learn and Earn: Using Humor in Your Book

The more you laugh, the more you learn. The more your readers laugh, the more you earn. Best-selling author Norman Cousins believed that "laughter is inner jogging."

Humor makes books more enjoyable to read, which in turn makes them sell better. If you're writing an exposé or a serious book, humor might be out of place. Otherwise, the more depressing the subject, the more the book will benefit from the addition of humor. But don't feel that you have to become the next Dave Barry to use humor in your book. Search for material in:

- quote books
- joke books
- books of anecdotes
- biographies of people in your field
- other books about your subject
- cartoon books, although you'll have to pay for permission if you use the drawing instead of just the caption
- books on popular culture
- books on writing humor
- comedy clubs
- comedy CDs
- books by humor writers

Three other ways to obtain humor:

- Google it: Key in the word *humor* on Google, and you will find more than 12,000,000 links!
- Watch Comedy Central.
- If money is no object, hire a comedy writer to create material for your book. Where there's a wit, there's a way.

Hot Tip

When you see, hear, or read something funny, make use of it. Here are four ways:

1. Use it as is.

2. If it's not about your subject, build a verbal bridge between it and your subject to make it relevant. In my book on agents, I told the story of a man named George Bosque who robbed Brinks of a million dollars, spent it in a year and a half, and turned himself in. When the police asked how he managed to spend a million dollars in a year and a half, he replied: "Well, I spent half of it on gambling, drink, and romance, and I guess I squandered the rest."

> That has nothing to do with publishing, right? I tied the two together by saying that if publishers think they're getting the next Tom Clancy or Danielle Steel, they'll bet a bundle in the best-seller sweepstakes.
>
> 3. Change it any way you want so it is relevant. "Want to know how to make a small fortune? Start with a large fortune and write full-time." I first heard this when my partner, Elizabeth, and I were writing books about Victorian houses that need a lot of attention. There the punch line was "Start with a large fortune and buy a Victorian."
>
> 4. Use it as a springboard for creating new humor. Develop an instinct for comedy by looking for the funny aspects of everything you experience. This is a skill that will help you weather hard times as well as write successful books.

If you want to use humor, anecdotes, or other special features, include them consistently throughout the book. Decide on the number of jokes or anecdotes you would like in a chapter and how best to integrate them. Use humor, drama, compelling insights, or inspirational writing to move your readers and make your book as enjoyable as it is informative.

The punch line: The best and only hope most books have for being successful is word of mouth. The funnier a book is, regardless of who writes or publishes it or how well it's promoted, the better the word of mouth it will generate. In most cases, it's as impossible to make a book too funny as it is to prevent the success of one that is funny enough. As a bonus, the effective combination of humor and content will also lead to your success on the speaking circuit. And speaking enables you to test-market your humor.

Benefits for Readers, Royalties for You

Including a list of your book's benefits after describing its special features will help prove why your book is needed. Listing benefits makes sense for a how-to book, but it's not necessary for a biography or a picture book.

In their proposal for *Guerrilla Trade Show Selling*, Jay Conrad Levinson, Mark S.A. Smith, and Orvel Ray Wilson listed their book's benefits:

> *Guerrilla Trade Show Selling* will:
> - Enable readers to avoid image-damaging, business-killing show behavior. Some companies will be better off if they don't participate in trade shows.

- Give readers control over their trade show sales results, leaving little to chance. Include ideas to salvage shows with poor exhibit placement, wrong show selection, missing exhibits, and seven other problem situations.
- Enable small companies to compete with larger, well-established competitors. Large competitors often don't prepare their exhibit sales staff properly. A small, well-trained exhibit staff will beat a large, unprepared staff every time.
- Maximize readers' trade show investment. They won't waste their marketing budgets. The investment in this book will be repaid thousands of times over.
- Save time, money, and energy in creating in-house training programs or researching the scattered information on trade show selling. This will eliminate the need to hire sales trainers—perhaps inexperienced at trade show selling—or expensive consultants.

Example: Promoting a Book's Special Features

Communication and information are entertainment, and if you don't understand that, you're not going to communicate.

—John Naisbitt, best-selling author of the Megatrends series

At the beginning of his proposal, Wayne Lee was specific about his book because he had already self-published it. Being as specific as you can about what your book will be, even if it is not yet written, will help convince an editor of your confidence and authority.

Twenty-five years after an enthralled nation watched Neil Armstrong plant the American flag on the moon in July 1969, national interest in space flight remains strong. A survey conducted by Rockwell International shows that an overwhelming 88 percent of the American public continues to support funding for the space shuttle program and considers space exploration an important part of America's future.

The immense media coverage of the summer of the *Apollo* anniversary, the Shoemaker-Levy Comet collision with Jupiter, and continuing shuttle flights further demonstrate the public's interest in space.

To Rise From Earth: An Easy-to-Understand Guide to Space

Flight, written by NASA space flight engineer Wayne Lee, offers a look at space exploration. The 324-page book is the first to describe in plain English the inner workings of space flight and exploration.

Readers will find chapters about rockets, orbits, space maneuvers, the race to the moon, the space shuttle, the role of satellites in our daily lives, and interplanetary flight with robotic spacecraft.

The book ends with an exciting chapter that describes the methods NASA will use to send astronauts to Mars early in the twenty-first century. *To Rise* also offers more than theoretical concepts. For example, the book includes articles about the history of space flight, the *Challenger* accident, the Hubble Space Telescope repair mission, and flying missions on a tight budget.

The author designed the book with a visually appealing layout and included sixty-five pages of drawings he created using computer-aided design tools. Each illustration is self-contained and tells the story of the concept it presents. *To Rise* also contains 147 photographs from NASA operations and space missions. This presentation style of no math and many visuals will appeal to readers of all ages eager to learn with as little effort as possible.

Striving for Your Best Work

Sending anything less than your best work may increase the time it takes to interest an agent and sell the book. Like book buyers, editors are looking for solutions, not problems. The further your proposal is from being 100 percent—as well-conceived and crafted as you can make it—the less enthusiasm editors will have for it, and even if they buy it, the less they will pay for it.

Your agent may be forced to sell the book to a less-than-ideal editor and publisher. You may have to settle for thousands of dollars less in your advance and less commitment from your publisher. A deal is usually destiny. How publishers buy a book usually determines how they publish it, and a small initial sale usually lowers the prices paid for subsidiary rights and the next book.

Trust your instincts and reliable readers to know when your proposal is as good as you can make it. Then, and not a moment sooner, it's time to see if you are right.

You may want to give your book a superstructure by dividing it into several parts. Dividing a book into parts will help assure you that the different elements of your book fit together harmoniously. It adds to the impression that you have thought your book through well enough to give it a balanced structure.

Hot Tip | Speed is the enemy of quality. If you let yourself get caught in a speed trap, you may doom your proposal. Doing your proposal right is far more important than doing it fast. Don't send drafts, don't send the proposal in pieces, and don't submit your work before it's ready. Editors can tell when writers are more anxious to sell their books than to write them, a sin punishable by a speedy rejection.

You will have two opportunities to present the parts of your book:
- If it will help readers understand your book, describe with separate sentences what each part of your book will cover. Be brief to avoid repeating the outline.
- For most books, including the parts of your book in the list of chapters at the beginning of your outline will suffice. This is how the authors of the sample proposals in Appendix E showed the structure of their books.

A biography is usually structured chronologically. A how-to book starts with the simplest elements of a skill and leads readers to the advanced aspects of it. If the structure of your book isn't apparent from the nature of the project or how you have described it, tell readers about the structure of the book in a sentence. If you are proposing a picture book, describe the balance between text and illustrations.

Back Matter

In a *New Yorker* cartoon, a patient is on an operating table and a nurse is standing over him saying: "They're going to have to take you back to surgery, Professor. Dr. Bickel got confused and removed your glossary instead of your appendix."

The last thing to mention about the contents of your book is what comes last: the back matter. If books like yours don't have back matter, skip it, and go on to the next part of the overview.

If you will have back matter, list it in the order it will appear:
- Resource directory (including books, periodicals, organizations, events, Web sites, etc.)
- Appendix (one or more)
- Footnotes
- Glossary

Avoiding Technical and Legal Problems

This part of the overview is only for writers whose books deal with specialized subjects or may spark litigation. If your book will not present technical or legal challenges, say nothing about these. Skip this part of the overview, and go on to the next.

If evaluating your proposal requires a particular expertise, an editor will have a specialist review it. Unless you have absolute confidence in the material, find your own expert to read it first. If you do, indicate who that expert is.

Publishers receive threats of lawsuits that, more often than not, are settled without litigation. Nonetheless, they are wary of books with the potential to provoke a suit that may cost more than $100,000 before going to trial. Even if authors are innocent, the costs may be charged against their books, and a suit can stop a book dead in its tracks.

Among the potential sources of lawsuits:

- Making libelous statements
- Revealing information told in confidence without disguising the source
- Using copyrighted material without required permission
- Revealing government secrets
- Including instructions that can harm readers

There's a Mexican curse that says, "May your life be filled with lawyers." Avoid becoming a victim of this curse. If you suspect a potential legal problem, have an intellectual property attorney check the proposal and its supporting documents so you can assure editors that you have addressed the legal issue.

You can obtain the name of an attorney from the National Writer's Union and the Author's Guild.

- Bibliography
- Index

Estimate the number of double-spaced pages each part of your back matter will run, except for the index. Use comparable books as a guide. As noted in chapter three, you should mention in your book hook the total number of back matter pages you will have in your manuscript. Librarians like back matter because it adds to a book's value as a research tool. Publishers like to please librarians because school, college, and public libraries are major customers.

> ### The Golden Rule for Including Back Matter in Your Book
> Use back matter to make your book as useful to your readers as you can.

Writers can usually list in one sentence all of their back matter. However, if you need to describe your book's appendices, use a separate page at the end of the outline to supplement your mention of them in the overview.

The back of your book can also include any of the following: a one-page bio, a description of your products or services, a request for feedback from readers, and your contact information. You don't have to mention your bio, but when it's time to write it, use it to help consummate a working marriage between you and your readers. List as many reasons as you can to attract visitors to your Web site. Promising updates to your book will help.

Hot Tip

Two quick tips:

- Offer to put your back matter on your Web site. Your publisher may prefer this because it will shorten the book and lower its cover price.
- Avoid footnotes in your proposal. They are distracting and will make your proposal (and your book) look academic. If your book will have footnotes, make them blind footnotes, divided by chapter, that readers can find at the end of your book. If you use them in your sample chapter, include them at the end of the proposal. Avoid asterisks, which also interrupt the flow of the text.

❖ ❖ ❖

Keep in mind the distinction between special features and benefits: Features are contained in your book; benefits are what your features do for your readers. Features create benefits, and benefits will keep readers coming back to your books.

5 | Your All-Star Foreword and Cover Quotes

When you buy a nonfiction book, you want the author to be an authority on the subject, to have enough experience in the field and as a writer to write the book. As an author, you become an expert. How do you acquire authority before you write your first book? Here are three ways to gain the status of being an expert:

- **Establish yourself as an expert.** Get a degree, work in the field, or give talks, and write articles about the subject.
- **Collaborate with an expert.** Finding an authority on a subject or a professional who wants to write a book can be an easy way to break into publishing. Choose a person who is promotable and with whom you will enjoy a happy working marriage. Rosalynn Carter admitted that the closest she and Jimmy ever got to divorce was when they collaborated on a book.
- **Find experts to write a foreword and give cover quotes.** Though the least effective, this is the easiest and most common way to gain authority. Ideally, the foreword should come from someone whose name will give your book credibility and salability with book buyers around the country where your book is published.

Because Elizabeth and I know science fiction star Ray Bradbury from the Santa Barbara Writers Conference, we were able to get him to write a foreword for Stan Augarten's *State of the Art: A Photographic History of the Integrated Circuit*. Like the rest of Ray's writing, his foreword was poetic, passionate, and visionary—and at a dollar a word, it was light-years away from the penny-a-word stories Ray used to write for science fiction magazines. The irony is that Ray is not a fan of computers. When he signed a guest book at the Los Angeles Public Library after Bill Gates had spoken there, Ray added: "I don't do Windows!"

According to speaker and author Sam Horn, best-selling authors receive between fifty and one hundred requests a week to read manuscripts. That's another reason to start cultivating relationships with opinion makers in your field.

The less qualified you are to write your book, the more you need experts to vouch for you. If you want to write a book about health, psychology, or some other subject that requires an academic imprimatur and you don't have an M.D. or a Ph.D., find someone who does to give your book that professional seal of approval, and mention it in your proposal. In this case, the person doesn't have to be widely known.

The Fortunate 500

If the expert you find is not well known, give his or her credentials, and indicate how long the foreword will be—five hundred words will do. An expert's name can have value either because book buyers know it or because the person is affiliated with a well-known business or institution. If the expert you find is not well known, state her credentials. The CEO of a Fortune 500 company, a professor at Harvard, or a member of the cabinet will give a book instant credibility.

The time to approach opinion makers for a foreword and quotes is after you've written your proposal and received feedback from your network but before you share it with agents or editors. Your proposal must prove to the opinion maker that you both will benefit from the endorsement.

The two reasons to ask someone to do a foreword are equally important. First, the person's stature in the field should lend authority to you and your book. Second, the person's fame should help convince browsers who see the name on the jacket to buy the book. If book buyers notice endorsements by people or institutions they know, that will lessen their sense of risk in buying a book by someone whose name they don't know.

People usually write quotes and forewords after they have read the manuscript. If the person feels strongly enough about the project or you, he may do the foreword in exchange for just the publicity and an autographed copy of your book. On the other hand, a well-known authority may ask for and deserve a dollar or more per word.

Your editor may think a foreword isn't necessary or may have a better suggestion for who should write it. The editor may be able to obtain a foreword from someone the house already publishes, which might save you money. The trade-off is that industry insiders and knowledgeable book buyers will know it's an inside job, so the quote will carry less weight.

Finding the "Write" Names

You know you need endorsements from instantly recognizable names. How do you decide who might help you? How do you approach such people? Your first step should be to contact your networks; they can help you make a list of likely prospects. Then you face three challenges:

1. The more well-known people are, the more besieged they are with such requests.
2. They may not be receptive if you contact them without a referral from someone they know.
3. They may prefer to wait until you have a publisher or a manuscript before they will commit to giving you a quote.

Commitments for a foreword and quotes from key people in your field will be valuable ammunition. The most valuable people are those who don't usually give quotes. Use your proposal to obtain quotes before you submit it to agents or editors. In your cover letters to authorities, state that you would appreciate any suggestions they have regarding editors, publishers, and other opinion makers you can contact for quotes.

Once you decide to write your book, meet likely prospects at events or write to them to praise their work. You can write to authors in care of their publishers. Publishers send authors' mail to the authors' agents, so you also may find an agent. Assume that anyone you want a quote from has an e-mail address, if not a Web site, so make Google eyes at them. If you find something by them worth quoting, mention that you will be quoting them in your book. Include a postcard marked so they can check off whether they will look at your proposal or manuscript. Be creative and resourceful in meeting this challenge. For example, if you are writing about the environment, ask Robert Redford as well as the head of the Sierra Club for a quote or foreword.

If you cannot approach prospects with your proposal, list the ones whom you will approach after your manuscript is finished or accepted. If they're not well known, identify the people you will contact and list them in descending order of their value to your book. This indicates that you at least know the people to ask.

Hot Tip | If your book will provoke controversy or present a new take on a subject and you do not have enough credibility in your field to overcome the disbelief of skeptics, getting quotes that support your book will be even more important. Publishers are wary of writers who want to go out on a literary limb without the safety net of authorities in their fields. Also look outside your circle of support for quotes; those from people opposed to your thesis will carry extra weight. If, for example, William Buckley endorses a book by a liberal author, the quote will carry extra weight.

Example: Name-Dropping

When we sold Rick Crandall's self-published book, *Marketing Your Services: For People Who Hate to Sell*, editors were impressed with the names he had on the cover of his book as well as the sheer quantity of testimonials he had collected for it. Here's what Rick's proposal said about the testimonials. (Note also the money-back guarantee, the author's way of expressing confidence in his work.)

> The three stars featured on the cover—Harvey Mackay, Ken Blanchard, and Tom Peters—will impress buyers in stores. They are three of the biggest names in business books. The colors and size of the book were chosen so that it stands out on the shelf. And the 100 percent money-back guarantee is unusual, encouraging browsers to buy.
>
> The book also has strong testimonials from Jay Conrad Levinson, the biggest selling marketing author (the Guerrilla Marketing series), and Don Peppers, the hottest name in high-tech marketing (*The One to One Future: Building Relationships One Customer at a Time*).
>
> The book opens with twenty-four different testimonials from service providers, in alphabetical order, from accounting, advertising, and architecture to stock brokerage, surveying, and window

washing. Following these are fifteen more testimonials from experts. More comments are coming in all the time, so a new edition will have even stronger testimonials.

❖ ❖ ❖

You have hooked agents and editors on the concept of your book. Your next challenge is to get them excited about all the lucky consumers who are waiting to rush into their nearest bookstore to help you live in the style to which you would like to become accustomed.

6 | The Markets for Your Book

Zeroing In on Your Readers

A book has two kinds of markets: readers who buy it and businesses that sell it. After you describe your book, tell editors who will buy it and where. Starting with the largest group of potential readers, describe the buyers for your book. You can present your book's readership with data such as:

- age
- gender
- income; "upmarket" (*The Truffle Sniffer's Cookbook*) or "down-market" (*473 Ways to Use Spam to Stuff a Turkey*)
- occupation, including the number of professionals in the field
- interest in hobbies, sports, or other leisure activities
- marital status
- location
- education
- religious or other beliefs
- memberships in organizations
- statistics on sales of related books, magazines, services, or merchandise

- the growing awareness of your subject because of television, films, advertising, the news, or electronic media (Include supporting articles with your proposal and underline key passages.)
- the number of people who have the problem your book addresses
- attendance at events
- the number of links the subject has on Google

Use round, up-to-date figures verifying that your book's regional, national, or special interest audience is large enough to justify publishing it. Keep the sources for your numbers handy in case editors ask for them.

Your reference librarian can point you to the best sources for the figures you need. You may also be able to find the numbers you need online. How can you suggest a large number of potential readers when you can't provide numbers? One way is to write that your book will appeal to readers "personally or professionally interested in [your subject matter]."

Women buy—for themselves and others—78 percent of books sold, so a book that caters to them has a head start. If it's not clear to you what kinds of consumers buy the type of book you are writing, ask a bookseller, a librarian, or other members of your networks.

Including a statistic in your subject hook will give editors a sense of the market for your book. For instance, in the subject hook quoted earlier for *Claiming Your Share*, Michelle Saadi mentions that eighteen million auto accidents occur each year. She discusses that number in her section on markets.

Figures lend credibility and authority to your assertions, but you may not need them. This may be the case if you refer to a large enough number of groups of potential readers or if there are obviously enough book buyers in the groups to assure a market for your book.

This is what William Paxson wrote about markets in his proposal for *Write It Now: A Time-Saving Guide to Writing Better Letters, Memos, Reports and More*:

> The market for this book consists of everyone in business, government, and nonprofit organizations who writes daily, or who is self-employed.

Since editors like to jump on bandwagons, mention a pattern of growth if there is one in the numbers you present. For instance, if your book will be about DVDs, the statistics on the growing number of consumers who are buying them will give editors ammunition for buying your book.

Example: Your Book's Markets

Ted Allrich described the markets for a book that was finally called *The Online Investor: How to Find the Best Stocks Using Your Computer* like this:

> *Win Big: Think Small* will give everyone with a personal computer a compelling financial incentive to go online. It can be sold in bookstores, computer stores, software stores, mail-order catalogs, individual investor newsletters, book and computer clubs.
>
> Owners of personal computers, estimated at more than 100 million worldwide, constitute an educated and prosperous market. They constantly seek to maximize use of their computers, particularly to earn money. They are also likely to have the financial means and intellectual curiosity for investing.
>
> Combine PC users with 51 million individual investors, 84,000 stockbrokers, 17,500 money managers and my immediate family, and the numbers indicate how huge the potential market for this book is. Even discount brokers like Schwab, Fidelity, and Quick and Reilly may purchase it as a premium to attract new accounts.

Because of the book, Ted has a site on America Online called *The Online Investor.*

If you plan to approach niche publishers that specialize in a subject such as computer books or travel books, you don't need to include market information. If your aim is a large publishing house, market information will be an important part of your proposal. While editors at large houses know about the markets for their specialties, the other people whose support they need, such as sales and marketing directors, may not. And publishers want to know that you can accurately assess the markets for your book.

Example: Mentioning Television in Your Markets

Television, a major source of competition for readers' time, provided strong ammunition for Dennis Hauck's self-published book which Penguin bought and called *Haunted Houses: The National Directory: Ghostly Abodes, Sacred Sites, UFO Landings and Other Supernatural Locations:*

Surveys show that tens of millions of Americans believe in ESP, reincarnation, encounters with angels and similar ideas once thought to be the sole province of "New Agers." One out of every four of us believes ghosts exist, and more than twenty million Americans believe they have seen a ghost. Never before have so many Americans believed in the paranormal. More than half of Americans from eighteen to thirty-five believe that UFOs are real.

According to *TV Guide*, "Television's hottest trend is reality-based programming targeting unreality." Dozens of new series and specials on everything from angels to UFOs have premiered in the last year. "TV is both a shaper and a reflector," noted Dr. Will Miller, host of NBC's *The Other Side*, "but first it reflects. The motivation is to respond to cultural trends."

But the recent wave of TV shows, movies and books devoted to paranormal phenomena are actually part of a larger trend incorporating alternate realities, a realm media analysts call *hyper-reality*.

The National Directory of Haunted Places is a travel guide to the realm of supernatural experience. It will appeal to general readers, leisure travelers, New Age enthusiasts and serious researchers. Because the book is a national directory with a bibliography, there is strong potential for large sales from the $1.5 billion library market that is always looking for quality reference books in this area.

The book also has a built-in market, since most of the 2,000 hotels, inns, campgrounds and other establishments mentioned in the book will want their own copies. Nearly a third of the entries are tourist centers with their own gift shops that will want to stock the book. Since the scope of the book is nationwide, there will be opportunities in every state for free publicity and promotions.

In addition, there are more than six hundred organizations devoted to the study of the phenomena described in these pages. There is no single database, paper or electronic, that provides them with the scope and wealth of information offered in this work. Most of these organizations have journals with book review sections and mailing lists. The organizational, individual and library sales of this book will provide a continuing market for updated editions.

Going Through Sales Channels

Four market channels—ways for your book to reach your readers—are:
- bookstores and other consumer outlets
- schools
- libraries
- special sales

Let's take a look at each:

Bookstores and Other Consumer Outlets

Trade paperbacks and hardcover books are sold through bookstores and other consumer outlets. Bookstores, drugstores, airports, and supermarkets are among the fifty thousand outlets that sell mass-market books.

If your book will have crossover potential—the potential to sell on more than one shelf in a bookstore by appealing to more than one group of consumers—mention that. On the back of trade paperback covers you will see the shelves where publishers recommend books be stocked. Here are three examples:
- *Guerrilla Marketing Online: The Entrepreneur's Guide to Earning Profits on the Internet*: Business/Computers
- *Lost Star: The Search for Amelia Earhart*: Biography/History
- *The Sierra Club Guide to Safe Drinking Water*: Health/Environment

Other consumer outlets include:
- stores other than bookstores
- online booksellers
- television shopping channels, such as QVC
- warehouse clubs
- conventions

Chicken Soup for the Sale

One of the ways that have enabled Jack Canfield and Mark Victor Hansen to sell more than eighty million books is bypass marketing: getting stores other than bookstores to sell their books. Beauty parlors, gas stations, and other outlets that don't sell books do sell the Chicken Soup books. It's a win-win deal: The stores profit and so do the authors.

In your proposal, list specialty stores such as music, sporting goods, hardware, stationery, or gourmet cooking stores that sell similar books. Check with stores to see if they can sell your book. If they can, ask them how many such stores there are in the country and how they buy their books. You may not find a large selection of books in specialty stores, but if your book has that potential, use the information.

Say you want to write a book called *Snore Your Way to Total Fitness: 101 Exercises You Can Do While You Sleep*. Mentioning in your proposal that fitness centers will sell your book is gravy, not the meat of your push for your book. Assume that publishers don't sell books to fitness centers and don't know how to do so. Give this tidbit value by explaining how *you* will sell to the fitness centers. Find out if whoever sells to fitness centers will carry your book. If you can, make the sale in advance by telling the publisher how it can be done.

Example: Markets for a Self-Published Book

Wayne Lee test-marketed his self-published book on outer space, so he was able to draw a well-defined portrait of the markets for his book:

> To gauge the market potential of *To Rise From Earth*, a test was conducted under the sponsorship of the Texas Space Grant Consortium, a nonprofit institution of thirty-one corporations and universities that promotes space education and research. This test involved printing one thousand copies of the book and offering them for sale to individuals and organizations.
>
> Through word of mouth alone, all of the copies sold in five months. Customers included:
> - many individuals without backgrounds in science
> - parents looking for gifts for their children
> - sponsors of summer space-education programs for high school and college students, university and high school classes
> - science museum gift shops around the country, including the National Air and Space Museum in Washington, DC
>
> A list of organizations that purchased the book is included with this proposal. The material on how space flight works and the history of space exploration will never be dated. This will help make the book appealing to high school, university, and public libraries.
>
> Museum gift shops represent another market for *To Rise*. More than three million tourists a year pass through the visitors' center gates at the NASA Kennedy Space Center in Florida and the NASA Johnson Space Center in Houston, Texas.
>
> The Association of Science and Technology Centers also re-

ports that more than five million people visit the nation's one hundred major science museums every year, all of which have gift shops.

The book has been used in programs for high school students such as Lift-Off and Spaceship Earth in Texas and the NASA Space Life Sciences Training Program in Florida. The United States Space Academy, popularly known as Space Camp, has expressed an interest in providing the book to its one thousand students a year.

Course Adoptions

If your book will have adoption potential in schools or other institutions, identify the courses and academic levels for which it will be suitable. To make this market valuable instead of just an idea that may or may not come to pass, name the professors and their schools— ideally, both well known—who will adopt your book and the courses they will use it for—the more courses, the better.

Libraries

School, college, public, and corporate libraries are collectively a large potential market for books. If your book will have special appeal to any of these libraries, double-check this with librarians and mention it in your proposal.

Special Sales

Special sales are bulk and premium sales to corporations or institutions that buy large quantities of books for internal use or to give away or sell. A savings and loan in our neighborhood once gave away a series of Bantam's ethnic cookbooks over a period of time to encourage prospective savers to start accounts. A corporation might buy copies of a book on business writing for its employees. This kind of sale is more likely with a mass-market book than a more expensive trade paperback, more likely with a paperback than a hardcover, and more likely still when a company can see the successful book.

Noting what kinds of companies use books and discussing this possibility with friends who know marketing will help you decide if your book can generate special sales. Only a tiny percentage of books are used this way, so don't spend much time investigating it unless you can deliver a sale yourself. Major publishers have special sales departments, and if a business buys enough books, publishers customize the cover and text to suit the buyer's needs.

Example: Closing in on Niche Markets

For *Making Videos for Money: Planning and Producing Information Videos, Commercials and Infomercials*, Barry Hampe cited the increasing number of video makers and other markets that added to his credibility as an authority on the subject:

> The primary market for the book will be the new wave of video makers, both professionals and newcomers to the field who need help. Making information videos, commercials and infomercials will be bread and butter for virtually all video makers.
>
> This market includes:
> - professional production people who face the need to expand their skills into new areas and recognize the need for resource information
> - professionally trained camera operators who need to structure a video production.
> - writers who face the need to write the script for an information video, an infomercial, or a television commercial
> - newcomers to the field or trained professionals who want to make video productions and don't know how
> - colleges, libraries, and professors who adopt the book
> - video equipment and supply stores
> - readers who have discovered the author's previous two books on writing and producing video

❖ ❖ ❖

Proving that the frontlist and backlist markets for your book are large enough to justify publishing it is essential to selling your proposal. The larger the markets for your book, the more eager publishers will be to buy it. The next chapter, on subsidiary rights and spin-offs, will show you how to keep checks heading in your direction.

7 | Your Book's Subsidiary Rights and Spin-offs

One reason why now is the best time to be a writer is that there are more ways than ever to make money from your ideas. Every book has primary and subsidiary rights. Publishers acquire the primary rights to a book and as many subsidiary rights as they can. Subsidiary rights can make the difference between profit and loss on a book, so publishers are increasingly eager to protect their investments by retaining as many rights as they can. Agents, on the other hand, want to enable their clients to keep as many subsidiary rights as they can.

The following list will show you why your book may generate income long after publication.

Primary Rights

Publishers expect to acquire a book's primary rights, enabling them to sell the book as is or in adapted and condensed form. These rights include:

- Publishing and selling the book in hardcover, trade paperback, and/or as a mass-market paperback
- Selling permission to excerpt part of a book within another work
- Book club rights

- Second-serial rights to excerpt the book or condense it or serialize the whole book in a periodical after publication
- Reproducing the text in a large-type and a royalty-free Braille edition
- Reproducing the text in other forms and media, such as microfilm and microfiche
- Publishing and selling the book in unbound sheets, outside the United States, for example
- Selling school editions of the book, adapting it as needed
- Photocopying rights to all or part of the book for internal use by a school or business
- Selling the book through direct-response marketing channels such as direct mail, television ads, and infomercials
- Selling the book as a premium to businesses or nonprofits as a promotional tool
- Selling the book in bulk quantities to customers outside of the book industry
- Granting the right to use part of the text to promote the book for example, in a review

American Association of Publishers President Pat Schroeder has observed that we create technology faster than we can create a business model for selling it. This explains the turmoil in the music business created by rock fans downloading music for free, a fear that also has movie people scrambling to protect their work. Bill Gates has predicted that the pace of change will accelerate six and half times in this decade, so the problem of ensuring that consumers pay for creative work will not disappear soon.

Electronic rights to books have created a tug of war between agents and publishers. Such rights allow the text of a book, as is, to be published online; made available through an electronic database using print-on-demand technology; or handled through other electronic storage, retrieval, and output systems. Agents and publishers are struggling to establish a model for who should own these rights and how authors should be compensated for them.

Subsidiary Rights

Subsidiary rights are all other rights, including:

- First-serial rights to excerpt the book before publication
- British and translation rights
- Rights to produce abridged, unabridged, and dramatized audio

and video versions of the book

- Performance rights for feature films, television movies, videocassettes, plays, and radio broadcasts
- Merchandising rights for items such as T-shirts, coffee mugs, note cards, toys, and calendars
- Electronic rights, for items including text-based software and multimedia CDs, that involve changing or adapting the text and using other material, such as illustrations

Mentioning your book's potential subsidiary rights will add to an editor's interest in buying your book. If you hire an agent, your agent will try to retain as many subsidiary rights as possible for you. These usually include at least performance and merchandising rights.

Fiction has a greater likelihood of generating merchandising rights. But the likelihood of selling merchandising rights to any book approximates that of getting on *Oprah*. So listing them won't sound realistic. It will have the negative effect of making it seem that you are reaching for the stars instead of proving that you have a clear vision of your book's potential.

Two exceptions:

- If you are talking to enough people a year to warrant doing cups or caps yourself to sell at your presentations, mention what you will produce.
- The six painted ladies books never hit the best-seller list, but after they had sold hundreds of thousands of copies over a fifteen-year period, we were able to sell the rights to produce calendars, note cards, and puzzles. So the steady sale of enough books over enough time may make merchandising rights a reality for your book.

Only bestsellers and successful series with recognizable graphic elements that lend themselves to translation into other forms and media generate merchandising rights. Children's book agent Andrea Brown has found that merchandising can be especially lucrative for children's books. And the Chicken Soup books have licensed twenty-nine products. But one hundred companies made one thousand products to tie in with the movie version of Michael Crichton's *Jurassic Park*, and they sold more than one billion dollars' worth of them. Do we dare estimate the number of products that will over time be generated by Harry Potter if J.K. Rowling said yes to all comers? And why, pray tell, isn't there a Hogwarts Amusement Park where kids in costumes get in free?

Translation rights are more likely to be exercised, and there are more countries than are buying translation rights. Reading the Hot Deals column in *Publishers Weekly* and logging onto www.publishers marketplace.com will help you keep track of who's selling what to whom and for how much.

Know Your Book's Potential

Because you have more opportunities to profit from your ideas than ever, when you're thinking about what to write, take into consideration a book's potential for subsidiary rights. They may be the key that unlocks your book's success.

A first-time novelist once came to us with a humorous novel about a dying multimillionairess who lives in a penthouse. To go on living, she hires an Indian guru who, at the moment she dies, is going to transfer her soul into the body of her beautiful young nurse.

But, the guru slips, and the vessel containing the soul of the multimillionairess falls out of her penthouse into the body of a drunken bum in the alley below. I immediately envisioned Katharine Hepburn and Lee Marvin for the movie. However, the first producer to see it bought it and turned it into a hilarious movie called *All of Me*, starring Steve Martin and Lily Tomlin. Humorous novels by unknown writers are tough to sell, so we were never able to sell the book rights. The only money the author made on the book was from the movie.

Spin-Offs

Editors and agents don't want literary one-night stands. They want to discover writers, not just books. Writers who turn out a book a year, each book better and more profitable than the last, are the foundation of successful publishers and agents. If your books become best-sellers, you will be one of your publisher's most prized authors, a "repeater" who produces at least one best-seller a year.

Look at your ideas with the broadest perspective. If your book has the potential to be a series, it will make you and your book more important to your publisher. While unusual for first-time authors, you may even be on your way to a multibook deal, which will increase the house's commitment to you and your book.

Books often lend themselves to other books on the same subject or with the same structure. If you can develop your book into such a series, begin the spin-off section of your proposal with this statement: "[Your book's title] will be the first in a series of *x* books including A, B, and C." Don't overwhelm publishers with the scope of your idea; list up to about six books, starting with the most commercial idea. (I've been trying to sell a series of books about each day of the year, but I haven't found anybody who wants to commit to publishing 366 books.)

Will your book lend itself to sequels? It depends on how you answer the following questions:

- If you're writing a book for men, are variations for women, children, or young adults possible? (Writing for children is an art unto itself, but your agent or publisher may be able to find a collaborator if you need one.)
- If it's an introductory book, can you write additional books for intermediate and advanced levels?
- If your book is directed at corporate types, would it also be useful to entrepreneurs and nonprofit groups? Would it help people with their private lives?
- If you're planning a book that can be adopted for a college course, can you write other versions that can be used in elementary school, high school, graduate school, English-as-a-second-language classes, or the burgeoning field of continuing education?

Hot Tip
One way to help create a two-book deal is to make the last page of your proposal a one-page, single-spaced proposal for your next book. Give the book title and a list of chapter titles with a one-line description of each. At the bottom of the page, give the length of the book and how long it will take you to finish it. You may find a publisher who wants to start with your second book.

A series of books is enticing, but a publisher may hesitate to commit to more than one book—especially by a writer without a track record—unless the series promises to be a surefire success. The publisher may prefer to wait to see a complete manuscript or see how the first book fares before committing to the next one.

Nonetheless, if your idea lends itself to being extended into other books, mention them even if you don't want to write them. They will help justify publishing your book. If your first book is successful enough, you may change your mind and decide to write the spin-off books or work with a collaborator.

You will have many opportunities to generate ideas and copy for future books. You can use the last page of the book to ask for readers' reactions or experiences. You can also ask for feedback at your Web site and when you give talks and interviews. Fans will be eager to share their responses to your book and give you ideas for your next one.

Hot Tip

You may be able to expand a chapter of your book into another book. In *Guerrilla Marketing Attack*, Jay Levinson wrote a chapter containing a hundred marketing weapons and a two-line description of each one. For *Guerrilla Marketing Weapons*, he wrote two *pages* about each one. Once you finish your outline, ask yourself if any chapters are overviews of other books. This will increase the salability of your book.

❖ ❖ ❖

Establishing your expertise and how you will continue to use it in future books will help make editors eager to help you start or continue your career. The next chapter covers two new optional sections for your proposal that will make editors believe the promotion plan that follows them.

8 | Your Mission Statement and Platform

This edition of this book introduces two new *optional* overview sections
that can help you sell your book: a Mission Statement and the Author's
Platform. They lay the groundwork for the promotion plan that follows
and will help ensure that your proposal excites editors.

Overcoming the Power of No: Your Mission Statement

Publishing is driven by five Ps: pride, passion, profit, platform, and
promotion. Publishers want books they can be proud of. They also
yearn to be passionate about every book they publish, a luxury only
small houses can afford. The large and medium-sized publishers who
are independent or are part of the New York conglomerates need
nonfiction authors who already have a national platform, a word im-
ported from the speaking profession. Although a platform can be continuing national visibility in the media, it usually refers to authors who
make their living giving talks around the country. For most books,
what it takes for large publishers to turn a profit is an effective promotion campaign with an author who has a platform.

Money doesn't rule publishing; passion does. Author John Barth
once said, "My feeling about technique in art is that it has about the

same value as technique in lovemaking. Heartfelt ineptitude has its appeal and so does heartless skill, but what you want is passionate virtuosity." It's passion that seduces publishers into gambling millions on a book either because they love it, they think it's a gold mine, or both. Try to arouse such passion in all of the links in the book chain between you and your readers.

Ideally everyone involved with your book will be as passionate about it as you are. Passion is contagious, but it starts with you. Expressing your enthusiasm and commitment to your book will affect how agents and editors respond to it. Your idea, style, and promotion plan have to excite them, but your passion for your book has to inspire them to do their best to help make your book succeed and inspire the next link in the publishing chain.

Writing, researching, and promoting your books will take so much time, energy, and commitment that, for most books, your passion for doing it will be essential to your success. If you feel a sense of mission about your book, write one first-person paragraph about it.

The Chains That Bind

The most powerful book chain in the world is invisible: It's all of the people who come between writers and readers. The outline of the publishing process below will give you a sense of how complex and collaborative an enterprise publishing your book will be. At a major house, more than a hundred gatekeepers will come between you and your readers.

If you want to be published by a large or medium-sized New York house, it will usually take a year and a half to two years for your book to go from an idea in your head to a book on bookstore shelves. If your book is a hardcover, it will go through the publishing process again for the trade or mass-market edition or both and still more times if you revise it.

Jay Conrad Levinson believes that when people buy a copy of your book, they start a path on a straight line or a circle. If they don't read it or don't like it, they're on a straight line out of your life. If they do like it, they're at the start of an endless circle. Your fans will buy your other books and the products they generate, visit your Web site, come to your events, and become "sales reps" when they tell their networks about you and your work. Enlist enough of these angels and your future is assured.

On the following pages, the activities in the publishing process are listed in chronological order. At the end of it, you write another pro-

The Publishing Process

You write your proposal.

↓

You or your agent sells your proposal.

↓

Your editor likes it enough to
make a proposal to buy it.

↓

An editor in chief or the editorial board decides
whether to buy it and for how much.

↓

You write your book.

↓

Your editor edits your book.

↓

You respond to your editor's suggestions.

↓

Your editor accepts your manuscript.

↓

Your editor sends your book to
the production department.

↓

The production department
outsources the copyediting.

↓

You respond to the copyeditor's
notes on your manuscript.

↓

The art department creates or outsources the
design of the cover/jacket and the interior.

↓

A series of launch meetings, your editor and sales,
marketing, publicity, and advertising departments:
• Position your book on one of your publisher's
  two or three seasonal lists
• Create a trade and consumer marketing strategy
• Choose the print, broadcast, and electronic trade
  and consumer media to carry out the strategy
• Prepare sales materials for sales conferences

↓

Throughout the rest of the process, your agent and
your publisher's subsidiary rights department try to
sell movie, book club, foreign, and serial rights.

↓

You receive printed galleys to correct.

↓

The plans for your book are presented
to the sales reps at a sales conference.

↓

You receive corrected galleys to proofread.

↓

Sales reps sell your book to online and storefront
bookstores, specialty stores, warehouse clubs, and,
if it's a mass-market book, to the independent dis-
tributors who sell to 50,000 mass-market outlets.

↓

Your publisher's library sales rep sells books to school, college, and public libraries.

↓

Your publisher's education department sells books with course adoption potential.

Your publisher's special sales department sells books with potential for premium and bulk sales.

↓

The production department arranges for your book to be printed.

↓

Your publisher's warehouse receives books, ships orders, and later receives returns.

↓

Your publisher's advertising and publicity departments:
• Do prepublication trade promotion
• Send out copies of your book with a news release or media kit they prepare
• Carry out their consumer promotion plan

↓

Your book is on your publisher's Web site.

↓

Book reviewers and professionals in your field review your book.

↓

Your publisher promotes your book for as long as sales justify doing so.

↓

You promote your book for as long as you want it to sell.

↓

Readers love your book.

↓

They tell other readers to read it.

↓

Reprint meetings are held by your publisher to decide:
• When to reprint your book and how many copies to print
• When to sell or remainder part or all of the stock if sales fall below a certain point
• When to make your book available in a print-on-demand edition
• When to put your book out of print at which time you can ask for the rights back

↓

You write the proposal for your next book.

posal, and your publisher winds up at the beginning of the process with the decision to buy your next book, usually a decision based on what happens with your first book. If you write your manuscript before selling your book, adjust the list.

Putting a mission statement here wasn't my idea. I learned it from writers. Previous editions of this book gave writers the chance to write about their commitment to their book at the end of their bio, but writers felt compelled to place it at the beginning of their promotion plans. They were right. Your promotion plan is an expression of your commitment to your book. The more passionate you are, the more your plan must reflect your passion.

You may not need a mission statement for your book. If, for example, you are writing an A-to-Z reference book, you may not feel inspired to write a mission statement, nor will editors expect one. Editors will judge your book on your ability to research and write the information and on the book's potential for backlist sales. If your book doesn't need a mission statement, please skip to the platform.

But editors love to get excited about their books, and your passion for your book will help inspire their passion to buy it and help them justify buying it to the executives who have "the power of no." The mission statement is a new idea, so I don't have examples to share with you. The proposal for *It's More Than Money, It's Your Life* by Ginita Wall and Candace Bahr, which is included in Appendix E, has one. Here is a mission statement for this book:

> *A Mission Statement*
>
> I get a great deal of creative satisfaction from helping writers shape their ideas. That's one reason I like agenting, which includes working with writers to develop their proposals and books. My passion for making each edition of my book better is also fueled by the letters from writers thanking me because my book enabled them to sell their proposals.
>
> I'm proud of these letters. They inspire me and help me to keep making my book as helpful as I can. The book is an endless dialogue with the writers it serves. It will never be as good as I want it to be, but every edition will be better because writers keep telling me how to improve it. (Now if only they would tell me how make it shorter!)

The Author's Platform

What little promotion publishers do for most books, they do around the time of publication. If a book takes off during its one- to three-month launch window, they'll promote it to sustain its momentum. If it doesn't, which is what happens more than 95 percent of the time, they will move on to the next book; so if authors and readers don't keep books alive, they die.

Your platform is what you have done and are doing to give your ideas and yourself continuing visibility around the country in the media or through talks—ideally both. Large houses want writers ready to break out as successful authors. For books that depend on author promotion, the level of an author's visibility around the country on a continuing basis is an essential factor in determining whether to acquire a book and how big a bet to place on it. John Gray, Deepak Chopra, and the kings of Chicken Soup are poster boys for successful promotion. They are tireless promoters who crisscross the country seizing every opportunity to promote themselves and their work.

The authors of reference books, gift books, or serious books won't be expected to have a national platform. If, like most first-time authors, you don't have a platform or you are writing the kind of book that doesn't lend itself to speeches or publicity, please skip to the promotion plan.

But if you are writing a book that you will promote by giving talks around the country and you want to be published by a large or medium-sized New York house, you need to have a national platform before you sell your book. The promotion plan that follows must be a believable expansion of what you are already doing to promote yourself.

Here are three compelling reasons to build your platform:

• Giving talks enables you to give your ideas some air by test-marketing the title and the material in your book.

• You need to prove that you can and will promote your book around the country. If you already have a platform, a book will enable you to increase your speaking fees and sell books at your talks. Publishers will know that you'll have all the incentive you need to stay on the road—and you will have still more incentive if your book is to be the first in a series.

• Your first book's sales will determine your second book's value, who publishes it, and how.

Writers sometimes promise publishers they will give talks around the country and then don't. What recourse does a publisher have if writers renege? None. So publishers will not believe that you will do fifty talks a year around the country if you have only done five locally. Having a platform is essential for convincing a big publisher that you can promote your book and that you will continue to build your platform after your book is published.

Publishers want authors who will keep building the readership for their books. Once you do this, your publisher will have the confidence to keep buying your books; they will know that enough readers will buy your work to justify publishing it. Publishers hope that the first printing of every book you write will be bigger than that of the previous book because of your growing readership; new readers will buy your previous books, making them "evergreens"—backlist books that continue to sell.

When a book by an unknown writer is published, the challenge of reviews and promotion is to create a critical mass of passionate readers who will convince enough other readers to buy the book. The speed with which your book flies out of stores determines whether it makes the best-seller list. At the low end of the scale is the minimum number

A Recipe for Success

What does your book need to succeed? Here is a list of ingredients for a successful book:

- An author with craft, commitment, a good idea, networks, national visibility, a knowledge of how publishing works, and professionalism
- An irresistible proposal
- An agent who makes sure the proposal is 100 percent before publishers see it
- The best possible editor, publisher, and deal
- A manuscript as close to perfect as you and your editor can make it
- The perfect title and cover
- The passion of all the links who come between you and your readers
- Large subsidiary rights sales
- An effective promotion campaign
- Rave reviews
- Being published at the right time
- Word of mouth and mouse—readers who tell everyone they know to read your book
- An author who is a relentless promoter
- Luck

of books that your publisher must sell to justify keeping your book in print, even if it's only available as a print-on-demand book.

Your Trade Platform

If you are a doctor, lawyer, historian, psychologist, or another professional whose members are a secondary market for your book, publishers will want you to have a platform in your field. Every field has its own set of media, organizations, events, and opinion makers. Big publishers will expect you to be wired to it. A trade-off: The smaller a field is, the fewer sales people in it will generate, but the easier it is to reach them. To build "the big mo" (momentum), get to the MOE in your field: media, organizations, and events.

Publishers will want you to have published articles in trade journals and to have spoken at trade shows or conferences. They will expect you to be a member of professional organizations—good advice for writers in all fields. Being in a leadership position locally or nationally will be better still. Publishers are impressed with writers who have built their networks (which is discussed in chapter twenty-two).

Nailing Down Your Platform

To translate your platform into prose, write a list, in descending order of impressiveness, of what you have done and are doing to promote your work and yourself. Include:

- The number of talks you have done on the subject and the number you do in a year
- The number of people you speak to a year
- The names of major corporations/nonprofits you have spoken for
- Your speaking fee
- If you are selling anything, how much you average in sales at your talks or in a year's time
- Significant media exposure you have gotten and how much media you get a year, which enables you to send clips and a video with your proposal
- The articles on the subject you've had published
- The size of your e-mail list
- Anything else of comparable importance that will impress editors

The numbers on this list must make editors believe the numbers in your promotion plan. Your platform must convince editors that:

1. Your visibility will make your book failproof.
2. You will make your book as successful as you and they want it to be.

Another reason to build your platform before trying to sell your book is to make sure you're not constructing a scaffold. But as you will see in chapter twenty-three, talks are a great way to test-market your book.

❖ ❖ ❖

By the time editors finish reading your mission statement and platform, your book may be as good as sold if they're convincing enough. By this point, editors will know that you can write, that you have a salable idea, and that you already have enough visibility to make your book failproof. Now on to your promotion plan, your open sesame for getting the agent, editor, publisher, and deal you want.

9 | Your Promotion Plan

"My book will promote itself."

"Once a publisher buys my book, they'll promote it."

Elizabeth and I have heard vain hopes like these for more than thirty years. Sure, it's possible for word of mouth alone to make your book a hit, but you don't want to risk the success of your book on it. Sure, it makes sense that if a publisher buys a book the publisher will promote it, but the reality is that large houses publish too many books to do justice to all of them.

The chief complaint authors have about their publishers is lack of promotion. The eagerness and optimism with which publishers buy most books isn't backed up by their eagerness to promote them. They can't be if a house is publishing hundreds of books a year.

If you want to write a book aimed at a wide national audience, and if you want it published by a major house, and if you want it to be successful, you will need to create a promotion plan as long and strong as you can make it. Your promotion plan is one thing and one thing only: a list in descending order of impressiveness of what you will do to promote your book.

To write your plan, list what you will do to promote your book during its one- to three-month launch window, while it is still new, and as far into the future as you can see. For most books with a large potential audience, this list is far more important than the content of a book in determining the editor, publisher, and deal that authors get.

Choosing Goals That Get You Going

As you develop your proposal, establish literary and financial goals for your book. For example, what size publisher do you want to publish your book? How much of an advance do you want for it? How many copies of your book do you want to sell?

You may answer these questions any way you wish. The only right answers are the answers that motivate you to produce your best work, but they must strike a realistic balance between what you want to write and what readers want to buy. If you want a million-dollar advance for a no-holds-barred look at cotton candy, think again. Looking at other books on your subject and learning how well they sold will help guide your decisions.

Your goals will affect how you prepare your proposal, and gather the information editors need about your book and competitive books so they can see your book's commercial potential. If you're trying to build your career, your efforts in writing and promoting your book must enable you to achieve your financial goals. If they can't, reconsider your goals or your idea.

A Quick-and-Easy Promotion Plan

This book grew out of our experience selling books to New York houses. As mentioned earlier, the premise of this approach is that you want to sell your book to a major house for as much money as you can get. For a how-to or other nonfiction book aimed at a wide national audience, it will be difficult for you to gain the interest of a large New York publishing house unless you have a solid track record or a national platform.

But, less than 10 percent of new writers have enough promotional ammunition to interest large publishers. However, your promotion plan will be of less importance if you plan to sell your book to a small or university press or a medium-sized house outside of New York. With no layer of middle management or a midtown-Manhattan monolith to support, these publishers don't have to sell as many copies as large houses do to profit from a book.

If you or your book meets the following three criteria, you only need a one-sentence promotion plan:

- The market for your book is too small to interest big houses
- The market for your book is large but you don't have the platform or promotional skills needed to reach it
- Your writing ability isn't professional enough for your book to interest editors at big houses who may not have enough time to edit their books as well as they would like to

Your one-sentence promotion plan may be as simple as this:

> The author is eager to do what ever he can to promote the book and will cooperate with the publisher in every way possible.

If you can, add your speaking or media experience and contacts, and anything else you think will impress editors. Read what follows to get a feel for what large houses like to see, and get ideas for what you can include in your promotion plan.

What Publishers Can Do For You

After *Chicken Soup for the Soul* was published, Jack Canfield said he had "too much month at the end of the money." When books arrived in the stores, he visualized crowds flocking in to buy it. Unfortunately, it was, as he put it, "the calm before the calm." Then Canfield and Mark Victor Hansen promoted their book for fourteen months, and it hit the best-seller list. No matter who publishes your book, think of it as being self-published. For most books, publishers do at least some of the following:

- Include the book in their catalogs and in their list ads in the seasonal announcement issues of *Publishers Weekly*
- Send out review copies to trade and consumer media
- Send a news release with review copies
- Post information about the book on their Web sites, and perhaps a link to the author's Web site
- Give promotional copies to authors and perhaps to a distribution list the author provides
- Send authors on a regional tour and gauge the effect on sales
- Contact local and national media
- Piggyback on authors' travels for x months to y cities by contacting media in those cities

If you were publishing seven hundred books a year, how many of these things could you do for all of your books? How would you decide which books to promote more heavily?

If your book maintains a high enough level of sales, your publisher will be a distribution service that helps keep your book in stores. Your publisher will include your previous books in its promotion of your future books. If booksellers are selling enough copies, they will keep at least one copy on hand.

If you are not driven to succeed, you'll be run over by competitors who are. This puts the future of your book in the hands of the person who knows more about it, cares more about it, and will benefit more from it than anyone else: you. No matter who publishes your book, sooner or later its fate will come to rest in your hands, and in the heads and hearts of your readers.

It's been said that judgment is what you get from experience and good judgment is what you get from bad experience. Books tend to be big or small: best-sellers or everything else. New authors usually learn through experience the unhappy truth about writing a small book for a big house.

The more publishers pay, the more they push, but even a six-figure advance is no guarantee that a large house will promote a book. In fact, no matter how much publishers pay for a book, they will promote it only as long as they think that their investment in promotion will pay off.

Bottom-Up Books

Doubleday prints more than two million copies of a John Grisham novel, sends them to bookstores, and dictates a lay-down date—the date on which all booksellers can start selling them. Then Doubleday primes the pump with a six-figure trade and consumer marketing campaign for the book knowing that these efforts will pay off. The explosion of immediate sales gets Grisham not only on the best-seller list but at the top spot. This illustrates how "top-down" books, which start at the top of the best-seller list and work their way down, are born.

Bill and Elaine Petrocelli's Book Passage in Corte Madera, California, is one of the best bookstores in the country. Bill believes that less than 1 percent of the books they sell are "top-down" books. This means that more than 99 percent of books are "bottom-up" books, those that authors and publishers have to build an audience for.

The following advice works for self-help, how-to, and inspirational books; it also works for books about people whose fame, infamy, or achievements will interest the media as well as book buyers. If this model isn't right at this time for you or for what you write, do what works best for you, but make your plan as potent as you can. Chapter twenty-three will tell you how to test-market your book to see if the techniques you want to use will work.

Six Crucial Commitments to Consider

The Irish playwright, George Bernard Shaw said that every profession is a conspiracy against the laity. Writers are entitled to feel that way when it comes to selling their books and getting the commitment they think their books deserve. Here are six ways to get large publishers to turn the spigot and let promotional money flow:

- Have a successful book.
- Be famous.
- Convince them to spend a fortune to buy it.
- Make a publisher fall in love with your book—no matter what your advance is—so they will do whatever they can to promote it.
- Convince them that your book is a potential best-seller, so they will stay with the book as long as sales warrant it—even if they start with a small budget.
- If you aren't in one of the five previous situations, make the biggest promotional commitment you can.

Editors will be more likely to take a chance on your book if they see how professional you are and how committed you are to your book's success. Your proposal is a business plan in which you want one lucky publisher to invest. Your promotion plan is the part of that plan that must convince the publisher that its investment will pay off.

The Big Four

Four figures are the most important commitments you can make in your promotion plan:

- Your promotion budget, if you will have one. Most writers can't afford one, so they don't include it. Large publishers won't buy your book because you have a budget or reject it just because you don't. But with or without one, the next three numbers are crucial.
- The number of major markets and their satellite cities where you will speak and do publicity after publication
- The number of talks you will continue to give each year
- The number of copies of the book you will sell each year, assuming that one out of four listeners buys one

For a book that requires author promotion to succeed, I can tell from these four numbers whether I can interest a major house in the book. If the numbers are large enough, they will arouse the serious interest of agents and publishers.

Let's take a closer look at these numbers. At the top of a new page, type the word *promotion*, the subhead for your plan. Don't use the word *marketing*; the marketing department will think you're trying to infringe on their territory. Use "to promote the book, the author will" to begin your plan. Starting each part of the list with a verb, list in descending order of impressiveness what you will do to promote your book. (Omit the quote marks and the numbers that I include for clarity. Use a bullet before each item.) Let's look at six key commitments for you to consider:

1. "Match the publisher's out-of-pocket, consumer promotion budget up to $x on signing." If you plan to use all or part of your advance to fund promotion, you are fortunate. But don't write "Use x percent of the advance for promotion." You won't know what your advance will be so you can't use that number to determine how large a budget you will have.

If you will use the money you earn from speaking, mention it, but your platform information should show that you are already making enough money to carry out your plan. Do include in your budget the costs that you will incur getting yourself around the country unless your speaking clients will reimburse you for them. Only offer a budget to large houses even though they may not match it. Small and medium-sized houses won't expect one and won't match one.

2. "Hire [name of publicist] to publicize the book." *Literary Market Place* (LMP) and your networks will provide you with the names of publicists to approach.

Because publishing has a network of organizations, events, and trade and consumer media, you need a publicist with the contacts to do justice to you and your book. Ideally, the publicist will have publicized books on your subject for publishers like those you want to buy your book. Check with a publicist's clients about the publicist's experience, competence, and reliability before choosing one.

If you approach large publicity firms, the people you talk to will probably not be the ones you will work with, so be sure to meet whoever that is. Request written proposals from publicists that balance cost and effectiveness.

If you can, mention who your publicist is—ideally, someone whose name will impress publishers. Naming someone will make the idea real, and naming someone publishers are aware of will make you look more professional because you know what it takes to get the job done right.

3. "Give talks in the following *x* cities upon publication." List as many major markets and their satellite cities as you can. For example, the San Francisco Bay Area has five distinct areas that each have one or more bookstores worth visiting: the city itself, Berkeley, Marin County, the Peninsula, and San Jose. For a book on politics, it will be worthwhile to go to Sacramento, the state capital.

Research has found that people are more afraid of public speaking than of dying. As best-selling author and comedian Jerry Seinfeld once said, "That means that at a funeral, you'd be better off in the coffin than giving the eulogy." Despite this, if you can get paid to speak, take your act on the road.

If you can arrange to be paid for talks, you will be giving yourself a free national tour. If you are already giving presentations, you may be able to choose the most advantageous places to make them when your book is published. If not, don't worry. You don't have to know where you will speak in each city. Once your manuscript is accepted, you will have at least nine months to set up places to speak.

4. "Give talks at the following conferences/conventions." List trade and consumer conferences and conventions that you know you will be able to speak at during the year after publication. If the events are large enough, note the number of people who attend. If not, cite the combined attendance at all of them if it will impress editors.

Don't mention speaking at BookExpo America (BEA); your publisher will arrange that if it's possible. (Do go to BEA, held annually around the end of May. It's a unique opportunity to get a sense in one big room of what's going on in the industry.)

The publication of a book is usually an opportunity to make money. Between speaking fees and back-of-the-room sales, set a goal of at least breaking even, with publicity as a bonus. The relationships you create, the publicity you generate, and the new fans and clients you find will help you build your career.

If you are already giving talks, your book will enable you to raise your speaking fees and profit from book sales and products and services you sell. Your ability to profit from speaking will grow over time. Use your networks to help you set goals for yourself and your book, then do what you must to achieve them. When you command four-figure speaking fees, enlist as many speaking bureaus as you can to help you. *Literary Market Place* lists speaking bureaus.

Podium Pointers

New to the speaking scene? Never considered how conference talks might boost your book sales? Start thinking about it.

- Writers often think that they need a book before they can give talks, but thousands of organizations that meet regularly need speakers and will welcome you if you can talk about something that will interest their members. Talking to different kinds of organizations will help you learn the art of customizing your talk for different audiences.

- If you are writing a how-to book, you can get feedback on your advice by asking audiences to write to you about their experiences using the information you give them. Also, you should always ask people to give you their e-mail addresses so they can receive your newsletter or updates and information about your products and appearances.

- Bookstores may let you give a talk before your book is published. They will be more willing if you tell them about other books you will recommend in your talk. This allows you to test-market your talk, handouts, and business cards and establish relationships with the event coordinators who will book you to speak when your book comes out.

- Get testimonial letters from happy bookers, and at the end your talks, ask audiences if they know of other groups that might be interested in having you speak.

- Joining Toastmasters will give you the chance to learn how to speak at a professional level. Joining the National Speakers Association will enable you to build a speaking career. (Both groups are listed in the Resource Directory.) Mentioning in your bio that you are a member of a speaker's organization testifies to your commitment to your career.

- Speakers rarely begin their careers receiving five-figure fees to give keynotes to corporate audiences. They build their careers by doing training, seminars, workshops, and consulting. At the start of your speaking career, being able to offer clients more than one kind of service and speak about more than one subject will generate more opportunities than doing just one kind of event on one subject.

- Persuade other speakers to sell your book at their talks. This has an added benefit: If they express interest, they will have an incentive to give you feedback on your proposal and manuscript.

- Sell other people's books, products, or services at your talks. This is perhaps most helpful before you have your own book to sell.

5. "Continue to make *x* presentations a year." Writers constantly tell us that they're "willing to give as many talks as it takes." This is no help to publishers, especially since it can't help you pinpoint the next number.

6. "Sell *x* copies of the book a year." Publishers always want the biggest "buyback" that authors will commit to, the number of books authors will buy to resell. Business authors sell books to 25 to 30 percent of their audiences. That stat isn't true for all kinds of books, but 25 percent doesn't seem unreasonable for most nonfiction.

If you give a talk that inspires and excites your audience, they will want your book. Corporations understand this, which is why they sometimes buy copies for everyone in the audience. If you can sell a four-figure quantity of books a year, cite a round number. Assume that your publisher will include the number in your contract, so only commit to the largest round number that you know you can sell.

Base this quantity on the number of talks you give and the average attendance at your talks. Your quantity should equal 25 percent of the average attendance number. A large house will want that number to have four digits and won't be impressed by a number smaller than two thousand. Small and medium-sized houses will be satisfied with whatever number you provide or, if you don't specify a quantity, just knowing that you will sell books.

Selling your book will help you pay expenses and make a living, but remember: If your book comes out in hardcover, it will be more expensive to buy than the paperback edition that usually comes out a year later. The hardcover price may warrant being cautious about the number of hardcovers you can sell. On the other hand, first-year sales may be higher than sales you make after that because your book is new. But then again, the better known you and your books become, the more copies you will be able to sell. (Confused? You should be!)

So depending on your goals, the number of competitive books, how many related books you will write, and how long you will continue to give talks, you will have to balance optimism and realism in picking a number. You may want to say that you'll sell *x* books a year for the first *x* years and *x* books after that.

Talk to speakers in your field to see what they sell. Members of the National Speakers Association are willing to share information like that. So weigh the conflicting possibilities and commit only to what you are absolutely sure you can deliver.

Four Keys to Promising Promotions

Here are four ways to meet publishers' expectations in your promotion plan:

1. Exaggerate nothing. Assume that your publisher will insert your budget and the number of copies you will sell a year into their contract. Publishers respond best to the word *will*. They want to know what you *will* do, not what you are eager, willing, or available to do.

2. Use round but accurate numbers. If you write "Will give talks," publishers won't know whether you will do two or two hundred. Give the publishers one number, not a range of numbers.

Wrong: "Will give 40-60 talks a year."

Right: "Will give 50 talks a year."

Pick a number that is a reasonable expansion of what you're already doing. By building your platform before you sell your book, you will know how many talks you can give a year without burning out. Including numbers will make your commitments seem definite instead of like guesswork.

3. Use the active voice. Look at the examples below. Which one sounds more professional?

Passive: "Cookware stores will be contacted."

Active: "The author will promote the book to cookware stores."

As in the second example, tell publishers what you will do rather than what will happen to others. The sentence will carry still more weight with a more specific target: "The author will promote the book to the nation's 1,000 cookware stores."

4. If it's not obvious, tell publishers how you will do what you promise. To further improve that sentence above, explain how you will promote the book to cookware stores:

"The author will send a brochure to the nation's 1,000 biggest cookware stores." That's telling editors what they need to know.

Setting Your Promotion Budget

When you're deciding whether to invest in promotion, keep your eye on the doughnut, not the hole the expenses will make in your wallet. Here are five payoffs for having a budget for your book:

1. If your publisher will match your budget, you have a good case for requesting an advance at least the size of your com-

bined war chest. A buck for promotion should justify a buck in advance.

2. Your combined budget will affect:
   - How your publisher positions your book on its list
   - How many copies bookstores order and the quantity of the first printing
   - How the media, book buyers and subsidiary rights buyers view your book

3. The more promotion your book receives, the better it will sell.

4. The better your first book does, the more your second book will be worth and the more your publisher will promote it.

5. The more visible you and your book are, the more business you'll attract, if a goal in writing and promoting your book is to get clients or build your business.

Hot Tip | The lowest budget that will impress a large house is twenty-five thousand dollars. A budget less than fifteen thousand dollars isn't worth mentioning. Just indicate at the beginning of your plan that you will pay for the commitments that follow, but cost out the expenses to be sure you can.

Your budget must make sense in relation to how you will use it. An exaggerated example: You can't say that you will have a promotion budget of one thousand dollars and that you will mail ten thousand books to opinion makers. Editors know that you won't be able to do this for ten cents per book, and you will lose your credibility instantly.

If you know, regardless of your advance amount, how much you will spend, use that number and the following four steps to decide the best way to spend it:

1. Determine the size of the markets for your book.
2. Figure out the most effective ways to reach those markets.
3. Get ballpark costs for the materials and services you will need.
4. If the estimated costs are more than you can afford, scale back your plan until it fits your budget.

If you use your advance for promotion but the advance isn't big enough to cover your budget, scale down your plan and your budget when a publisher makes you an offer.

We represented an author willing to spend seventy thousand dollars to promote her book, but we weren't able to sell it. As I wrote earlier, no publisher will buy your book simply because you have a budget or reject it if you don't. As helpful as a budget is, equally important is convincing editors that you know how to get the biggest bang for the fewest bucks.

Make your budget available only on signing. If your publisher doesn't match your budget, you are free to spend whatever you wish. Assuming that you have a salable idea and your query letter is well written, mentioning your budget in your query letter will be an additional inducement to see your proposal.

Publishers may not be willing to match your budget or commit to any budget. On the other hand, we once had two publishers who wouldn't bid more than thirty thousand dollars for a book, but only one of them was willing to match the author's twenty-thousand-dollar promotion budget. That publisher got the deal, and the book benefited from a forty-thousand-dollar promotion campaign. If you find a publisher willing to match your promotion budget, they will decide how to spend their half.

Hot Tip | You may be able to get your promotion budget back by agreeing on a number of your books sold in a certain time or your book hitting a bestseller list. Make this commitment part of the clause in your publisher's contract about your matching promotion budget.

Getting Your Book's Sales off the Ground

My brother Ray, who's in the toy business, says, "Business doesn't go; you have to push it." Building momentum for a book has been compared to getting a 747 off the ground. It takes a lot of gas and runway, but once you have liftoff, the sky's the limit. Publicity is the most cost-effective form of promotion, but no matter how big a publisher's commitment to a book is, publicity is never guaranteed. Even authors who get on *Oprah* don't automatically see a huge spike in sales.

Warner spent $7.1 million for *Jack—Straight From the Gut* by former GE CEO Jack Welch. Welch was supposed to be on the *Today* show and the cover of *Newsweek* for the week of September 11, 2001. Figuring out how well the book would have sold if the tragedy of September 11 hadn't happened is impossible, but one thing is clear: Because of this setback, the book did not earn back its advance.

Publicity is essential to the success of most books. But three certain uncertainties of publicity—getting it, getting it when you need it, and

Four More Chances to Promote Your Book

Your book may present four more opportunities for you to launch a new promotion campaign:

1. The paperback edition of your book. Ninety percent of the hardcover books that survive their first year are published in paperback. If your book is published first in hardcover, it will have a second chance to be a new book when it's published as a trade paperback or a mass-market book. This will give you the chance to promote it again.

- If your book will be republished as a trade paperback, it will appear again in your publisher's catalog as part of one of its three seasonal lists, and the reps will sell it again.
- Hardcover sales will determine the zeal with which your publisher will promote the paperback edition or if it even decides to a reprint it. So another goal of your promotion is to help ensure the hardcover sells well enough to warrant a paperback edition.

Push the paperback edition as hard as you can. It's the format in which you want your book to have a long, profitable life. Use everything you learned and the connections you made from promoting the hardcover to help sell the paperback.

2. A new edition of your book. If your book has to be updated and revised, or if you have enough changes to justify a new edition, the publication of either will give you another opportunity to promote your book. (See chapter thirteen for more on updates, revisions, and new editions.)

3. The publication of your next book. If you're writing a series of books, you and your publisher will promote previous books in the series when the new books are published.

4. The sweet spot in the calendar for your book. A sweet spot on a baseball bat is the place that enables batters to hit the ball the farthest. Your book may benefit from having a "sweet spot" in the calendar: a day, month, or season every year that gives you the opportunity to promote your book. Books about love come out around Valentine's Day. For books about people, birthdays or other important dates are possible publication dates. Books about baseball hit the field in April. Every Halloween, Dennis Hauck Smith gets airtime for his books about haunted houses. May and June is grads-and-dads time.

whether it affects book sales—haunt authors and publicists.

But there was also an immutable Larsen Law at work: No matter what happens, it's good for somebody and bad for somebody. The calamity of 9/11 also made bestsellers of books that would otherwise never have made the list. At one point, there were five books on the subject on *The New York Times* list. (The royalties of some of them were donated to help the victims.) What this means to you and your book is that luck and the right timing are essential to success.

Nonetheless, hire a publicist if you can. Freelance publicists are more accountable and more motivated than staff publicists to produce results to:

- Justify their fees
- Maintain their reputations
- Do a good job so you will hire them for future books
- Deserve recommendations to other authors

Since major houses publish too many books to give each of them the attention they need, publishers concentrate on those they believe have the greatest potential to repay their effort:

- Books that have cost them too much to lose
- Books they fall in love with, even if they haven't spent a bundle on them
- Books that have a shot at making the best-seller list but that publishers have to push, hoping that reviews, a small promotion campaign (that publishers will increase if sales warrant), and word of mouth from readers and independent booksellers will build sales momentum
- Books that unexpectedly show signs of life: reorders from independent booksellers, early rave reviews, or subsidiary rights sales

Publishers have short- and long-term perspectives on promotion. They will be especially concerned about maximizing the opportunity for promoting your book during your book's launch window, the one- to three-month window of opportunity starting on the publication date, when your book is in stores and reviews appear. The challenge for you is to make the promotion upon the publication of your book as explosive as you can so your book's growing sales momentum will convince booksellers and your publisher to stay with it. After your book's launch window, your publisher will want you to continue to promote and sell your book as long as you can walk and talk.

If this approach to promotion is not right for you or your book, then follow Theodore Roosevelt's advice: "Do what you can with what you have where you are." Take the long view as well as the short view. Look at your career not as one book but as ten or twenty, each better than the last. In the context of your career, where you are now is less important than the direction in which you're heading.

Even with limited funds, you can still:

- Analyze the nature, size, and location of the markets for your book and how to reach them effectively and inexpensively.
- Join writer's organizations and go to writer's conferences. Ask your publishing network to share the techniques they find effective and help you figure out how to apply them to your book.
- Read books on publishing and promotion.
- Have a promotion potluck. Invite writers and have a brainstorming session on one another's books.

❖ ❖ ❖

From the moment you decide to write your book, think on both sides of your brain about how you can promote it. Cultivate the knack of thinking in a creative, anything-is-possible way. Develop a promotion reflex. Look at every person, place, fact, event, trend, institution, and story in the media and ask yourself: How can I use this to promote myself or my book?

When it comes to books, the big bucks often come not from royalties, but book sales and talks. So answer these questions:

How much do you like to travel?

How many talks can you give a year without burning out?

How much money do you want to earn a year from your books and talks?

Only you can answer these questions, and your answers will dictate your itinerary. If you have a salable idea, if your proposal proves that you can that write it, and if you can make your promotional numbers big enough, big publishers will want you and your book. It's unusual for a writer who is working on her first book to have the big numbers big houses like to see, but persevere and one day you will have them.

10 | Your Promotional Partners

You probably know bank robber Willie Sutton's famous answer when asked why he robbed banks: "Because that's where the money is." How would you like to do just one thing that will guarantee the sale and the success of your book? Securing promotional partners, an optional element to add to your promotional plan, will enable you to leapfrog over the problems of lacking a platform or a strong promotion plan. It will make any publisher want to acquire your book. However, this idea may not work for your book. If a partnership doesn't make sense for your book, go on to the next chapter.

Rick Frishman is a co-author of *Guerrilla Marking for Writers* and the president of Planned Television Arts, the industry's oldest and largest book publicity firm. According to Rick, everyone's favorite radio station is WIFM: What's in It For Me? Publishers can't spend enough money to promote most of their books, but corporations and nonprofit associations and foundations can and will promote your book if you can show them what's in it for them. If an organization can benefit enough from being associated with you and your book, you will be able to partner for profit with O.P.M.: other people's money. You supply the mind power and leg power; they supply the platform and the money power.

Because of the value of the Guerrilla Marketing brand, Microsoft's small-business Web site hired Jay Levinson, the other co-author of *Guerilla Marketing for Writers*, to write a book about how to use technology to market a small business. A new chapter appeared every month. Two months after the last chapter appeared, Addison-Wesley published *Guerrilla Marketing With Technology: Unleashing the Full Potential of Your Small Business*. This is an excellent example of what Jay calls fusion marketing—the e-book promoted the traditional book, and Jay got paid twice for writing it!

How a Business or Organization Can Help You

The challenge is to use your proposal to find a business or nonprofit that will benefit from being associated with you and then your book and obtain a written commitment. With luck and tenacity, you will be able to amend your promotion plan to show that it will "integrate the support of [name of organization], which will promote the book in the following ways . . . "

How can an organization help you? The organization can:

- Give you a grant to write the book
- Buy books to sell or give away
- Create a publicity and advertising campaign based on your book and show you and your book in its ads
- Include a copy of your book when consumers purchase its products or services
- Have its publicist set up a national tour for you
- Arrange for you to speak while you travel, perhaps for the organization's chapters or branches
- Include in its in-house newsletter and on its Web site an article about you and an excerpt or serialization of your book
- Add a link to your Web site from its Web site
- Put its name on the book's cover, if adding it will help your book's credibility
- Have the head of the organization give a quote or write a foreword for your book
- Open the doors to its networks

Besides being associated with a book that makes an organization look good, what's in it for a partner that supports you?

- If the partner buys enough books, your publisher will be happy to customize the cover and text. Bringing with you just a written commitment for a big enough bulk or premium sale when you sell your proposal will assure the sale of your book because your partner will underwrite your publisher's first printing as well and promote your book.

- If your partner will bear the costs, your publisher will include in the book a blow-in postage-paid reply card readers can use to request information, a free sample, or a special offer from the partner. (A *blow-in card* is a card that is literally blown into the book rather than being inserted by hand or machine. Your budget permitting, you can use a blow-in card to make a special offer to your readers.)
- They can use blank pages in the front or back of the book as they wish.

This is just a starter set of ideas. You, your partner, and your publisher are limited only by your imaginations.

Picking a Partner

Seek a partner with whom you will enjoy collaborating. Be sure you and your readers will feel comfortable with the partner's products, services, or beliefs. Avoid a partner that could undercut your credibility.

Let's suppose you are writing a book on how to stop smoking. Who are likely partners for you to approach? You could try:

- Kaiser or Blue Cross
- The American Medical Association
- Health or life insurance companies
- Manufacturers of products people use to wean themselves from cigarettes
- A hospital chain
- A medical school
- Organizations people join to kick the habit

On the other hand, even if Philip Morris were willing to help you (don't hold your breath), accepting their help would destroy your credibility as surely as smoking on *Oprah*.

Fusion marketing is a tremendously powerful idea, but it will be valuable to publishers only if you can convince the partner to make its commitments in writing and on its own letterhead and make the letter the last page of your proposal.

Such a partnership may or may not be a possibility for your book.

Even if it is, you can't assume it will happen easily or quickly, especially if you haven't yet written your proposed book. You are more likely to make a partnership happen:

- after you sell your proposal
- when your manuscript is accepted
- after your book gets published
- after your book is successful

If these things haven't happened yet, don't let that keep you from making the attempt. You will be publicizing your book and getting feedback that can help you make your book better and your next attempt more effective. You will also plant seeds that may one day bear fruit. If your partner stays with you for future books, you may have all you need for a successful career. A bonus: You can have as many noncompeting partners as you want.

Hot Tip

You may be able to accelerate the process of partnering by taking it as far as it can go online before you meet with anyone. You can determine the contact person, e-mail a query that includes a hyperlink to your proposal, and answer the contact's questions. Note that travel expenses may become a factor, and you shouldn't approach an organization if you don't have the means to meet with their executives if they ask you to.

A catch-22: When you're starting to write your first book, you may want to use fusion marketing. Unfortunately, first-time authors don't usually have the credentials or connections they need to form a promotional partnership—another reason to start building your networks immediately.

First-time authors face this problem in other ways. Obtaining quotes, interviews, and a foreword can be easy if Random House is publishing your book. But the more promotional ammunition you have before you approach Random House, the more likely it is that Random House will buy your book.

Since your name and credentials may not impress potential partners, try to find a successful author, opinion maker, or group who will vouch for your character and credibility with a letter you can include at the end of your proposal and quote from in your initial letter.

You know you're making progress if an organization tells you to come back when you have your manuscript or your book. This enables you to say that an organization has seen your proposal and expressed interest in your book. That's better than nothing, but barely because it's impossible to predict whether the interest will blossom into a partnership. *Guerilla Marketing for Writers* offers more information on fusion marketing.

Example: Promotional Partners

For his book about online investing, Ted Allrich provided a strong plan. But it wasn't until he obtained the following commitments from Prodigy that we received two offers for the book:

> On the basis of the proposal, Prodigy is willing to promote the book extensively. They will:
>
> • Purchase twenty-five hundred copies a month as a premium to attract new members as long as the promotion is effective. In one year, that will be thirty thousand books.
>
> • Sponsor a seminar in four eastern cities for current and potential subscribers. The author will be one of three or four featured speakers. If these are successful, Prodigy will present them nationwide. The book will be available for sale at the seminar or bought by Prodigy as a premium.
>
> • Promote the book online as part of the investment library. The provider of the library service will buy books. There are two million Prodigy subscribers; if half of 1 percent buy the book, that's ten thousand books.
>
> • Set up a bulletin board for the author where he can answer questions about investing and refer subscribers to the book.
>
> • Place the book in Sears and IBM outlets and wherever Prodigy software is sold.
>
> • Provide a cover quote by the head of the investment information services of Prodigy who has said Prodigy is willing to use its services to the fullest extent to make the book successful.
>
> While the author welcomes Prodigy's involvement and acknowledges the databases used on its service are the most affordable and practical for an individual investor, he is writing an independent, objective book about investing. The book will include other services and research databases.
>
> The author understands the importance of promotion to the success of the book. Coordinating his efforts with those of the publisher, he will devise and carry out a campaign that is carefully planned and enthusiastically pursued. The author makes the following commitments:
>
> 1. Because the book will be the marketing tool for the au-

thor's firm and will help him establish an audience for his next book and a newsletter, he will match the publisher's consumer promotion budget up to x dollars.

2. The author has hired book publicist Blanche Brann, a former director of publicity for Holt, as his publicity consultant.

3. On publication, the author will make presentations in fourteen cities: Seattle; Portland; Sacramento; San Francisco; San Jose; Los Angeles; San Diego; New York City; Boston; Washington, DC; Philadelphia; Chicago; Dallas; and Austin.

He will spend two days in each city to allow time for radio and television interviews, a lunch seminar, and an evening seminar. The Charles Schwab Company has expressed an interest in hosting seminars.

The author is also soliciting The Learning Annex and Computer User groups.

4. Brann will create a press kit that will contain:

- A pitch letter
- National and San Francisco Bay Area press releases
- The story behind the book, a history of how the author came to write the book and his dedication to investing
- An author photo
- A brochure about the author's firm
- Reviews and articles about the book
- Questions on investing, computing, and the stock market

Print

The author will send press kits to the print media:

- **Magazines:** While avoiding duplication of the publisher's efforts, the author will send press kits to all business, investing, and computer publications including *Business Week*, *PC Magazine*, *PC World Magazine*, *Money Magazine*, *Fortune*, *Forbes*, and *ASAP*, its publication for computer users.

- **Newspapers and news wires:** The author will send a book and press kit to business and computer editors in the thirty-five large markets and nationally syndicated business and technology columnists and feature writers. All other newspapers with a business or computer editor will receive the packet and a response card for requesting the book.

- **Special interest publications:** Editors of specialty publications for investors, such as the *American Association of Independent Investors*, and advisory newsletters, such as *Personal*

Finance, *The Prudent Speculator*, and computer-user newsletters, will receive the press kit.

Broadcast
- **Network:** A proposal for a network or local news show will show how the visual presentation will interest their investor, computer, and business viewers. Ideal programs are CNBC, Moneyline and Wall Street Week.
- **Phoners:** The author will do radio telephone interviews.

The Seminar
Using a laptop computer and a projector, the author will present talks, to give them an overview of investing. The first speech will be at the Stanford Business School annual Alumni Investment Seminar. The author is the chairman of this event and will repeat the presentation the following year.

Sales and Distribution
The author will send press kits to the hundreds of investment and computer clubs. He will send promotional copies of the book and a press kit to two hundred opinion makers in investing, politics, business, computers, and academia. The author will supply the copies the publisher can't.

Among the opinion makers the author knows are:
- Richard Hoey, chief economist of the Dreyfus Group
- Maria Ramirez of Ramirez Capital Consulting, often on CNBC with analysis on the stock market
- Tom Peters
- Walter Shorenstein, the largest landowner in San Francisco
- Tom Guba, managing director of Smith, Barney, who will recommend it to Sanford Weill, chairman of Primerica Corp.
- Tony Frank, former postmaster general
- Brad Child, senior investment officer of the government of Singapore

❖ ❖ ❖

Strategic alliances are a wonderful idea. If you can make one happen, it may be all you need to make your book successful. The next page describes one of civilization's greatest gifts to writers; something, in fact, no writer can be successful without.

11 | Additional Promotional Efforts

The following eight weapons are powerful, but you can't quantify the book sales that they will generate. I begin with the greatest source of continuous, worldwide visibility 24/7: your Web site.

Developing a Web Site

Begin your promotion plan's discussion of your Web site with this: "Use a Web site to _____." Follow this with a list of the ways that you will use your site to promote you and your book. You can use your site to:

- Post your media kit, a description of which follows
- Post your book's cover, the table of contents, and a chapter
- Post a teacher's guide, if your book has the potential to be adopted for use in schools
- Include a book club guide
- Update your book and add new information to it
- List your past and future media, speaking, and teaching appearances
- Exchange reciprocal links with as many sites as possible

- Sell your book directly or through a link to an online bookstore that will pay you commission on the sales your site generates
- Give your readers the chance to share their experiences with your book and give you ideas for changes and additions, and what they want to read next
- Post new articles to draw people back to your site
- Provide a resource directory, the one from your book or one created for the Web site, that you keep up-to-date

Convince visitors to return to your site for the unique and valuable information their visit proves they will find. Encourage them to forward material from the site and recommend the site to their networks.

Guerilla Marketing for Writers has a list of nineteen ways to use a Web site. Even if your site is not up yet, register the domain name for it. Choose one that makes use of your title so you can use it to promote all of your books, products, and services. A safe bet: Buy your name as a domain name, and you'll be able to use it for everything you do.

Developing a Media Kit

Include anything that will excite the media about you and your book, including:

- A news release about your book (updated periodically.)
- A list of questions that you will rehearse answers for, including a few that have nothing to do with your book but might intrigue media people
- Your bio
- A black-and-white glossy photo of you for print media and television shows
- Reviews and articles about you, with the good parts underlined, to be added to your media kit as they appear
- An impressive audio or video clip of you speaking or being interviewed
- A pitch letter tying all this material together and explaining why you will make a good subject for an interview
- A page of quotes from notable people (which is discussed in chapter five)
- A paper folder—printed especially for the kit or bearing a postcard copy of your book's cover—with two pockets to hold the contents

A no-budget alternative: Jill Lublin who, along with Jay Levinson and Rick Frishman, is a co-author of *Guerrilla Publicity*, believes that a great news release is a great media kit. To slash costs, send just a press release—an e-mail or a hard copy—to the media. Tell them that your kit is on your Web site. Include a hyperlink if you're using e-mail. Include a postage-paid reply card if you send a hard copy. Also indicate on the postcard that they can call or e-mail you if they want a printed media kit and a copy of your book.

Before you contact the media, be sure that you don't duplicate your publisher's efforts. Your publisher may be willing to produce the kit, or at least have the staff publicist give you feedback on your copy.

In your proposal, write, "The author will send x copies of the media kit and a book to y media people." Give round numbers for x and y. The publisher will supply promotional copies; what's unpredictable is how many. A low three-figure quantity is reasonable. If you are able to fulfill this promise, write, "The author will provide the copies that the publisher can't."

Sending Review Copies

If you plan to mail promotional copies of the book to opinion makers or important publications and organizations in your field, give a round number of copies that you will mail with a cover letter. Your list has to convince your publisher that mailing these copies will be justified by their potential for promoting your book and generating sales. Your publisher may be willing to mail copies to at least part of your mailing list or reimburse you for the cost to mail them.

Hot Tip | Staff publicists are trained on the job, are overworked and underpaid, have no strong incentive to promote your book, face no consequences if their efforts fail, and may change jobs at any time. Put someone on the list that you can check with so you will know when the kits and books have been sent.

Securing Interviews

If you have appeared on shows that have invited you back, and if their names or stations will impress potential publishers, mention them. If you've only had contacts with media people, you can mention them at the end of your plan. Contacts alone are not ammunition because who knows whether they will come through.

More Ammo

Here is more ammunition to include if you can:
- Special-interest magazines may be willing to trade an ad for a

story. If you can get a commitment for such a trade, mention in your proposal the ad's size and cost and the magazine's circulation.

• Mention magazines that will do per-order ads, for which the magazine supplies the space, your publisher supplies the books, and they share the profits. What will really impress publishers is this: "*X Magazine* (include the circulation if impressive) will run full-page per-order ads (value *x* dollars) as long as they continue to sell enough books."

• Mention a commitment to write a column, online or not, that will give your book as much exposure as possible. Write the column in exchange for cash and/or for a bio that will help promote your book.

• When they're researching stories, media people use Profnet and the Yearbook of Experts, Authorities and Spokespersons to look for experts. (The resource directory in Appendix B has contact information.) If you have a promotion budget, contact them for their prices to list you, and ask your publishing network and authors who use them to help you decide if the cost is justified.

End your promotion plan with this sentence: "The author will coordinate her efforts with the publisher's."

Example: Making Promotion a Family Affair

In their twelve-point plan for *The Family Business: Power Tools for Success*, Russell and Roger Allred locked onto schools around the country that offer courses on the subject to help assure continuing national exposure.

> After publication, the authors will:
> • Conduct seminars in the following thirty-five cities: [list of cities followed]. Most of these cities have universities with family business departments that sponsor seminars
> • Continue to present forty seminars a year to family business departments at universities; chambers of commerce; small-business development centers; and associations of accountants, consultants, attorneys, and independent business owners
> • Sell *x* books a seminar, or *x* copies a year
> • Encourage the universities to stock the book as a resource for their family-business departments and course syllabi
> • Visit bookstores in cities where the seminars are held to encourage them to stock the book
> • Produce a videotape of a *Power Tools* presentation for distribution with press releases and media kits

- Prepare and distribute press releases and media kits to include a video- and audiotape, bios, a book cover, and a business reply card for a book
- Appear on business-related interview shows in cities where the seminars are held. The authors work with a media consultant who has access to the major television shows nationwide.
- Conduct at least forty-five telephone interviews a year on radio shows in smaller markets
- Write articles on a continuing basis for *Family Business Magazine, Inc., Entrepreneur*, and *Independent Business Magazine* in exchange for a byline promoting *Power Tools*. The editor of *Family Business Magazine* has already promised an article on the book when it is published.
- Conduct a forum on America Online
- Obtain endorsements from family business advisors

As you will see in the sample proposals in Appendix E, the longer and stronger a promotion plan is, the better. Consider doing a second one-page lifetime plan of what you will continue to do to promote your book. Use a separate page for it unless it fits on the last page of your promotion plan. If your plan is longer than five pages, add a title page and place it in the left pocket of the folder in which you submit your proposal.

Seven Virtues for a Best-Selling Author

You will be creating your promotion plan eighteen months to two years before your book is published. The goal of your plan is to convince a publisher to buy your book, but the plan is a theory. After your editor accepts your manuscript, it's time to put it into practice. Your plan is really two plans in one: a vertical plan and a horizontal plan. Because your proposal is a selling tool, the plan in your proposal is vertical. It lists what you will do in descending order of importance and your ability to help sell your book.

When your book goes into production, it's time to get horizontal: Create a time line that begins when your book goes into production, usually nine months before publication. Glossy, long-lead magazines plan their issues six months ahead of time. At the other extreme are news media that decide what to cover every day. The need for promotion is perpetual. Jack Canfield and Mark Victor Hansen advise writers to do five things every day to promote their books. Promoting your work may be the biggest challenge you face as a writer; but even with its inevitable pitfalls, it can be fun, exhilarating, and profitable. Take the long view: Everything you do is helping you build your career.

Promising less than you deliver and doing more will elicit smiles; doing less than you promise will cause frowns. The gap between promise and delivery may affect your relationship with your publisher and the sale of your next book. So make delivering more than you promise one of your goals.

What virtues does your plan need most to help it sell your book? They include these seven:

1. Enthusiasm
2. Creativity
3. Practicality
4. Comprehensiveness
5. The proven ability to carry out your plan because of your platform
6. A professional perspective on what you must do to make your book succeed
7. A plan that proves that you understand the value of the techniques you will use

The Golden Rule for Approaching Agents or Editors

Contact agents or editors only when two things are in place:

- Your networks tell you that on a scale of one to ten your proposal is as close to a ten as you can make it.
- Your promotion plan is as long and strong as you can make it.

Your promotion plan will affect a publisher's decision to buy your book and the strength of its commitment to it. If you have the right plan, agents and editors will be eager to work with you. Once again, this approach to promotion is based on what we have found works for selling books to New York publishers, the conglomerates that have the resources to do whatever they want with your book. If these suggestions are too ambitious, at least for your first book, don't be concerned. Align your efforts with your goals and do what works best for you and your book now.

❖ ❖ ❖

For best results, use *Guerrilla Marketing for Writers: 100 Weapons for Selling Your Work* to supplement this guide. Because publicity is the most cost-effective form of promotion, you will also find help in *Guerrilla Publicity: Hundreds of Sure-Fire Tactics to Get Maximum Sales at Minimum Dollars* by my *Guerrilla Marketing for Writers* co-authors, Jay Levinson and Rick Frishman, along with Jill Lublin and Mark Steisel.

But enough about your book. Now it's time to check out the competition.

12 | Competitive and Complementary Titles

If in your book hook, you can write that your book will be "the first book to _____," then you will face no competition and may skip to the section on complementary books.

However, we get calls about books that face competition, and one of the first questions I ask is: "How many books are out there on the subject?" Sometimes the writers have no idea what books will surround theirs on bookstore shelves, a response that proves those writers are not ready to begin their proposals, let alone contact agents.

Competitive Titles

The more books that have already appeared on a subject, the larger the market has to be to justify another book on the subject and the harder it may be to find the gap that your book will fill. Your proposal must prove that you and your book can survive and thrive despite the past and future competition.

Fortunately, subjects like cats, the Civil War, and saving or making money are timeless. Enterprising writers are always coming up with new ideas about them and writing successful books. A fresh angle, a fresh face, a well-written book, and enough promotional support will make any book sell.

Editors and their colleagues in sales and marketing will want you to do their market research for them. Once you've told them everything they need to know about your book, make use of the data you gathered when you researched competitive books to ease their fears about the competition.

You must convince publishers that:

- You're an expert on the subject who knows about the competitive books.
- You're being professional in the way you are approaching the project.
- Your ability to assess the competition objectively helps prove that you can judge your own book accurately.
- You have used your knowledge to come up with a new slant that justifies another book on your subject.
- You know that editors need this information, for their colleagues if not for themselves. Assume that they will check the information in competitive books with bricks (on land) and clicks (online) booksellers.

At large publishing houses, editors usually work on a range of subjects, but they also have specialties. There's usually at least one editor whose job is to take care of the house's sports books, while other editors acquire the house's business, cooking, and science books.

Starting the description of each book on a new line, list competitive books in order of importance, supplying for each the following:

- Full title
- Author
- Publisher, without the location or Inc.
- Year of publication
- Number of pages
- Format (hardcover, trade paperback, mass-market)
- Cover price, stated in whole dollars (e.g., $21, not $21.00)
- Trim size of the book, if you are proposing an art or photography book

Avoid starting descriptions with "this book," "it," or the title. Write two sentence fragments, incomplete sentences, starting each with a verb. First describe what competitive books do, then what they fail to do. Keep these descriptions as short as possible.

End the list with a statement about why your book will be different and better than the competition. You may use a list of reasons that begins: "[Your title] will be better than the competition because it _____."

Then list the reasons, starting each with a verb. You may repeat what you wrote in your book hook, but change the wording.

If you're writing about dieting, parenting, relationships, or psychological self-help—subjects about which there are hundreds of competitive books—describe only the most competitive half dozen or so. Provide just the basic information listed above, no descriptions, about the six next important competitors.

Keep this section as short as you can, no more than two pages. The proposal is about your book, not the competition. You must, however, convince editors that you have a knowledgeable, realistic perspective on what's out there, and that you have done justice to the competition.

Here are four ways to determine best-seller status:
- Check book covers.
- Talk to booksellers.
- Check the category "Bestseller" under the "Books" tab at Amazon .com.
- Call Ingram, the nation's largest wholesaler at (615) 213-6803. Provide a competitive book's International Standard Book Number (ISBN) to find out how the book is selling.

Another figure you can include in your description is the number of printings a competitive book has gone through. You can find this information on the copyright page. Look for a row of numbers in descending order; the number of printings is at the end of the row. For example, this row of numbers

$$10 \quad 9 \quad 8 \quad 7 \quad 6$$

appears in a book in its sixth printing. A book may also have a list of numbers like this

$$02 \quad 01 \quad 00 \quad 99 \quad 98$$

to indicate the year of the printing, which in this case is 1998.

Here is the closing of Rick Crandall's overview for his self-published book *Marketing Your Services: For People Who Hate to Sell*:

> None of the competitive books are well distributed or visible, and all of them are dated. For instance, the Internet is not mentioned as a new marketing medium. Despite their shortcomings, several of the above have gone through many printings. So the niche is wide open.
>
> The strategy of *Marketing Your Services* is to give readers a book that is streetwise, practical, action-oriented, and state-of-

the-art. In short, *Marketing Your Services: For People Who Hate to Sell* is a better value.

Be factual when noting the deficiencies of competitive books. Assume the editor either has seen them or knows about them, and may even have edited one or more of them. Will your book be more thorough, timely, beautiful, comprehensive, or up-to-date than its predecessors? If you think your book will be written better or have a more commercial angle, your proposal must prove it.

Pamphlets, most self-published books, scholarly books, and professional books from specialized publishers—such as those for doctors, lawyers, and real estate salespeople—don't count as competition because of their limited bookstore distribution, so don't include them in your proposal. Also skip out-of-print titles and other books that aren't aimed at the general public.

Editors are concerned about the titles that will compete with your book on booksellers' shelves. They want to avoid bookseller and reader resistance to your book because of similar books that have national distribution. You have to convince them that these books have not saturated the market for the subject so they can convince their colleagues.

Example: Competitive Titles

Here is how Sam Horn described competitive books in her proposal for her successful book *Tongue Fu: How to Deflect, Disarm, and Defuse Any Verbal Conflict*:

> *Tongue Fu* has only three major competitors:
> - *The Gentle Art of Verbal Self-Defense* (310 pages, Suzette Haden Elgin, Dorset Press, 1980). Contains useful information, but difficult to read. Small type and academic jargon. Published in eight languages with four follow-up books.
> - *Verbal Judo: The Gentle Art of Persuasion* (222 pages, George J. Thompson, William Morrow, 1994). Claims to help readers control the outcome of every dispute in the home, classroom, and boardroom. By a former policeman who created his methods for fellow officers. Focuses primarily on what to do when faced with volatile and potentially violent situations.
> - *The Magic of Conflict: Turning a Life of Work Into a Work of Art* (254 pages, Thomas Crum, Touchstone, 1987). Shows how to apply the martial art of aikido to daily conflicts. Emphasizes the importance of being centered and outlines how

to use this "New Age stress-reduction strategy" to turn struggle into success.

Your competitive books section doesn't have to be that long, but I hope it will be as effective.

Agents' and editors' opinions vary on whether to include information on competitive books. Even if your agent doesn't want you to include it in your proposal, you must know the competition so you can improve on it and be prepared to discuss it if an agent or editor asks you about it.

Hot Tip | Were all of the competitive books on the subject about which you're writing published by small or university presses? If so, this may mean that your subject may lack sufficient commercial appeal or be too far ahead of its time to be published by a large house. You must supply strong enough evidence to the contrary if you want to target a major publisher.

Complementary Books

Even if no competitive books on your topic exist, every book will have complementary books. The success of books on the same subject or of the same kind as yours that won't compete with yours will help convince editors of the need for your book. If the books aren't well known, indicate what they cover. Give the title, author, publisher, and publication year for six books or less.

If you are preparing your proposal for a specific publisher, mention books on its list that complement yours. Close with a statement on how the existence of these books proves the salability of yours. And before you start your proposal, also check to see if the publisher has proposal guidelines you can follow.

❖ ❖ ❖

Finally! This is the end of your overview, the first part of the introduction in your proposal. By now you have convinced an editor that you have a publishable idea, and a promotion plan that will help ensure the success of your book. In the last two parts of your introduction, you will prove that your idea is practical and that you have the experience and ability to write your book.

13 | Resources You Need to Complete Your Book

You have completed your overview and proved you have a salable idea. Now it's time to prove that you have made a realistic assessment of the resources you need to complete your book, including the most important resource of all: you.

On a new page titled "Resources Needed to Write the Book," describe the out-of-pocket expenses, starting with the largest, that will affect the size of the advance you need to finish your book. Out-of-pocket costs are those that you will incur in writing your book.

Calculating Your Expenses

Your largest expense may be travel. If you indicate that you need a certain sum for a trip, a publisher may offer you that sum. Mention where you're going and how long you'll be there but not how much it will cost. For example, write: "Researching the book will require a two-week trip to New York." This may give you or your agent wiggle room in negotiating the contract. If the reason you're going isn't obvious, explain it.

Include round figures for the cost of artwork, photography, a foreword, and permissions to use text or illustrations. If you will use a freelance editor to help you write the book, have the editor estimate the cost. Give the total for each kind of expense: "The book's photography budget will be $500."

If you have more than three types of expenses, list them in column form with the type on the left, the cost on the right, and the total at the bottom of the list. (Don't mention your time or the cost of office supplies.) For example:

Completion of the book will require the following expenses:
Permissions: $1,000
Thirteen photographs: .... $ 650
Freelance editor: $3,000

Total: $4,650

The author is usually responsible for using the advance to provide everything that goes into a book. Publishers may provide a separate advance for large expenses. A publisher that wants a book badly enough will pay for all or part of the expenses. The trade-off: If the publisher folds expenses into the cost of producing the book, the cover price may be higher and hinder sales.

Here are the resources Bill Yenne needed for *A Treasury of Treasure*:

Resources needed to complete the manuscript:
Travel: $7,500
    (to concentrations of treasure sites and lost
    mines in the West)
Equipment for fieldwork: $2,500
Charts and maps: $1,500
Photos: $1,500

Total: $13,000

Association of Authors' Representatives members Susan Ann Protter and Sheree Bykofsky are among the agents who think that, except for a permissions budget, it's easier to negotiate for expenses if the resource list does not include dollar figures. Your agent may prefer to omit resources entirely.

Because expenses will become part of the negotiation for the book, research them in advance. This will save you time later and add to your credibility as a professional by showing you've thought the project through and know the expenses that will be involved in completing it. Knowing the resources you need will also minimize the possibility that you will encounter unexpected sources that require more re-searching time, or that you will find illustrations or permissions that can't be obtained without additional money.

Permissions

To excerpt copyrighted material—a passage, a page, a chapter, a short story, or an illustration—in your book, you may need to obtain per-mission. Excerpts of 250 words or less from a book have traditionally been considered fair use: They may be used without the permission of the copyright holder. But publishers vary in their approaches to permissions and the doctrine of fair use.

To establish the cost of permissions to use quotes and illustrations from books, look up the books' publishers in *Writer's Market* or *Literary Market Place* and contact the rights-and-permissions person. For permissions on material not in books, contact the copyright holder. Syndicates and magazines charge flat rates for permissions. Make sure, if you can, that the copyright holder will let you use the material and that the cost won't be prohibitive.

You may not be able to obtain an exact price until you know the publisher, format, price, and first printing of your book. Nonetheless, try to get a range of prices for what they charge for similar permissions and use the midpoint for your estimate. If, for example, they charge between one hundred and three hundred dollars, use two hundred dollars as your estimate.

Ask about the price for "the United States, including its territories, dependencies, and military bases; Canada; the Philippines; and nonexclusive rights throughout the rest of the world except for the British Commonwealth." This is the basic grant of rights your publisher will expect to buy.

In addition to the cost of these rights, copyright holders will want either a flat fee for world rights or a fee for each country to which the book is sold. Depending on the costs involved and your book's potential for foreign sales, it may be more efficient to buy world rights when you know what material you need, and after you receive the acceptance check from your publisher. Whoever retains foreign rights will arrange for permissions for a British edition and then translations when they become necessary.

If you're doing an anthology, obtaining the right to use copyrighted material is essential to writing your book. If you expect the cost of permissions to run more than one thousand dollars, find out as much as you can to be accurate about permissions costs in your proposal.

Learning everything you can in advance may prevent you from proposing quotes or illustrations you can't obtain or afford.

If you're just using a short quote from a book, it may fall under the fair-use doctrine. If you must obtain permission, mention in your proposal that completing the book will require permissions costs for x quotes or illustrations. If you are willing to pay for permissions and write them off as a business expense, write: "The author will pay for the cost of permissions." Your publisher won't have to be concerned about the cost, but you should be confident that you can cover the cost with your expected advance and potential book earnings.

As with other expenses, permissions costs may be a bargaining chip when you negotiate your contract. If you're in the fortunate position of having more than one publisher bidding for your book, one of them may be willing to pay for all or part of the permissions, give you a separate advance for them, or handle the paperwork on them.

Publishers' permissions forms vary. After your book is sold, ask your editor for a copy of the permissions letter that you can photocopy as needed. You won't pay for permissions until after your manuscript is accepted, so you can use the acceptance portion of your advance for them.

Packaging Your Book

If you're proposing an illustrated book and you want to package it—that is, provide the publisher with bound books or the book ready for the printer—include the costs involved and your experience as a packager along with the publishing experience of anyone who will help you.

Suggest packaging only if you have experience in the field or you can work with an experienced packager. Even then, the publisher may prefer to take care of the editing, design, and production.

Determining a Budget and a Timeline

In addition to making a list of out-of-pocket expenses for writing your book, make a budget of your living expenses for your own benefit. Keep in mind that publishers may regard an advance as a sum of money enabling a writer to meet expenses involved in writing a book. But you need enough money so you can devote all of your time to completing your book. Editors know that the smaller the advance, the more time it may take you to turn in your manuscript if you have to work to support your writing habit.

Hot Tip

Unless your book will be complicated to research or is large in scope, don't explain how you will write it. Let your proposal prove that you know what you're doing. If an agent or editor is working with another writer on a similar project, valuable information may wind up in a competitor's hands. If editors have questions about your research techniques, they'll ask.

Two exceptions: If your book requires access to celebrities or VIPs, your proposal must prove that you have it. If you're writing a biography, indicate your access to the person or to information about the person. If the subject is dead, note whether the bio will be authorized and whether the estate will give you access to the person's papers.

The time it takes you to research and write the proposal, especially the sample chapter, will provide a basis for judging how long it will take you to write the rest of your book. Another way to estimate your writing time, once you have finished your proposal, is to go through your outline chapter by chapter, use the time you spent on the sample chapter as a criterion to guess how long it will take you to write each chapter, then add the results.

Publishers want to start recouping their investments as soon as possible. They also want their books to be well written. Unless your book is on a hot subject and must be completed quickly, don't commit yourself to writing 50,000 words in two months. Unless you have a strong track record, editors will not believe you can do a professional job in that time frame, and they may offer you less money because of your short deadline.

The time you allot should make sense in relation to your writing experience, the time it takes you to write the sample chapter, and the book's subject and length. After you decide how long writing the book will take, add a month or two as a cushion to allow for unexpected problems that may force you to veer off course. Six months, nine months, and a year are common deadlines. Make yours what you feel will enable you to produce your best work.

Here are three variations on how to write the last sentence about resources:

- "The author will deliver the manuscript *x* months after the receipt of the advance." If time is the only resource you need, this is the only sentence you need. Add it to the end of your overview.
- "The author has finished, in draft form, *x* chapters of the book.

The rest of the book will be completed *y* months after receipt of the advance."

* "The manuscript is complete in draft form, and the author will deliver the final manuscript. . . . "

You can use one of these sentences as the last one on resources if you already have a partial or complete manuscript.

Updating Your Book

Publishers want to publish a book and have it sell forever without having to be changed. They're reluctant to publish books that have to be updated every year, unless—as with almanacs, consumer guides, or tax guides—a large enough readership needs the information.

If your book holds the promise of continuing sales but will require updating, write: "The author will update the book every *x* years." Try to avoid including anything in your book that will become outdated before you revise it.

To be considered an updated and revised edition, at least 10 percent of a book must be new information. For a new edition, 30 percent of the book must be new.

A new edition is treated like a new book. It appears in the publisher's catalog again, the reps resell it, and you have another chance to promote it. Meanwhile, you can also update your book on your Web site.

Chin Up: Surviving the Exercise

Sometimes writers must feel like the guy in the cartoon who asks a bookstore clerk for a book on suicide and the clerk says, "Why don't you try self-help?"

It may sound like you have to know everything about your book before you have fully researched it. But, what you do have to do is convince editors that:

* You know your subject.
* Your idea won't require too much time or money to write and publish.
* You're giving them an opportunity to latch on to a winner.
* You will do a superb job writing your book.

Editors understand that you are presenting your book only on the basis of what you know now. Once the project is sold, you and your editor will have an identical interest in producing the best possible book, and you will be free to improve on what you propose in any way that you and your editor agree will help the book. Despite this opportunity, a well-thought out proposal may save you grief later by ensuring that you write the same book the editor bought.

You don't have to be an expert on your subject when you begin researching it. Starting a proposal with just an open mind and a passionate, insatiable curiosity is better than setting out with misconceptions or prejudices. One joy of the writing life is the opportunity to learn new things that enable you to grow both as a person and as a professional. Another is getting paid for the opportunity.

❖ ❖ ❖

After you've finished the proposal, you will probably know more about your subject than an agent or editor does. The research you do for your book will elevate you toward the status of an expert. Let the bio that follows prove you're a pro.

14 | Your Bio

The last part of your introduction is the About the Author section.
Start on a new page, and describe in descending order of relevance
and importance everything about you that will prove you can write
and promote your book. Don't repeat what you include in your
platform.

Eleven Elements of an Author Bio

These are the eleven most important elements to cover in your bio:

1. If you have had a book published, give the title, publisher, and
publication year. Include sales figures, if they're impressive, and subsidiary rights sales.

2. Editors won't take the time to read complete reviews unless your
books have received raves in major periodicals, so include up to a
page of favorable quotes on a separate page with the heading "From
the Reviews of [title of book]." If editors are not likely to be familiar
with the source of a review, describe the periodical and note its circulation if impressive.

3. If your previous book received favorable reviews in important
magazines or newspapers, underline the good parts and enclose the
reviews at the end of the proposal or in the left pocket of the paper

folder in which you submit your proposal. Include the cover of the magazine if it's 8½" by 11". Don't staple the pages if you or your agent will photocopy them.

4. If your book was blessed with a half page or more of quotes from opinion makers, include the quotes in descending order of the words' or the source's impressiveness.

5. If it will impress editors, give the number of articles on other subjects that you've had published, and the range of subjects you've written about.

6. Name the online and offline media in which your work has appeared.

7. Include impressive articles about yourself with the significant points underlined, particularly if they're also about the subject of your book. These will prove the acceptance of you and your idea in the media. Articles about the subject will also help your cause. Include them in the left pocket of your proposal folder.

8. Include every facet of your personal and professional experience that adds luster to you as a person and a writer: published work on other subjects; education; awards; travel; hobbies; and special skills. Include writers conferences you've attended and contests you've won or received honorable mention in.

9. Mention memberships in writers organizations. You will get extra points if you have served as an officer in the organization and more points still if you have been an officer of a national organization.

10. If you have received letters about you or your work that will impress editors, include up to a page of quotes from them.

11. If you have audio or video clips of interviews, send them to agents and editors with your proposal.

If you plan to write books on other subjects, list up to three ideas or titles in the order of their commercial potential. As noted earlier, agents and publishers are eager to discover authors who can be counted on to turn out a book a year, and every idea that editors like is another reason for them to work with you. You might wind up selling another book you plan to write instead of the one you propose. Editors may have their own book ideas, and if they're impressed enough with your proposal, they may give you a writing assignment.

If you have a brochure about the business you own that will impress editors, include it. If you have a family, mention it along with where you live. If you wish, mention hobbies or other activities you enjoy.

Hot Tip

Pretend you're an editor at the house you would most like to have publish your book. What would you want to know about the author? Every word in your bio must prove why buying your book is the right decision.

Here are three mistakes to avoid in your bio:

1. Avoid the extremes of hype and false humility, even if you have a lot to be modest about. In *Book Editors Talk to Writers*, Farrar, Straus & Giroux senior editor Rebecca Saletan notes that "in literary nonfiction or memoirs—books that are more like fiction—credentials are less important."

2. Don't be cute or overly creative. It's okay to let your personality shine through in your bio—especially if it will help you sell the proposal or promote your book. For example, the first line of one writer's query letter was "I've been collecting rejections on a city-by-city basis, and San Francisco has come up," a funny, attention-grabbing line. But cute is out, as is humor unless you will use humor in your book. Avoid far-out approaches to telling your life story. And don't offer sympathy for agents and editors, as in "I know that many books pass your desk, but . . . "

3. Avoid the terms *currently* or *at present*.

Example: Third-Person Bio

Dennis Hauck's bio in his proposal for *The Emerald Tablet: Message for the Millennium* proves that he has the credentials, including speaking and media experience, that large publishers want. This was written before I started to recommend writing a platform, but you can see how Dennis included his platform.

> Dennis William Hauck is an internationally recognized authority on the paranormal. A respected consultant and investigator for three national organizations, he remains at the forefront of modern research into unexplained phenomena. He has personally experienced a variety of paranormal manifestations and has interviewed hundreds of witnesses to events ranging from apparitions to UFOs.
>
> A founding editor of the *MUFON UFO Journal*, Hauck was editor for six monthly newsstand magazines (*ESP*, *Phenomena*, *Sea Monsters*, *Ancient Astronauts*, *UFOlogy* and *Official UFO*).
>
> For four years, he wrote a weekly syndicated column and

has written dozens of articles. Hauck lectures extensively about Fortean phenomena and has appeared as a featured speaker at a dozen international conferences. He is one of the leading advocates of treating all paranormal experiences as part of a larger phenomenon that parapsychologists call "exceptional human experience."

Hauck has been interviewed on nearly three hundred radio programs, as well as more than twenty television talk shows. He was featured in William Shatner's *Mysteries of the Gods* (Hemisphere Pictures, 1976) and has consulted on several motion pictures, including *Close Encounters of the Third Kind* (Columbia Pictures, 1977). He was a paid consultant for Hollywood production companies to work on three TV movies based on true-life ghost stories. Hauck also works with television shows such as *Sightings, Encounters, Hidden Lives,* and *The Other Side.*

He attended Indiana University and pursued his graduate studies at the University of Vienna in Austria. Today he works as a full-time freelance author/lecturer, as western regional director for the Mutual UFO Network, and as California state director for the Ghost Research Society. He is also an active member of the American Society for Psychical Research and conducts scientific investigations into claims of paranormal activity.

Hauck translated a series of medieval German alchemical manuscripts, which led to this proposal. Hauck is listed in *Who's Who in California, The Dictionary of International Biography, The International Authors,* and *Writers Who's Who.*

Hot Tip

Avoid using a résumé instead of a biography. Résumés are too formal and contain information editors don't need. Through your proposal you may be applying for work, but you're not applying for a job. If you are an artist or professor and you think your résumé is also necessary to prove your qualifications, make it an appendix to your proposal. Make your bio a clear, concise description of your life and work. If you are writing a humor book, be funny.

The first two sentences of Ted Allrich's bio provide all the credibility he needs to write *The Online Investor:*

A professional investment advisor registered with the SEC, Ted Allrich is a graduate of the Stanford University Master of Business Administration program. He launched his own advisory firm in 1991 and manages more than $22 million for individuals, trusts, and IRA accounts.

Example: First-Person Bios

Write your bio in the third person as if you were writing a news release about yourself. Editors will appreciate your modesty, and it will read better than a page full of *I*s. That said, a first-person bio can be effective if it's well written.

The bio that follows proves that Francesca De Grandis brings immense authority to her book, and that what she writes about is an integral part of her personal life as well as her professional life. An editor will also be impressed by her media savvy, her teaching experience, and her personality, which comes through in the first five words.

> Raised by a Sicilian witch, I learned that spirituality must be practical. That earthiness is a tenet of Goddess spirituality and is expressed in *Be a Goddess!*
>
> I completed rigorous training with Victor Anderson, a Master of the Faerie Tradition, to become a Celtic shaman. I was adopted into Victor's family, which had kept the old ways intact. Few Wiccan traditions today have such lengthy, in-depth training. Mr. Anderson has called me "one of the very few . . . who has shown understanding of the endangered mysteries of my people. . . . "
>
> I am one of only five people in the country who earn their living as a witch. My prosperity as a professional witch is remarkable since I work in San Francisco, where the market is glutted with first-rate teachers like Starhawk and Luisa Teish. Religious leaders refer students to me.
>
> In 1986, I established The Third Road in San Francisco for Goddess Spirituality. Through the oral tradition—my classes and counseling—my teaching has been successful for more than a decade. My national and international work has also been successful. In 1992, I taught in England for six months.
>
> When a National Public Radio program in which I was featured was marketed as an audiotape, its review in *The Whole Earth Review* mentioned my name along with Z. Budapest and Starhawk. My work on ABC's San Francisco affiliate, KGO radio, where I hosted an occult special, helps prove the marketability of my approach to shamanism. I was a regular guest on KSFO; on KPIX, San Francisco's CBS television

affiliate; and I have shared my magic on Voice of America. Z. Budapest called me "a real musical talent . . . haunting." And Starhawk called my thesis for the New College of California "a personal and magical journey by a witch who knows her stuff." I was the subject of a documentary aired on PBS.

I led workshops at the Massachusetts Rites of Spring and the Middletown, California, Ancient Ways Festival and led one of the main events at the Wiccan Conference in San Jose as well as one of the larger events at the Covenant of the Goddess's national conference.

An interview with me appears in *People of the Earth: The New Pagans Speak Out* by Ellen Evert Hopman and Lawrence Bond (Inner Traditions). Other presentations include an interfaith ritual at the six thousand-member Chicago Parliament of World Religions, a storytelling performance at the Intersection for the Arts in San Francisco, and a lecture on Mysticism and Art at the San Francisco Art Institute. The online magazine, *Witches' Brew*, published a feature article on me in late 1996.

Picture Yourself Published

Affix a 5″ × 7″ or an 8″ × 10″ black-and-white photo of yourself at the end of your bio or centered on a blank, unnumbered page after your bio. Your photo can help sell you as a professional, promotable author. Make the photo relate to your book. For example, if you are writing a book about fly-fishing, aim for a photo of you standing in your waders and casting into a stream.

If you can't use your computer to print your photograph, a high-resolution photocopy will be fine for a multiple submission. A photo that makes you look "mediagenic" in a story about you will suffice.

If you are sharing authorship with a writer, photographer, or illustrator, include a bio and a photo of each of you on a separate page. If you are just using someone on a work-for-hire basis and paying her a fee for all rights to her work, include a bio but not a photo.

If Your Book Is Complete

If you have a complete manuscript, read chapter eighteen to see if you should submit all of it. You don't have to prepare anything described beyond this point if you're submitting a complete manuscript, but you should include information on future expenses such as artwork and permissions in your cover letter. If you're submitting a self-published or out-of-print book, plan to include the first part of the proposal and information about the sales of books and subsidiary rights, how many pages of changes you want to do, and how long they'll take to write.

❖ ❖ ❖

It may take you a lot of time and effort to get to this point in your proposal, yet your introduction may add up to less than ten pages. The next challenge is to prove that you can use the information you've gathered to produce a book that's worth putting between covers.

15 | Your Outline

"It's not a book, it's an article." The following pages will prevent you from hearing this fatal complaint. After you have marshaled the ammunition for your book, the next challenge is to convince editors that you have researched the subject well enough to prove that there's more than enough information in your idea to fill a book.

The outline of your book is the bones, the pieces of information that fit together to form a harmonious structure that enables you and your editor to envision the finished book. Your outline must prove that you have come up with the most effective way to present your information, and it must make editors want to read the sample chapter.

Writing your outline also gives you the opportunity to prove:
1. The quantity and quality of information you uncover will merit the publication of one and ideally a series of books.
2. The book will be commercial enough to justify writing and publishing it.
3. You will enjoy writing and promoting it.

Your List of Chapters
The first page of your outline is a double-spaced list of chapters. The best time for editors to see the list is just before they read your outline.

At the top of the first page, center these two double-spaced lines:

The Outline
List of Chapters

Along the left margin, type the number of the chapter, then the title, and flush right, the number of the page the outline begins on:

Chapter 1: Title (and subtitle if you use one)   11

Give each chapter a title as clear, compact, and compelling as the title of your book. If you wish, give chapters catchy or intriguing titles, then use subtitles to tell and sell: Tell readers what the chapter is about and convince them it will be worth their time to read it. If your subtitle will spill over to the next line, type the whole subtitle on the next line. Include the number of the page on which the outline begins flush right on the same line.

Make your titles flow naturally, resulting in a sense of continuity in time, tone, and structure. Whet the editor's appetite for the outline that follows. Make them read like headlines of ads that compel people to read the copy that follows. If you are writing a humorous book, make your titles funny.

Consider giving your book a superstructure by dividing it into parts. Give each part a title and use Roman numerals to number them. Deciding to divide your book into parts and creating chapter titles are two more opportunities for you to emulate successful books. Type all titles and subtitles in upper and lower case.

Example: List of Chapters

The chapter titles for Steve Capellini's *The Royal Treatment How You Can Take Home the Pleasures of the Great Luxury Spas* (Dell) capture the engaging, down-to-earth tone with which he wrote the book. The range of topics makes the book look comprehensive. Note the superstructure Steve gives the book by dividing the chapters into two parts.

The Outline
List of Chapters

Introduction: Your Own Royal Treatment   15

PART I: Creating a Ritual

> Chapter 1: She Sells Body Scrubs by the Sea Shore:
> Sans Souci Spa, Ocho Rios, Jamaica   16

Your list of chapters is not the complete table of contents of your book, so don't include your book's front or back matter. Instead, just include the titles of the chapters that editors are about to read.

Constructing the Best Outline for Your Book

If you find it difficult to create a book outline or impose a structure on your material, one of the following three techniques will help you:

1. Use your computer to list your chapters and then what each will cover. Your computer makes it a breeze to change and move copy to your heart's content.
2. Use a more portable technique: index cards. You can shuffle them until they fall into the right order.

3. Do what author Sam Horn recommends: mind-mapping.
   - Draw a circle that symbolizes the book and then draw gently curving lines going off from the edge of the circle like strands of hair waving in the breeze.
   - Along one side of each line, write a word or phrase describing the idea for each of your chapters.
   - Draw perpendicular lines off those lines to list words or phrases for the parts of each chapter.

You'll be surprised at how this stimulates your creativity. You can also use mind-mapping to create the title of your book. Listing phrases that capture the benefits of your book. Then abstract the essence of your book in the one title that belongs inside the circle.

Certain kinds of books such as cartoon books or picture books may not lend themselves to being outlined. But like readers, editors expect books to have a unified, harmonious structure. When I wrote the proposal for *Painted Ladies*, instead of just proposing a book of photographs of houses, I gave the book a structure by dividing it into four sections covering parts of the city. Later, we added another element to the structure of the book by arranging the photographs in the order of an architectural tour.

Ray Bradbury condenses the writing process into two verbs: Throw up and clean up. There are two basic ways you can ease your way into writing your outlines—from the outside in or the inside out.

- **From the outside in.** Use the left side of your brain to burrow your way in. As suggested above, list your chapters and the bare bones or subheads of each chapter on index cards, in a notebook, or on your computer, then flesh out the bare bones with connective tissue.
- **From the inside out.** Use the right side of your brain to create a body of information for you to draw on. Let at least one draft of your manuscript pour out, then create a separate file for each chapter. Whittle away until you create a chapter hook and one-line of outline for every page in each chapter.

The second approach is more likely for a memoir than a book about the history of a country that you've researched enough to know what each chapter will cover. Other books, by their very nature, suggest a structure. A biography is structured chronologically; a how-to book starts with the simplest elements of a skill and leads readers to the advanced aspects of it.

Discovering What Your Book Wants to Be

Michelangelo believed his statues were waiting for him inside the blocks of marble he carved with hammer and chisel. Imagine that you are a sculptor and that your idea is an enormous block of marble inside of which is a magnificent edifice, the perfect embodiment of your idea. Your job is to use your craft and vision to chip away the superfluous until only an effective, organic structure remains in which form and function are inseparable. One sign of great art is that the artist's technique is so effective that it disappears into the work.

You can also think of the outline of your book as the blueprint of the cottage or castle you will build with your royalties. (Even if you can only imagine building a hut, stay with me here.) Just as you would not leave a room out of your blueprint, your outline must provide an overview of what your book will cover. And just as you want your new home to be as beautiful as the design you have created for it, your blueprint must reflect the unity and harmony that you want your home to have.

Your outlines are not showcases meant to dazzle editors with your style. They are an opportunity for you to show how well you can research, organize, and outline your book. In your introduction and outline, content will count more than style.

But even though an outline cannot be a stylistic triumph, every word still counts. Providing a sound structure for your chapters and the book as a whole demonstrates your knowledge of the subject and your ability to transform your idea into a book you and your publisher will be proud of.

A skimpy outline will have editors asking: "How do I know this is a book and not just an article?" A thin outline also invites unexpected problems. By not thoroughly investigating what's involved in writing your book, you are more likely to encounter more books to read, places to go, people to interview, illustrations, or permissions to obtain than you thought. A comprehensive outline is the best way to prevent costly, time-consuming surprises.

The German poet Rainer Maria Rilke believed that "prose should be built like a cathedral." When you set out to construct an enduring edifice of prose, give yourself a solid foundation on which to build.

A One-Sentence Overview

To help an editor grasp the essence of a chapter quickly, consider beginning each outline with a one-sentence overview of the chapter. Here are three ways to do this:

1. This chapter covers . . .

When a Detailed Outline Isn't Necessary

Here are four simple ways of outlining a book you may be able to use:

1. If you're planning to submit your complete manuscript, you can just write a two-page synopsis instead of an outline.

2. If your book will have short chapters, don't use complete sentences for your outlines. Use phrases beginning with verbs the same way you describe competitive books. Vary the verbs as much as you can. You will also use this technique if you abbreviate your outline for the mini-proposal discussed in chapter twenty-four.

3. If your book will consist of a series of chapters, each with the same structure and presenting the same kind of information, you don't have to prepare an in-depth outline. Just list the chapters and then list what each will contain in the section on special features. For example, if you were going to write a guide to Europe's ten greatest cities, you would list—in order—the cities the book will cover, then—also in order—the resources you will describe in each city.

4. If you are planning a compilation of information such as an almanac, a dictionary, or an encyclopedia, list the topics the book will cover.

2. The goal (aim, purpose, object) of this chapter is to . . .

3. This chapter has or is divided into *x* parts. This alternative has the added virtue of telling the editor about the structure of the chapter. If you do this, you can write a paragraph about each of the parts, starting each with a catchy subhead if you wish.

Here are the first sentences of the outlines for two chapters in Michael Lillyquist's book, the final title of which is *Sunlight and Health: The Positive and Negative Effects of the Sun on You.*

> The second chapter serves as an introduction to the knowledge about the nature of sunlight and its effects.

> The final chapter describes four advances civilization has made with the advent of artificial lighting as well as the problems encountered along the way.

How Much Description Does Each Chapter Need?

Outlining a chapter with only a series of one-line topics, set off with letters or numbers, looks academic, raises questions a list can't answer, and doesn't explain enough about the chapter. The exception to this is if your book will be a compilation of information in chapter form.

For other kinds of books, start each chapter outline on a new page, and describe the contents of the chapter: the instructions in a how-to book, the characters and events in a history or biography, the development of a book's thesis.

Aim for one line of outline for every page of manuscript that you envision. For a chapter with nineteen pages, write nineteen lines of outline. This is a goal, not an absolute, but it does make the length of your outlines relate to the length of your chapters. You will learn how to guesstimate the length of your chapters below.

A chapter outline may run from one paragraph to two pages or more, depending on:

- The kind of book you're writing
- How much information you have
- How long the chapter will be
- Whether you use an anecdote at the beginning of each chapter
- Whether you will include a sample chapter with your proposal
- How long an outline your agent prefers
- The guidelines of the publisher you plan to submit your book to

For most books, a page of outline for each chapter is enough. Use as few words as necessary. If you're not planning to include a sample chapter, consider compensating by doubling the length of your outline.

Hot Tip

Establish literary goals for each chapter as well as your book:
- What effect do you want the chapter to have on your readers?
- How much humor, if any, do you want in a chapter?
- How many anecdotes?
- Will the anecdotes you plan to include have the desired effect?

Write the outline your book needs. If your book calls for outlines of a half a page or less, let them run one after the other instead of beginning each outline on a new page.

Outline every chapter, including the one you submit as a sample, so an editor can see how the chapters flow into one another, and how an outline relates to a completed chapter.

Outline Style: Format and Length

Start the first page of each chapter outline like this:

Part #
Title

(The above go only on the first page of each new part.)

Chapter #

Chapter Title   # Pages, # Photos
(Flush left)   (Flush right)

Chapters usually range from fourteen to thirty-six manuscript pages. Once a chapter starts running longer than thirty-six pages, consider dividing it into two chapters, but follow your models.

If your chapters will be the same length or your chapters will average *x* pages, make this point in the overview in the section on special features. Then you don't have to give page lengths in your outlines, and you can center your chapter titles.

If the salability of your book depends on the new revelations that you are adding to the record, your outlines give you another chance to mention them. Weave your revelations into your outlines by writing, "This chapter/The next part of the chapter will be the first to . . . "

When you mention a person, place, event, fact, or instruction you plan to illustrate, add the word *photo*, *graph*, *map*, *drawing*, or *chart* after it in parentheses. An alternative: Skip a line after the end of the chapter outline, type the word "Illustrations," then list them in paragraph form in the order they will appear and what kind of illustration each will be, if they will vary.

Your Page Count

Your manuscript pages will have:
- About 10 words to a line
- Sixty 12-point characters to a line
- Twenty-five, 5″ lines to a page
- About 250 words to a page

But when your manuscript becomes a book, the page count will usually be cut by at least one-third, so, 180 pages of manuscript will become 120 pages of text. The number of words, pages, and chapters in books you want to emulate will help you decide on the numbers for your book.

Add up the number of illustrations you envision in each chapter.

Then add the number of pages in your chapters to the page count for the back matter that you included in your overview and you will obtain the figures you need for your book hook (described in chapter three). Your agent may prefer to have only these totals in the proposal without including the numbers for each chapter.

Editors know you are guesstimating. As mentioned earlier, you'll be free to make whatever changes you and your editor agree will help your book. But a proposal that presents a clear vision of every aspect of the book makes you look like the professional you aspire to be. Writing your sample chapter will give you a sense of the relationship between outline and manuscript. As you write your sample chapter, you will develop an understanding of how an outline corresponds to a finished chapter.

After you have written your sample chapter and completed your outlines, go through the outlines paragraph by paragraph, and, based on your experience of how an outline evolved into your sample chapter, estimate how many pages of manuscript each paragraph of your outlines will be. You will usually be able to tell whether a paragraph in the outline will turn into three, five, seven, ten or more pages.

Hot Tip | Avoid having all of your page counts end in five or zero. If you use just those numbers, it may seem like you are just picking the first number that leaps to mind instead of thinking through how long your chapters need to be. Using 19 or 21, instead of 20, will convince editors that you considered the length of your chapter with at least the same care as the numbers they will choose for their P&L (profit-and-loss statement) for your book.

Fast Fixes for Four Problems

Be as specific as your research allows you to be about your ideas, facts, people, statistics, dates, advice, instructions, incidents and anecdotes. Take care to avoid these four problems in outlines:

• Because you are preparing your outline for agents or editors, avoid the word *you* as if you were talking to your readers. One exception is if you will include a list of suggestions for readers in the outline. Here's an example: *This chapter explains ten suggestions for getting along well with agents: Remember that your agent works for you, you don't work for your agent.* The word *you* makes sense here, because this suggestion will be used both in an outline and in the book.

• Put your quotes into context. Identify the sources of your quotes. If the book, person, or periodical is not well known, include additional information such as a date, place or circumstance, to place the quote in context.

- If you mention a person or incident, include enough information so an editor understands what you're writing about and why.
- Avoid asking rhetorical questions. Questions editors can't answer don't help sell your proposal. The purpose of the proposal is not to ask questions, but to answer every question an editor may have about you and your book. The only part of the proposal in which questions make sense is your sample chapter, in which you're free to address your readers.

Example: Chapter Outline

Here's an outline from the first edition of the book I wrote that later became *Literary Agents: What They Do, How They Do It, and How to Find and Work With the Right One for You*:

Chapter Twelve

Good Fences Make Good Neighbors:
How to Handle Agency Agreements   13 Pages

This chapter starts by balancing the pros and cons of agency agreements. Then it covers eleven essential points that should appear in any agreement, as well as five clauses for writers to avoid. Four representative agreements follow, including the author's.

The discussion of agreements concludes that since no agreement can encompass every potential contingency, the most important basis for any agreement is the good faith of the people who sign it.

The next part of the chapter presents a separate Bill of Rights for authors and agents stating their responsibilities to each other whether or not agents have an agreement.

The chapter ends by analyzing the causes for changing agents and the three-step procedure for doing it:
- Try to find a mutually satisfactory solution to the problem.
- If that is not possible, notify your agent in writing that you are leaving the agency.
- Find another agent.

❖ ❖ ❖

Now that you have an overview of preparing your outline, you are ready to learn about the four keys to making your outline effective.

16 | Keys for Effective Outlines

The Golden Rule for Starting an Outline
Use a quote, event, revelation, anecdote, statistic, idea, surprise, or joke to entice editors to read your outlines.

Here are four essential keys for writing effective outlines:

1. Create Hooks That Keep Readers Reading
Just as the beginning of your proposal has to hook editors, so must every chapter outline. Start every chapter outline with the most captivating anecdote or slice of copy from the chapter that captures the essence of it.

Put your chapter hooks in quotes and skip an extra space between them and your outline. Don't repeat the anecdotes in your chapter hooks. Don't use the anecdote you placed at the beginning of your proposal or in your sample chapter. If you don't have another story you can use, write at the beginning of the outline: "The chapter begins with the anecdote at the beginning of the proposal." You could, if you are saving an anecdote for the beginning of your sample chapter, write a one-line synopsis: "This chapter begins with a story about . . . "

Roger Crawford, whose proposal is in Appendix E, has such a wealth of stories that he has both opening and closing chapter hooks in his outline. Make one of your goals to entice readers into reading the next chapter by making the end of your chapters as seductive as their beginnings.

Consider these factors in choosing your hooks:

- Quotes can draw readers into a chapter, but make them fresh, concise, and enjoyable to read. Avoid Plato, Shakespeare and The Bible. Editors have seen the old standbys too many times.
- Try a short passage of dialogue from a biography, history, or another kind of narrative nonfiction book for which the quality of the writing will be essential to its success.

Starting your outlines with the strongest slice of prose from each chapter will help:

- Prove that you can write the book
- Make your outlines enjoyable to read
- Show editors how your style complements the subject
- Excite editors about your book

If your hooks are strong enough, editors may just skim the outlines. They'll believe that if you can write well enough and zoom in on the strongest parts of your book, you know how to structure and outline it.

2. Give Chapters a Structure

If you simply summarize your chapters, the outline will read like an article or short book, and editors will reject your proposal, thinking that the idea doesn't have enough substance for a book. Giving each outline a structure makes your outlines read like outlines instead of summaries. You will find these three approaches effective:

- Use a number in the title, like *10 Steps to . . .* or a time by which readers will gain the book's benefit. *Thin Thighs in 30 Days* is such an example.

Your chapters can be part of the metaphor you use in the title of your book. As mentioned earlier, for *Guerrilla Marketing for Writers: 100 Weapons for Selling Your Work,* we divided the book into 100 short pieces. Each chapter title includes the number of weapons we cover. If you were going to write a book called *The House of Love,* your chapters could be the rooms in the house and what's in them.

You can divide chapters into parts, chunks, modules, steps, ways or stages that are the organizing force of the chapter, and that you can also mention in the title of the chapter, as I did in this chapter. Unless your title indicates that your book is structured around numbers, using numbers for every chapter will make your book seem formulaic.

- Structure each chapter like a little book with a beginning, middle, and end. Indicate the structure by introducing each part of the chapter.

Here are alternative openings for the successive parts of a chapter:
First, the chapter . . .
The first (opening) part (section, segment) of the chapter . . .
The chapter begins (starts, opens with) . . .
. . . starts (begins, opens) the chapter.
In the opening part (section, segment) of the chapter, . . .
Next comes (is) . . .
At this point in the chapter, . . .
The next (following, middle) part (segment, section) of the chapter . . .
The chapter then (or, Then the chapter) . . .
In the following (next, middle) section (part, segment) of the chapter, . . .
. . . follows (comes next).
The chapter's next (middle) section (segment) . . .
In the last (final, closing, concluding) part of the chapter . . .
The rest of the chapter . . .
The chapter ends (concludes, closes) with/by . . .
. . . ends (concludes, completes) the chapter.
The chapter's conclusion . . .

Outlining your first book is a new skill, but you will get the hang of it, and a thorough outline will help you even more than your publisher. Three quick tips:

1. Don't write *this chapter*, write *the chapter*.
2. Don't write *the reader*, write *readers*.
3. Be creative in how you vary your wording.

• Conceptualize the information in your chapters in the form of an image or symbol that captures the essence of the chapter in a unifying, memorable way. Is it possible to visualize the material in your book as a shape like a circle, a triangle, or a pie, the slices of which constitute the substance of each chapter? Could the information be compared to a jewel, a plant, an activity, a machine, a person, a place, a period or an event in history? Like an evocative title for a book, the right image can convey the tone and structure of a chapter.

For example, my book about literary agents has separate chapters about a terrible day and a terrific day in the life of an agent. Starting in the morning, I made up a composite of the horrible and wonderful things that have befallen our agency over the years. And judging from the comments I get, those are the two most memorable chapters in the book. The search for the proper structure for your chapters and your book is another example of how reading comparable books will spark your creativity.

3. Use Outline Verbs

Another way to make your outlines read like outlines is to use outline verbs that tell what each part of the chapter does. For instance, instead of writing a description of the Left Bank in Paris, write: "The next part of the chapter describes the Left Bank in Paris. . . . "

To give you a better feeling for outline verbs, here is an alphabetical potpourri. You don't have to read the list now, but keep it handy as you do your outline.

address	continue	express	list
advance	convince	focus on	lock horns
advise	debunk	follow	look (ahead,
advocate	defend	forge	around, back,
affirm	define	form	closely, for-
agree	deliver	give (voice to)	ward) at (into)
analyze	demonstrate	go (ahead, back	maintain
appraise	deplore	to, into, on,	mark
argue	describe	over, through)	marshal
assert	(is) designed (to)	guess,	mention
assess	develop	guesstimate	mobilize
assist, assists	discuss	hammer	motivate
readers in,	dispel	harmonize	move on to
associate	dissect	help (readers)	name
attack	distill	highlight	narrow
attests to	document	identify	note
balance	dramatize	illuminate	observe
blast	drive home	illustrate	offer
blend	elaborate	include	orient (readers)
broaden	emphasize	incorporate	outline
build (on, up)	enable	integrate	paint
center (on,	encourage	introduce	pepper
around)	establish	investigate	persuade
challenge	evaluate	join	pinpoint
chart	examine	judge	place (readers, in
clarify	expand	justify	perspective)
complete	explain	lay out	point out
confirm	explore	lead (readers) to	portray
confront	expose	link	predicts

prescribe
present
probe
proceed
  (with, by)
prod
prompt
propose
prove
provide
puncture
put (an end to, be-
  fore, in perspec-
  tive, into
  context)
question
raise
recommend
reconnect
reconstruct
recount

reinforce
refer (readers to)
refute
reject
relate
remind
reply
report
resolve
respond
reveal
review
say
scrutinize
set (forth, up)
shake up
share
shift
show
sort out
specify

speculate
(re)state
stimulate
stress
strive
suggest
summarize
sum up
supply
surprise
survey
tackle
take [advantage
  of, a (closer)
  look at, a stand
  on, issue with,
  place, up]
talk
tease
teem
tell

thrill
tie (together, up)
uncover
undertake
unearth
unify
unmask
unravel
unveil
uphold
urge
use
venture
vindicate
voice
warn
wax
weed out
widen
work out

To expand the list, try adding the prefixes dis-, re- or un-; see if the opposite of a verb fits; or if you can use it as a noun.

To keep your outlines from reading like formulas, avoid using the same verb twice in the same chapter or more than four times in the outline. If you use a verb more than once, vary its form. Vary your verbs as much as accuracy allows.

You can use many of the verbs above in three ways:

1. The middle section of the chapter reveals . . .
2. Begins by revealing . . .
3. Begins with the revelation that . . .

You can use verbs that involve readers or characters:

1. The chapter opens by encouraging (warning) readers to . . .
2. The following section takes (leads) readers to . . .
3. In the last part of the chapter, readers learn (discover, find out, meet, see) . . .

If you're writing about people, you are free to use verbs that describe their actions. In a biography, however, avoid a string of sentences beginning with he or she.

Avoid the passive voice.

Wrong: The issue of drunk drivers is examined in the chapter.

Right: The chapter examines the issue of drunk drivers.

I know, I'm using formulas to tell you how not to write in a formulaic way. But do as I say, not as I do!

Hot Tip

Since your book doesn't exist yet, write about it in the future tense, but write your outlines in the present tense. Your chapters don't exist yet either, but your outlines use many verbs, and they will (oops) read better without all those *wills*.

Example: Chapter Outline

Barbara Geraghty opens this outline from *Visionary Selling How to Get to Top Executives and How to Sell Them When You're There* (Simon & Schuster) with a short paragraph that establishes the rationale for the chapter:

Chapter Nine

Building Credibility and
Trust . . . Quickly   14 Pages, 1 List, 1 Cartoon

The purpose of this chapter is to provide tools and techniques for building credibility and trust in every encounter in the prospect's organization.

The chapter begins by exploring corporate team dynamics and the importance of being perceived as a competent and trustworthy ally by everyone who may have an influence on the decision to buy or use a product or service.

Next comes a discussion of the importance of preparation for sales success and customer satisfaction, acknowledging salespeople's tendencies to improvise with two humorous anecdotes and a cartoon. Then it explains the vital importance of asking questions, listening intently and asking additional questions to penetrate to a deeper level of need.

Then the chapter cites three examples of top salespeople losing business because they didn't do their homework and began sales presentations without understanding the real needs and issues of everyone involved in the decision.

The chapter concludes by providing twelve ways to build credibility in the prospect's organization.

4. Provide Continuity

Maintain continuity within and between chapters so there is a natural flow of ideas, incidents, and information. If you're writing a narrative that unfolds over time, include enough dates so readers can understand the progression of events and see how each chapter advances your story. If you can divide your book into periods of time, consider indicating the time period at the beginning of each chapter.

If you are writing about a person, historical period, issue, system, or endeavor, the subject will have a past. Put its past into context by providing a historical perspective. By the end of the outline, an editor should have a clear sense of continuity in the subject's past, present, and future.

This doesn't mean that you have to start your book at the beginning. Start with a powerhouse first chapter that hooks your readers with as much intensity as you can deliver. Then you can backtrack to fill in the information readers need.

Besides placing your subject in the context of time, also establishes its relevance, if any, to what is happening in the field elsewhere in the United States and the world. This will be an expansion of the perspective you gave the editor in the subject hook of your overview.

To help provide unity and continuity within the entire outline, begin and end chapters with introductory and concluding remarks. For the same reason, books often require bookend chapters:

- An opening chapter that tells readers what you want them to know and excites them about reading it
- A concluding chapter that summarizes your book, speculates on the future, or inspires readers to act on your book's advice

Your outline should be so teeming with ideas and facts that editors will easily be able to visualize the proposal expanded into a full-length manuscript and be delighted at the prospect.

Example: Outline Anecdotes

With both their sample anecdote and their list of the chapter's other anecdotes, Peter and Susan Fenton did an excellent job giving editors a provocative, humorous glimpse of what *I Forgot to Wear Underwear on a Glass-Bottom Boat: Real People, True Secrets* (St. Martin's Press) will be like. This story is longer than I recommend, but is a book of stories, so it is representative of what the book will contain.

Chapter Two

Love and Sex   18 Pages

Your First Chapter

If you want the book to start with an introduction about what you want your readers to know before launching into the text, make it the first or second chapter. Outline it just as you would a separate chapter. Since the introduction may be a shorter chapter than others, make the outline for it shorter.

Just as the beginning of your proposal has to hook the editor, the first chapter of your book must be the subject hook for your book, and must convince readers to read your book. If it doesn't, why would they continue? Would you? Your first chapter may be short, but make it as enticing as you can. Think of it as an ad, a brochure, or the proposal to readers for your book. Like your title, it must tell and sell.

When I revised my book about literary agents, our assistant Antonia Anderson read the book and asked, "Why do readers have to wait until chapter five to find out how to get an agent?" You learn more by not being able to answer a question; my silence was instantly enlightening. Now readers learn how to get an agent in chapter one.

Your first chapter has two goals:

- To excite your readers about what your book will do for them and how enjoyable reading it will be
- To start delivering the benefit of your book so your readers get immediate help if it's a how-to book

For some people, it's flowers and a gourmet dinner in the best restaurant in town. For us, dancing The Twist unlocks the door to romance!

My husband and I are Baby Boomers who met as teens in high school. We did all the fun things kids did back in the sixties—sock hops, midnight movies and endless cruising.

Our absolute favorite activity, though, was dancing at parties. We'd turn the lights low and slow dance for hours. But one night our pals introduced us to a brand new sound—Chubby Checker's version of "The Twist." It hooked us. We spent hours mastering the art of "The Twist," even practicing in front of a full-length mirror to get our moves down. Our friends really admired our style.

We fell in love and made plans for marriage after our high school graduation. We exchanged vows when we were both just nineteen. Then married life began for real: four babies in a row, a husband who was establishing his own business and had plenty of money worries.

Without wanting it to happen, passion took a back seat to the pressures of everyday life. Although we still adored each other, we somehow lost the sexual bond that keeps a man and a woman together.

That is, until the day we heard The Twist again—after twenty-five years. A radio station was playing the song as we were driving home from the kids' track meet.

My heart suddenly skipped a beat. The music stirred up emotions that I thought had long since died. I glanced over at my husband and saw his eyes light up with love.

When we got home, we twisted our way to the bedroom and to the most wonderful night of passion we've ever known. Since then, whenever we want to set the mood for love, we turn the lights down low and turn on with The Twist!

The eight tales in this chapter prove there's more to love and romance than wine and roses. Secret-tellers share their most intimate confessions, such as the fitness pro who sees sex as an opportunity for an extra workout.

Other Secrets in this chapter:

> Fitness Nut's Secret Intercourse Workout
> I Wear a Surgical Mask When I Make Love
> I'm with 32-A: Boyfriend's Secret T-shirt Has Her Fuming
> Marriage Made Me a Hit with Men
> My First Orgasm Sent Me to the Emergency Room

Hot Tip | Separating sections of chapters with subheads breaks up an endless procession of paragraphs. Subheads will also make your outline easier to read, and if they're clever, they will engage the reader's interest in what follows.

❖ ❖ ❖

When it comes to outlining a book, different kinds of books create different challenges for writers. The next chapter will help you solve the problem of outlining different kinds of books.

As you journey on the road from being a new writer to a successful author, place yourself in the service of your ideas, your readers, and your books. The more you devote yourself to them, the more successful you will be.

17 | Outline Strategies for Six Types of Books

In *Bird by Bird*, Anne Lamott said, "I started writing sophomoric articles for the college paper. Luckily, I was a sophomore." You can't use being a sophomore as an excuse for a shaky outline. But there are more ways than ever for you to approach these subjects: as a how-to, serious or pop, traditional or alternative, multicultural, high- to low-income. Or, in the form of a biography, a history, a look ahead, an illustrated book, a serious, popular or consumer reference book, a gift book, a novelty book, a humor book, an exposé, an issue book, or an inspirational book. Your book may be published as a hardcover, a trade paperback, a mass-market book or, in time, all three.

Different kinds of books present different challenges in writing outlines. Below are suggestions for outlining six kinds of books. If you are writing another kind of book, please skip to the next chapter.

How-To Books

How-to books are staples in the book business. Publishers and book buyers welcome fresh ideas that enable readers to lead better, richer lives. Successful how-to books present a new idea at the right time, or are written by an expert, celebrity, or promotable personality. With luck, a how-to book will have a strong idea, an engaging voice, and the right timing. People want to know, but they don't always want to learn, so your job is to make learning as easy and enjoyable as possible for them.

How-to books use five techniques to present their material:

- They have a down-to-earth, me-to-you tone. At their best, as in Anne Lamott's book about writing, *Bird by Bird*, the author has a distinctive, endearing, inspiring voice that helps keep readers turning the pages.
- They include jokes, quotes, cartoons, or anecdotes both to create a rapport with readers and to help make the book as enjoyable to read as it is informative.
- They give readers something to do along the way to keep them involved.
- If they are teaching a skill, they present it in a clear, step-by-step way that is reflected in the book's title and the chapter titles.
- They supplement the text with illustrations.
- The information is presented in a visually appealing way.

If you are writing an instructional book like an exercise book or a cookbook, start each outline by describing the chapter's introductory remarks and plan on including copy between exercises or recipes. Besides creating a rapport between you and your readers, it allows your personality to shine through, breaks up the instructional material, and makes your book a pleasure to read.

Biographies

In *Another Life: A Memoir of Other People*, Michael Korda's excellent book about his four decades at Simon & Schuster and his other career as a best-selling author, he wrote that "Jackie [Susann] taught everybody in publishing that what most people want to read more than anything else is a good story."

The success of *Angela's Ashes* by Frank McCourt, *Into the Wild* by John Krakauer, and *Longitude* by Dava Sobel helped unleash a flood of memoirs, adventure travel books, and books about history. These books were best-sellers because they enabled readers to live in other places and experience other people's lives by telling compelling stories. They also enlarged the market for all kinds of narrative books.

Biographies present the temptation to summarize a chapter instead of outlining it. "First, she did this, then she did this, and then she did this, etc." Starting outlines with brief passages of narrative or dialogue that convey your chapters' emotional impact will enhance your outlines. Below are two outlines: one written in the third person for a biography, the other written in first person for a memoir.

Example: Biography Chapter Outline

The following outline of the first chapter of Randy Shilts's proposal for *The Mayor of Castro Street: The Life and Times of Harvey Milk* (St. Martin's Press) shows that it is possible to outline a biography in the form recommended above. Randy gave continuity to the chapters by including the time period of each chapter. If this were being written now, I would suggest adding an anecdote at the beginning of the outline.

Part I: The Years Without Hope

Chapter One

The Men Without Their Shirts

Time: 1930-Korean War   29 Pages, 2 Photos

The chapter opens with the story of how police round up a teenage Harvey Milk with other gay men cruising Central Park, marching them off to a paddy wagon for the crime of taking off their shirts in a gay section of Central Park. The police march the group through a family section of the park where shirtless men are left unmolested. For the first time, Milk realizes there's something wrong in society's treatment of gays.

This opening symbolizes Milk's life as a homosexual growing up decades before the phrase "gay rights" was ever used, and it also indicates the social climate facing gays of that period. The chapter develops both of these themes.

On the personal side, this segment outlines Milk's early family life on Long Island and his college years in Albany. Many of Milk's personality traits are evident during these years: his lust for the limelight, his stubborn dogmatism, his sense of humor, and, most significantly, his intense interest in politics.

Milk's ramblings in New York's gay milieu of the mid-forties and fifties offer an opportunity to capsulize the social and political status of gays at the time. The chapter also touches on the homosexual emancipation movement in Germany, which thrived well into the 1920s.

After telling about an experience of four-year-old Harvey Milk, for example, the narrative shifts to Germany in the same year when, on "The Night of the Long Knives," Hitler wiped out Germany's gay subculture. That marked the beginning of the dictator's attempts to exterminate homosexuals.

The gay genocide, coupled with the holocaust, exerts a powerful influence on Milk's thinking. Through such historical digressions, the first chapter introduces the book's four levels [described earlier in the proposal].

The chapter ends when Milk, at the apex of a budding career in the Navy, is booted out of the service because of his homosexuality.

Photos: Milk at four on a pony and in Navy uniform.

Example: Memoir Chapter Outline

In the following page from her proposal for *Wild Child*, Linda Ashcroft (whom we discussed in chapter one), deftly blends writing a first-person outline with giving an appealing sense of the intimacy of her friendship with Jim Morrison:

Chapter Seventeen

Hands Upon the Wheel   28 Pages

The chapter examines our feelings for each other. I feel that Jim only asked me to marry him to liberate me from my father's control. Since I have vowed to my mother I will not marry until I am eighteen, there seems no reason for Jim to marry me. I free him of any obligation. He tells me he came to Maine not to save me, but to save himself from alcohol.

The next segment of the chapter shows us feeling lighthearted again. We decorate a rented room with a Kandinsky poster he bought on his European tour and start a collection of quotes for the wall with one from Rimbaud about the coming equality of women as poets. I go to school by day and sneak out of my friend's house after everyone has gone to sleep. Worn to exhaustion, I fall asleep amid my notes for a history paper. While I sleep, Jim writes the paper for me. He wants to mount a protest when it only receives a B+.

The chapter moves on with Jim and my mother making amends. Never before has Jim truly forgiven anyone, but he loves my mother enough to try to understand she meant to do the right thing [about an incident described earlier] and forgives her. After dinner, the three of us sit around the table while Jim reads his poetry. My mother only knows Jim as a poet. I ask if he might make the same gesture to his own mother. He walks away without an answer.

The remainder of the chapter is devoted to a drive along Highway 9 from Saratoga to Santa Cruz, where Jim starts humming the music that, in the course of the evening, will become "Roadhouse Blues." While I take the winding two-lane highway without so much as a driving permit to my name, Jim slouches down, knees on the glove box, writing in my diary, "Keep your eyes on the road/your hands upon the wheel."

Interview Books

If you plan to write a history of Los Angeles, the information you need is available. If you outline it well, editors can assess the proposal easily.

Books based on interviews, however, present problems:

- Predicting the value of future interviews is difficult, even if you provide editors with a list of interview subjects.
- You can't guarantee you'll come away with a book's worth of publishable material.
- Predicting the length of your chapters is more difficult.
- Asking everyone the same questions will yield repetitive answers.
- Publishers' sales reps cover fifty states and want books of interest to book buyers in their territories. If an idea has national scope, its examples should be from around the country.

If for example, you're profiling successful entrepreneurs, you can't just cover those in your area. Aim for as much diversity in location, background, type of product and service, experience, attitude and lifestyle as you can in those you interview. Editors will expect the book to be comprehensive in presenting the range of the entrepreneurial experience. Include people from major cities, which are also major book markets, and all regions of the country. The regional variations you encounter will add depth to your book.

You want to minimize your expenses for a proposal that might not sell. So interviews in your area, perhaps supplemented by telephone interviews, may suffice for the proposal. But indicate in your overview and outline that the manuscript will contain anecdotes from people around the country. A problem might arise later if your interviews don't yield the material you want, and you need more time or money to obtain additional interviews. Plan your research carefully and give yourself a cushion.

Interviewing as many people as you can in your initial research in person, by phone, or online will enrich your proposal, help teach you how to overcome problems you encounter, and provide leads for other interviews. After published articles, the most convincing argument for publishing an interview book is offering a hefty portion (a third to a half) of the manuscript.

Writers with interview articles to their credit may be attracted by the notion of doing a book of interviews, thinking, "Hey, I'll find twenty people who need publicity, do ten ten-page interviews, and I'll have a book." Well, editors aren't wild about collections of anything, including interviews, unless they meet one or more of three criteria:

- The interviews are wedded by a fresh, salable idea.
- The interviews are with celebrities or VIPs whom people want to know more about.
- The interviewer is famous.
- The author has a can't-miss promotional plan.

For editors, writing a book means taking an idea and developing it, structuring it, and using interview material to prove your points. Consider building your book around ideas that you can use quotes to discuss.

Humor Books

After he received a book from S.J. Perelman, Groucho Marx said to the humorist, "From the moment I picked up your book until I laid it down, I was convulsed with laughter. Someday I intend reading it."

Unless you have a track record writing humor, or experience as a stand-up comic, humor can be hard to sell with a proposal. It's difficult to prove that you can be funny for the length of a book, even a short one. So if you can't deliver all of the manuscript, try to submit at least a third of it to present a solid sampling of your sense of humor. If you're doing a cartoon book with captions, provide all of the captions, as many drawings as possible, and a description of the remaining drawings.

Exposés

Controversy can sell books if it's the right subject at the right time with an author who can publicize the book in a way that catches the attention of the media and the public.

Silent Spring by Rachel Carson, *The American Way of Death* by Jessica Mitford, *Unsafe at Any Speed* by Ralph Nader, *All the President's Men* by Bob Woodward and Carl Bernstein, and the surprising string of best-sellers about the Middle East since 9/11 have proven it.

Nonetheless, people don't like to get depressed, and they sure don't want to pay for the privilege. That's why unless exposés are written by a promotable author and about a hot subject—Hollywood, politics, big business, or some other juicy subject with built-in national interest—exposés don't sell well.

If your book will bring bad news, try to be prescriptive as well as descriptive. People don't want to buy problems; they want to buy solutions. They want to take a book like they take a magic pill. Swallow the pill—follow a book's advice—and enjoy the book's benefit. So if you can, develop a program for making the situation better. This will give your book a positive slant that will improve your title and your sales.

Anthologies

The amazing success of the Chicken Soup series proves the commercial potential of anthologies blessed with the following:

- A great idea for a seemingly endless series of books that sell each other
- A system for test-marketing the stories to ensure that they move readers and leave them craving more
- A huge potential readership
- Perpetual, powerhouse promotion driven by the authors' zeal, creativity, and speaking ability
- A title strong enough to become a brand and generic enough to support a certain kind of story collection

And since most anthologies also don't have the strengths listed above, they don't fare well unless they are used in the classroom. Even the word anthology is deadly. Avoid the notion of a collection in the title if you can.

If you're doing a treasury or celebration (less academic, more selling words), start with a strong concept, and make sure the selections are worth including, that they measure up well against each other. Make the case that the book will hold up over time. Try to make your selections flow naturally from one to the next. Splitting up the book into parts and chapters and writing an introduction for each section and perhaps each entry helps ensure this.

Include brief bios of your contributors, and include them at the beginning of their entries. If you prefer to include bios at the end of your book, place them at the end of your sample material.

Getting permissions, covered in chapter thirteen, can be time-consuming because copyright holders may be abroad, may not respond to your inquiries, may charge you an exorbitant fee or may refuse to quote a price until they know how your book will be published. Yet it's important that your proposal include as accurate an estimate as you can obtain.

Two reasons to do anthologies:

- They can usually be done to length. You can make them shorter or longer depending on the length your publisher wants.
- If one works, there is often the potential for a series.

A Final Thought: Laying the Foundation

Your outline is the foundation of your book. A sturdy, cohesive foundation will help convince an editor to back your proposal. A thorough outline may also prevent your book from being rejected.

Whether your finished manuscript matches your blueprint will depend upon how well you write your outline, the need to explore new avenues of investigation, suggestions your editor may make, and how cut-and-dried or open-ended the subject is. Your book may change unexpectedly because of new ideas or information or an unpredictable turn of events. But properly done, your outline will help you write your book.

Hot Tip

If you have concerns about any part of your proposal, including the structure, ask your networks about them when you send out your proposal for feedback. The more precise you are about the advice you need, the more helpful your readers will be. But friends may give you the worst advice with the best of intentions. So you must trust your instincts and your common sense.

Writers have told us that writing the outline was the hardest part of doing the proposal. However difficult creating an outline may seem, keep in mind that besides impressing publishers, you're doing yourself a favor. If you deliver your manuscript on time, and it lives up to what your proposal promises, your editor will have no legitimate reason to reject it.

If this is your first book, you will feel far more confident about tackling it once you've finished a chapter and have a clear vision of the rest of your book. Doing your outline will enable you to pick the best sample chapter to write. Ace freelance editor, Hal Zina Bennett, with whom I wrote *How to Write With a Collaborator,* believes that a well-written outline can make writing your book "almost as easy as painting by the numbers." After using the outline as a guide in researching your book, your outline is a roadmap guiding you as you write.

Learning to write outlines is less painful than learning to ride a bicycle, but it will last you as long. Like typing, the skill of outlining a book will help you as long as you need it. Like the rest of your proposal, it's a test of your commitment to your book.

❖ ❖ ❖

Your outline is the bones on which you are hanging the meat of your book, the manuscript. Everything you've written up to this point as an hors d'oeuvre for the main course that editors will sample next: your sample chapter, the proof that you can write your book well enough to reach your literary goals. Bon appetit!

18 | Your Sample Chapter

The four important elements in most proposals are the idea, the title, the sample chapter, and, if promotion is essential to a book's success, the promotion plan. Having a terrific idea and proving that you will make your book successful will be to no avail if you can't write the book. After your mission statement, your platform, your promotion plan, and your bio, your sample chapter is your last chance to answer the question, *Why you?* If you have a book's worth of publishable information but you're not a writer, you can use an editor, a book doctor, collaborator, or ghostwriter if you need help. What's essential is that when your proposal reaches editors, it's unassailable.

Your sample chapter is your audition for the role of author. If your introduction is the sizzle and your outline is the bones, your sample chapter is the steak, the meat of your proposal, a delectable sample of what's to come. It must be so substantial and enjoyable to read that editors will be convinced your book will be a movable feast.

Editors may only read a few pages of the overview, then quickly move on to the chapter, especially if it's a book in which style is important. If they like the idea and the writing, then you've got their attention. Your writing must deliver what your introduction promises. The last part of your proposal is the only chance you have to strut your stuff, to prove you have the craft to deliver what you promise.

Like the rest of your manuscript, your sample chapter must achieve the goals you set for it both in content and in its impact on readers. If it does, it will increase the value of your proposal by allaying an editor's anxiety about your ability to write the book. They long to find the same things in books that you do. An editor once said to us, "If it makes me cry, I'll buy it." A humor book must make editors laugh; a dramatic or inspirational book must move them.

Q&A Session on What to Submit

A cartoon in *The New Yorker* shows a sedan speeding away from the scene of the crime with a police car in hot pursuit, and the driver is leaning out the window reassuring a bystander, "I'm only doing this to support my writing." If you want your first book to support you, you will probably need to include a sample of your writing. The first decision you have to make about your sample text is the number of chapters you have to prepare. This will depend on:

- Your knowledge of the subject
- Whether you've had anything published on the subject
- Your track record
- Your time, energy, information, and other resources at your disposal
- How many sample chapters editors have to see to become as excited as you want them to be

Since you're working on spec on a proposal that may not sell, you want to minimize your time, effort, and expense. The answers to the following eighteen questions will help you understand how to prepare your writing sample:

1. **Can I get away with not sending a chapter?** If you've already written an article or a book on the subject, your track record is strong enough, or if your credentials are impeccable, you may not need a sample chapter. An outline submitted with previous work may suffice. You also may not need sample material if you have had several books published that attest to your ability to write the book you are proposing.

Teaching, running a professional practice, or being a journalist may also be enough to prove your credentials. But if you don't prepare a sample chapter, write a longer outline. If you must sell your book quickly because it's about a subject in the news, editors won't expect you to take the time to write a chapter.

2. How many chapters should my book have? As you string together the pieces of information that will become your book, they will fall into natural groupings that will become your chapters. Ten to twelve chapters are common for a 200- to 250-page manuscript.

The longer your book, the more chapters it will have. Take into consideration the trend toward shorter chapters and books, but adhere to the standard set by successful books on the subject.

3. How long should my chapters be? There has been a continuing string of best-selling self-help books that are short and have short chapters. One of the reasons why Chérie Carter-Scott's *If Life is a Game, These Are the Rules* became a number one bestseller is that the chapters in the book averaged two pages each.

Serious books have longer chapters than books aimed at a mass audience. Your chapters are the building blocks of your book. Like the book itself, your chapters should not be a word longer than it takes to say what must be said.

Maintain a balance between making your chapters so thin that readers will ask, "How could he leave that out?" and so long that they say, "How much more is she going to pad this thing?" Similar books and your networks will set you straight.

Hot Tip

Do not repeat information in your sample chapter that you will cover in earlier chapters. Cover only the information in your outline of the chapter. One of the goals of your outline is to enable editors to understand the context of your sample chapter. If you feel they need to know something from previous chapters to understand your sample chapter, include a comment in brackets that alludes to what you covered earlier and, if you must, explain it concisely.

4. How many chapters should I send an editor? The answer depends on how long your chapters will be and the kind of book you are writing. Editors expect to see about a tenth of a book, twenty to thirty manuscript pages. Here are three ways for you to judge what to send:

- If your chapter reads like it is worth the advance you want for your book, you can sell most books with one twenty-to-thirty-page chapter.
- Editors don't have to read every exercise or recipe to know if you can write a how-to book, especially if you teach the subject.
- If your book will be a series of chapters identical in structure

and with the same kind of information, one chapter will suffice. If you were going to write the guidebook to Europe's ten greatest cities mentioned earlier, editors won't get more jazzed about the book by reading about a second city.

5. How can I tell which is the best chapter to submit? The only chapter to send is the one that best blends freshness and excitement. Let it come from the heart of the book and be a shining, representative sample of what is innovative and stimulating about your subject.

Balance your passion for the subject and the time and effort you're willing to expend against what it will take to get editors so revved up about the book that they'll be outbidding each other to buy it.

If you feel certain that you will at least be able to sell an article on the subject, or better yet, get an assignment to write it, that will help sustain you as well as enable you to test-market your idea (an idea in chapter twenty-three).

The following cartoon appears in Jim Charlton's *Books, Books, Books*, a collection of cartoons about writing and publishing that appeared in *The New Yorker*. A man is standing at the counter of a bookstore about to buy a book and the clerk is saying to him: "You'll like this one, sir. It has a surprise ending in which the murderer turns out to be the detective."

If you have a chapter that's guaranteed to surprise editors, then that's the one to send. If you're not sure which chapter to use as a sample, preparing the outline will help you decide. Certain chapters usually stand out as being easier for you to write and more impressive for editors to read. Getting feedback on your proposal will convince you that you have chosen well.

6. Is it okay to submit parts of different chapters? Editors will want to see how a complete slice of your book reads, so make your sample material a complete segment or chapter, not part of one or more chapters.

If you are doing an anthology, and you can get pieces of each part of your book but not a complete section, list the entries of your book as thoroughly as you can, and then include one part of your book as complete as you can make it. Send at least 10 percent of the material from each section of your book.

7. What if my book will have short chapters? The shorter your chapters will be, the more of them editors will need to read. Again, submit twenty to thirty pages of manuscript.

8. What if I haven't had anything published? Then your proposal will be all editors have to go on. The less experience you have as a writer or as an expert on the subject, the more chapters editors may need to overcome potential opposition to your book. This will definitely be the case for a narrative book, the effectiveness of which depends on the writing.

Another circumstance that may require additional chapters is if your idea seems too ambitious in relation to your expertise or track record. Editors will want enough text to convince themselves and others that you are ready to tackle the project. As your in-house agent whose job it is to stir up interest in your book, your editor needs that confidence to fight for your book.

Hot Tip | Your relationship with your agent and editor will be a working marriage with personal and professional aspects to it. Test the chemistry for that marriage by meeting with them before you commit to working with them.

If you were writing your first novel, most editors would expect to see the whole manuscript. Only a whole manuscript can prove that you can you can develop character, plot, and setting for the length of a novel.

If you're writing a nonfiction book that you want to have the impact of a novel—a dramatic story with mounting suspense about the solution of a crime, or an inspirational book about someone heroically overcoming obstacles—an outline can't convey the emotional impact of your finished manuscript. If the emotional impact of your manuscript will be stronger if an editor reads the whole manuscript, be prepared to send it or as much of it as you can.

The goals of your proposal are to not waste an editor's time and to use a minimum number of words to generate maximum excitement for your book. So the criteria for deciding how much more than one chapter to send are:

- How much of the book are you willing and able to write before selling it?
- Will additional chapters generate enough additional excitement to justify writing them?

Hot Tip | Ninety percent of nonfiction books are sold with proposals. Here are five reasons why:
1. Writers need money to write the book.
2. Writers don't want to risk writing the book and then find that they can't sell it.

3. The book is on a subject in the news, so the writers want a commitment to publish the book before writing it.

4. Agents make a living selling books, so they want to sell them as profitably and as soon as they can.

5. Editors prefer to receive proposals for most books. They're faster to read, and editors enjoy the creative satisfaction of helping writers shape their books. A complete manuscript deprives them of that opportunity. Editors may also be more excited by what they imagine the manuscript will be than what it is.

9. What if my book is divided into three parts? If the three parts of your book are distinctive enough, and you think editors will need to see a sample of each, send them. They will read only far enough to reach a decision.

10. What if my book is depressing? Editors spend at least two years working on a book. They want to enjoy the time they spend working on a book with an author. This is even more important with a book that doesn't promise to become a best-seller.

So if your subject is depressing, try to balance the bad news with humor or good news. Make at least the last chapter or part of your book upbeat so that editors will finish reading your proposal feeling positive about the subject, your proposal, and the prospect of working with you on it.

11. What about a fill-in-the-blanks book? Send the whole manuscript. Librarians don't like fill-in books because their borrowers fill them in. If your book will require written responses, ask readers to use a notebook or their computers, unless it's essential for them to write in the book.

Do develop a workbook if you can use it in your seminars. If your book is successful enough, your publisher will be eager to make it available to your readers.

12. Should I send the introduction? Although your introduction has to seduce readers into reading your book, it may not be representative of what your book will cover. Also, you have introduced the book in your overview. In a how-to book, for instance, an introduction may not demonstrate how you will treat the instructional material that is the reason for your book.

13. What if I have finished more of the book than I submit? You will be mentioning on the resource page of the introduction how much

Twelve Reasons to Write Your Manuscript First

Here I am writing a book on how to do proposals, and I'm about to suggest that you write your manuscript before your proposal. You're probably saying, "Geez, Larsen, make up your mind! Should I write the proposal or the manuscript?" Will you settle for a definite maybe?

Writing the manuscript first will be an option for only a few writers because of three questions you have to be able to say *yes* to first:

1. Is time the only resource you need to write your book?
2. Are you the only person who can write your book?
3. Are your passion for writing your book, your faith in the quality and salability of it, and your ability to promote it great enough to risk writing a book that you may not be able to sell?

If you answered *yes* to these questions, consider these twelve reasons for writing your manuscript before writing your proposal:

• The best way to write your proposal is to write your book first, even if you just do a first draft. Outlining your book and picking the best sample chapter will be easier.

• If you are giving talks, you can test-market your information.

• Interested editors can read all of it immediately.

• Your book may be worth more because you have removed the risk of whether you can or will write your book.

• Your book will be published sooner.

• You will receive all of your advance sooner. Advances are divided into at least two parts: half on signing and half on acceptance.

• You won't need an outline if you use a complete manuscript to sell your book; a two-page synopsis will suffice.

• If editors want to see more of your manuscript than you include with your proposal, they can.

• You can use the manuscript to get feedback from your networks.

• You can use your manuscript to obtain quotes and a foreword.

• You will prove that you can write it if:
    – Your track record isn't impressive
    – If your book is ambitious in scope
    – If you need the cooperation of executives or celebrities
    – Or if your project will require a lot of time, money, or illustrations

• It will be easier to find partners if you have a full manuscript.

of the manuscript is finished "in draft form." If editors want to see more than you submit, they will ask.

14. What if I have finished the manuscript? Agents and editors are perpetually swamped. They need just enough text to judge whether you can write the book. They and the other people in the house who have to review your proposal will read a small pile of pages faster than a large pile. So even if you have more, don't send it unless an editor requests it or it's for one of the reasons mentioned above.

15. If I am submitting more than one chapter, do the chapters have to be in sequence? Your chapters don't have to be from the beginning of the book or in sequence.

16. What if my book has no chapters? If your book doesn't break up into chapters, an editor will still expect to see at least 10 percent of the complete manuscript. If you're proposing a picture book, make the project more substantial by writing the introductory chapter for your book and providing captions and perhaps a running text.

17. What if I'm doing an illustrated book? Unless a large national audience already exists for your work, or your idea is extremely commercial, your book will need more than just illustrations. Unless they're giving your book as a gift or feel they must own it, browsers may not buy your book if they can finish it in the store.

Editors are print people, people of the word. They want text to explain illustrations. They also want a compelling reason to go to the effort and expense of producing a picture book. As for the illustrations you include in the proposal, they should be gorgeous and, in their diversity, representative of the range of illustrations that will be in your book.

18. What if I want my book designed in a particular way? If you have a vision of how you want your book to look, and you are able to design sample pages on your computer, or you can obtain the services of an experienced book designer, include a cover design (which is discussed in the next chapter) and two facing spreads—four sample pages—as examples of the design you want for the book.

These are only worth including if they are of professional quality. Even if you envision a book larger than $8\frac{1}{2}'' \times 11''$, make your sample pages the same size as the rest of your proposal. They will be easier to prepare, reproduce, submit, and read.

Your publisher's sales and marketing staff will expect to have the final say on how your book is presented to the public. If you present a cover design or suggest a format for your book, it must be with the understanding that if the S&M crowd (sales and marketing) says it won't fly, you will have to compromise or seek another publisher.

❖ ❖ ❖

Now you know what editors expect to see in proposals. Once you start doing it, the pieces will start falling into place. Once you are committed to writing your proposal, your sense of excitement about it will grow as the project develops momentum and creates a life of its own.

Now that you have read about the information you need, let's zero in on features that will give your proposal an extra kick. The advice in the next chapter will help you make your proposal irresistible.

19 | Making Your Proposal Stand Out

To help ensure that your proposal is impeccable when you submit it, this chapter provides five ways for you to increase the salability of your proposal:

- Illustrations
- Clips of your work
- Cover art
- A professional format
- A surprise

Illustrations

Illustrations add to a book's salability, but they will also make a book more expensive for your publisher, book buyers, and you. If you will use illustrations, include the illustrations for your sample chapter.

We once sold a book called *Raven: The Untold Story of the Rev. Jim Jones and His People* for Tim Reiterman, a reporter for the *San Francisco Examiner*, who was wounded in Guyana. Tim didn't have to account for photographs because his publisher knew that Tim could obtain whatever pictures were needed.

If your book is about a subject in the news, photographs will be available, so you don't have to include them. Indicate where photos will appear and add the cost to the list of resources you need. Submit illustrations if they will be a major element in your book. When you plan to use an illustration of a person, place, event, or instructional point, indicate this in the text by typing "(Illus. X)" after mentioning what you will illustrate.

Number your illustrations consecutively. Make your pictures no larger than 8½″ × 11″ so they will fit in with your text. Affix illustrations to 8½″ × 11″ papers.

If you can, scan slides, photographs, and artwork into your computer and integrate them into your text. This will also enable you to print as many copies as you need. You can also scan additional artwork and text, and make them available online to editors.

If you're not scanning your artwork into your text, place each illustration on a separate page following the page on which you mention it. Give the illustration page the same number as the page of text preceding it followed by a letter of the alphabet: 27a, for example. If you have more than one illustration on a page, work your way through the alphabet. Below each illustration, indicate what number it is and provide a caption.

Four considerations will dictate how you handle captions:
- Your vision of the book
- How similar books use illustrations
- How much explanation your illustrations need
- Whether your illustrations will be grouped together or spread throughout your book

If you're sending duplicate slides, number them and insert them in a plastic sheet that holds twenty slides. Place the slides in the left pocket of the folder in which you are submitting your proposal. Behind them include a page with numbered captions.

If your book will contain black-and-white photos, use 8″ × 10″ glossies for the sample chapters. Color illustrations result in large production costs, so unless there's a need for color, stick to black and white, or consider a combination of the two. Line drawings are less costly to reproduce than photographs, so consider using them instead. As mentioned above, let your preferences and comparable books guide you in balancing cost, effectiveness, and aesthetics. *Always send photocopies of artwork and duplicates of slides until your editor requests originals.*

Publishers print illustrations in one of three ways:
1. In eight- or sixteen-page inserts on coated stock for better reproduction

2. Scattered throughout the book on the same stock as the text
3. A combination of the two

Gift books are printed on coated stock to enhance the illustrations and impart a more luxurious feel to the book. If it's not clear from the proposal how the illustrations should be grouped, and you have strong feelings about it, describe how you see them being presented in the special features section of your overview.

Sample Clips

Outstanding samples of your published work demonstrate its acceptance by publications and their readers. Besides proving that you are a professional, they show editors what you can do.

If you have clips that will impress an editor because of their quality, length, relevance and range of subjects—or because of the periodicals in which they appeared—include up to six of them. If it's a magazine piece, include the cover of the magazine. Originals are more effective than photocopies, but if you want to avoid the possibility of losing the originals, send photocopies. If you have more than one story about yourself or rave reviews about a previous book, underline the key points and include them.

Only send clips or a published book if they will help sell your proposal. Otherwise, wait until an editor asks to see more. If you find stories on your subject in major periodicals, such as a cover story in *Newsweek*, that will make your proposal more salable, underline the relevant parts and include photocopies of the articles.

Hot Tip

Small or poorly produced periodicals, which may be where a writer's early work appears, will not impress editors. Use your judgment about what to include. When in doubt, leave it out unless your networks advise otherwise.

Cover Art

Including cover art can help sell your proposal by giving editors a feel for the book and its marketability. A paperback cover or a hardcover jacket must be a felicitous blend of art and commerce. It must be attractive, but it must also sell your book.

Authors don't usually get involved with designing cover art, usually because of their lack of knowledge or interest. However, if you are an artist or a photographer, or have access to one, and you have a selling title and cover idea, include it.

Professionals in the field spend their lives creating cover art, and they still don't always get it right. The concept and the execution of the art and type must be of professional quality, or your artwork may backfire and give publishers a reason to reject your proposal.

Try out your preliminary sketch and the finished artwork on your networks, especially booksellers, before submitting it. If they say that, on a scale of one to ten, it's a ten, submit it. As with sample clips, when in doubt, make the artwork the size of the book you envision but no larger than 8½″ × 11″, so it fits as the first page of the proposal.

A Professional Presentation

Your Title Page

Type your title page and your table-of-contents page in upper- and lower-case letters on unnumbered, double-spaced pages.

About a third of the way down the page, in the center or along the left margin, type and center:

A Proposal for
Title (in Italics)
Subtitle (in Italics)
by (Yours Truly)

Include your degree or your position and employer if impressive:

Professor of Psychology, Stanford University

If possible, add either or both of the following two lines:

Foreword by *x x*
First in a Series of *x* Books

Near the bottom of the page, flush left, type:

Your street address
City, State, ZIP code
Day and evening phone numbers
Fax number
E-mail address
Web site

Hot Tip Because you don't number your title page and your table-of-contents page, you may want to make them a separate file so the first page of your overview is page one.

Your Table of Contents

After your title page comes the table of contents for your proposal. Besides showing an editor what's ahead, this page makes the proposal look carefully organized, like a miniature version of the book it aspires to be. It will also help editors find the parts of your proposal.

List the three parts of the proposal flush left, then indent the sections of each part. At the right margin, indicate the page on which each begins:

Table of Contents

Introduction
    Overview   1
    Promotion   5
    Resources Needed to Complete the Book   9
    About the Author   10
Outline
    List of Chapters   11
Sample Chapter   23

Enclosed separately in the folder:
    The author's brochure
    The author's articles
    Supporting documents
    Publicity material

As noted earlier, you do not have to mention front matter such as a dedication, epigraph, or acknowledgments in your proposal. You also do not have to list the back matter unless you are outlining it.

Hot Tip

Editors will not expect you to design your book. They just want to be able to turn the pages as quickly as possible. We once received a proposal from someone who had gone hog-wild with type fonts and had six different typefaces on one page. This made the page look like an amateur's attempt to dress up the proposal. Unless you possess proven design skills or have access to them, keep your proposal simple in appearance like the samples in this book.

The appearance of your proposal reflects the professionalism with which you are approaching agents, editors, the subject, and your career. It's the tangible evidence of the care you will lavish on your manuscript and it will affect readers' reactions to your proposal.

Agents and editors know that there is a relationship between how writers submit their proposals and how they write them. Writers are endlessly ingenious at finding wrong ways to submit their work. Here are thirteen dos and don'ts on preparing your proposal:

- Do type your proposal on one side of 8½″ × 11″ 20-pound bond paper.
- Do type twenty-five, ten word, sixty-character lines, about 250 words on a page.
- Do double-space everything, including quotes and anecdotes.
- Don't add extra spaces between paragraphs.
- Don't leave "widows," a subhead at the bottom of a page, or the last line of a chapter at the top.
- Do use a standard twelve-point typeface. Printers like Times Roman.
- Don't justify the right margin; the designer will do that.
- Do use running headers. Type your last name and the first key word from the book title, separated by a slash mark, on the upper left margin of each page. Type the page number on the same line, flush right:

Larsen/Write   11

- Do number pages consecutively, from one to the end of the proposal, not by section or chapter, so that if your proposal is dropped, it will be easy to reassemble.
- Do proofread your proposal carefully and get an eagle-eyed friend to check your work. Proofread a printout to catch what you miss on the screen, especially the extra spaces between words that can sneak in when you revise your work.

Here are some tips for proofreading and submitting your proposal:
- Run your index finger under each word as you read it aloud softly to yourself.
- Proofread your proposal from back to front so you can concentrate on the words and not be seduced into reading it.
- Always submit your work without staples or any form of binding. Paper clips are acceptable, but they leave indentations.
- For a more professional look and greater protection in case you have to resubmit the proposal, insert it in the right side of a double-pocket paper portfolio. You can use the left pocket

for writing samples, illustrations, supporting documents, and your business card if the left flap is scored. Put a self-adhesive label on the front of the folder with your title and name.

- As I suggested earlier, make everything in the proposal, including artwork, no larger than $8\frac{1}{2}'' \times 11''$. This makes it easy to reproduce and submit via mail or e-mail.

Every day, every agent receives letters and proposals that don't follow these guidelines. So one simple way to make *your* proposal look impeccable is to follow them.

A Surprise

If you can, include a happy surprise with your proposal to catch the attention of harried editors. The ideal surprise:

- Relates to your book
- Is imaginative
- Is inexpensive so it doesn't seem like a bribe
- Is humorous
- Lays flat
- Packs small
- Plays big
- Grabs an editor's attention so effectively that your proposal is read immediately

An author writing about *The Godfather* included a foot-long plastic fish wrapped in newspaper. He got our immediate attention. Less lucky was the woman who sent us an orange children's shoe with a letter that began "Now that I've got my foot in the door . . ." We mentioned this to an agent friend, and she said she got the other shoe! AAR member Jillian Manus once submitted a book on assertiveness for women, and she enclosed a whip with a note saying, "Submit to your editor." The book sold quickly.

Chocolate is always a safe bet (Elizabeth assures me it's the iron). But if your surprise is edible, it must be sealed.

❖ ❖ ❖

Before you go out to conquer the marketplace, your next step should be to revise and refine your proposal first with your own sharp eye, then through your networks and test-marketing.

20 | Getting the Words Right

The following three sentences are children's answers to questions they were asked in Sunday school. What do they all have in common?

The fifth commandment is humor thy father and mother.
Christians can have only one wife. This is called monotony.
It is sometimes difficult to hear what is being said in church because the agnostics are so terrible.

They show how even two letters in a word can transform the meaning of a sentence. Every word you write counts. Narrative nonfiction that tells a story has to seduce readers with its style and emotional impact.

Editors are delighted to find fine writing. You want agents and editors to read your proposal without stopping and with a growing rush of enthusiasm. Your book will only have two basic elements: your idea and the execution of your idea. So make the execution of your idea as strong as your idea.

Craft comes before art and before commerce. You have to learn to write before you can wring beauty from words. And just to sell your work, your writing must rise to a professional level. Craft leaps off the page instantly. Since editors and agents reject more than 95 percent of what they see, they will be delighted if after reading your first paragraph, they can say to themselves, "My God! This one can really write!"

Although style is more important in a literary biography than in a how-to book, the more pleasurable any book is to read, the better its reviews, and the more word-of-mouth and word-of-mouse recommendations it generates. When a fan recommends this book to writers, she says, "Use his format, but use your style." Good advice. Your writing will be an expression of who you are.

Playing for Keeps

It's been said that if at first you don't succeed, skydiving is not for you. But writing may still be. Writing is a forgiving craft that pardons all sins except one: not doing as many drafts as it takes to make your work 100 percent. Your final draft must be your very best if it's going to hold the attention of agents, editors and readers. Let your networks assure you that your last draft is your best draft.

Ernest Hemingway rewrote the last page of *For Whom the Bell Tolls* thirty-nine times. When someone asked him what the problem was, he replied, "Getting the words right." If you are serious about being a writer, strive to make your writing as lucid, flowing, creative, brilliant, moving, engaging, entertaining, passionate—in a word, irresistible—as you want your reviews to be.

"Wondering irresolutely what to do next, the clock struck twelve." This gem is from the indispensable guide to the prose of pros: *The Elements of Style* by William Strunk Jr. and E.B. White. It inspires as it teaches by example. Put its thirty-two golden nuggets on composition and style on the wall where you write. The relative calm before starting your proposal is a propitious moment to summon your muse by (re)reading it.

My favorite rule in *The Elements of Style* is "Omit needless words." The one key on your keyboard that will do the most for your writing is the delete key. If you delete all of the words you don't need, then the only words you have left are the words you do need.

Publishing is a business. Whether prose is good or bad is beside the point; only writing well enough for your readers is important. Amy Tan and Danielle Steel write differently, but their readers love the way they write. The need for style is greater in a literary memoir than an exercise book. Such differences are another reason to follow the benchmarks set by books you admire.

Reading and Writing at Bullet Speed

Agents, editors, media people, and consumers are deluged with information; they want to go through the reams of paper they confront as quickly as they can. Help them by using bulleted lists. You can't have list after list (which I may be guilty of), but when you discuss more than one thing in your proposal, manuscript, and publicity material, consider presenting it as a list.

Mention the number of items in a list, but don't feel that you have to use a number before each part of the list unless it's a long list or you have a reason to include it, such as using the number in your title. *Guerrilla Marketing for Writers* has a hundred weapons, so the numbers were the organizing principle for the chapters as well as the book.

Less is More; More is a Bore

Jazz trumpeter Miles Davis once said, "I always listen for notes I can leave out." This approach to his art is one reason why *Kind of Blue* is the greatest modern jazz album. Fine writing stands out because of its lack of faults. Books endure in part because their authors know when a word, sentence, or idea doesn't feel right, and have the craft and perseverance to revise their work until it shines. First-time authors may find it difficult to believe, but when it comes to prose, less is more. Good writing is simple, concise, not unnecessarily flashy; direct, not flowery.

Think of writing as having two stages: writing for fact and writing for impact. First you have to get your information down in the easiest and most pleasurable way you can, and then massage it into final form.

After you have the information down to your satisfaction, add "The Pleasure Factor": Enhance your prose with grace notes—humor, passion, inspiration, felicitous turns of phrase—anything that will add feeling and aesthetic value to your information. Grace notes are the value that you add to your information. They are an essential element in building the humorous, dramatic, spiritual, inspirational, intellectual, persuasive, even life-changing impact that you want your book to have. (Since I'm not setting the best example, you'll have to take my word for it.)

At its best, writing also has passion, vision, and vigor. Bantam executive editor Toni Burbank once remarked about a manuscript, "There was nothing wrong with it, but there was nothing right with it either." Author and teacher Cyra McFadden once lamented about another failed effort: "The prose just lay there, dead on the page."

Make your writing sing to an editor, who should be your toughest yet most sympathetic critic, and if you have a salable idea, your proposal will sell.

Rely on your instincts and reliable readers to know when your proposal is ready to submit. Then, and not a moment sooner, it is time to see if you are right.

Why Your Book Will Be a Masterpiece

Writing, like speaking, is a paradoxical art. Everybody talks and everybody writes, but the difference between talking well on the phone and giving a speech, or between writing a snappy e-mail and writing a book, is huge.

Writing is a virtue that merits encouragement, even if it doesn't lead to publication. But people who wouldn't think of just sitting down and playing in an orchestra, painting a picture or acting in a movie, think that they can just sit down and write a book. They may be right, but it will take far more effort than they can imagine.

The origin of the word *masterpiece* goes back to the medieval guilds. Novices would apprentice themselves to a craftsman for years without pay to learn a craft. The only way for them to prove that they were master craftsmen and were qualified to join the guild was to create a masterpiece.

Like the other arts, writing is also a craft that also requires an apprenticeship for about the same salary. If you have a lifetime's worth of ideas for books you want to write, then you have to learn your craft. And you don't have to create a masterpiece to prove you're ready. Having a job that requires you to write may suffice.

The apprenticeship for becoming an author is usually getting articles published, perhaps for free at first to get bylines, to develop one's craft, and build credibility as a writer. It reassures some writers working on their first books to look at them as collections of articles. Apprenticeship trains you to serve your readers while you develop your craft. Then when the idea, the skill, the opportunity, and the passion to write a book merge, you have to create and sell a proposal for your book.

When an editor accepts your manuscript, you have created your masterpiece, and you have earned the right to be considered a professional. Your book will elevate you above writers who haven't written one. Your masterpiece will enable you to join the Author's Guild.

❖ ❖ ❖

Being an author is something that you will be proud of for the rest of your life for three reasons:

1. Writing a book is the Mount Everest of writing. Proving that you have the craft, creativity, knowledge, stamina, perseverance, and professionalism to complete a book will set you apart from writers who haven't.
2. The world will respect you as an expert on your subject.
3. Relatively few writers get their books published by houses that pay for the privilege.

21 | A Style Guide

Like you, editors at big houses are overworked and underpaid. They do too many books and attend too many meetings to have all the time they would like to edit books. So if a proposal indicates that the manuscript will need too much work, they'll reject it.

This means that agents have to make sure that what they submit is as close to 100 percent as possible. Agents in turn will either request that writers keep doing drafts until the agents are satisfied or will suggest that writers get help to cure what ails their proposals.

Their interest in the craft of writing is only one reason why agents pay scrupulous attention to what they submit. Another is their interest in eating. Agents' reputations are on the line with every submission they make. If agents send work that isn't ready, editors will do the same thing that you do when people waste your time: ignore them.

This chapter is a guide to common mistakes that keep writers from getting book contracts. The two best times to refer to it are before you start your proposal and after you finish it. Also, when you send out your proposal to be critiqued, request that your readers note questions they have about word use, numbers, repetition, and the impact of your anecdotes. Ask them to rate humor or anecdotes as well as the emotional or inspirational impact of your work on a scale of one to ten. Also ask them to rate each example of these elements and your proposal or manuscript as a whole.

Adding Variety to Your Prose

Every word you write must convince readers to read the next word. For this reason, avoid:

- **Long words:** Keep them simple, but if a long word is the best one to use, use it.
- **Long sentences:** Long or complex sentences slow the eye. But don't go to the other extreme. By using sentence fragments. Or a succession of short sentences.
- **Long paragraphs:** The mind revolts when confronted with unbroken, page-long blocks of copy. If you're writing for a wide audience, aim for three or four paragraphs on a page. And unless similar books indicate otherwise, avoid paragraphs longer than about a third of a page.

Variety is as essential a virtue in prose as brevity. An endless succession of short words, sentences, and paragraphs will read like ad copy or a formula approach to writing. The art of writing is the ability to express and structure your ideas so that every word counts. Stick with the standards set by the best books in your field.

Here's more advice to keep in mind as you write and edit your book:

- Between your overview, outline, and sample chapters, an editor may read the same information three times. Avoid repeating yourself if you can. If you can't, change the wording.
- Assume editors know only what average Americans know about the subject; terms, concepts, and explanations must be clear.
- Avoid cuteness and gratuitous humor.
- Excite your readers' senses—sight, sound, touch, taste, and smell—to breathe life into the people, places, and events you depict.
- Dialogue is action. It breaks up the narrative and enlivens your prose as it develops the story, characters, and atmosphere.
- People enjoy reading about other people. Humanize your book by writing about people.

Stories and Fictional Techniques

The biggest challenge in writing anecdotes is cramming maximum impact into the minimum number of words. The longer a story is, the more impact it needs to justify your readers' time. If you want your book to read like a novel, write it like a novel:

- Use telling details to bring people, plots, and places to life.
- Make readers care about what happens to the people you write about.
- Give your prose the distinctive voice that only you have.
- Accelerate the pace of your story by jumping from scene to scene like movies do.

Overcoming Repetition With Restraint

Abstinence is better than perfect moderation.

—St. Augustine

Using a word, sentence structure, or punctuation, then using it again, and then, since it comes to mind quickly, using it again, is a nasty habit to which unwary writers fall prey. The repetition makes it stand out like a writing tic, a literary hiccup. Given the richness of the language, this suggests either a lack of writing skill or an unwillingness to find the most felicitous way to express a thought.

If you lapse into the repetition of a word, sentence structure, or punctuation, avoid the offending usage altogether so you won't be tempted to succumb to it, or limit yourself to using the culprit only once every twenty pages. It's an easier cure for hiccups than drinking a glass of water while you're upside down.

If you use two or more nouns or verbs together, make sure that all of them fit the rest of the sentence. I managed to provide an example of this mistake in a first draft of this manuscript: "For a more professional look, greater protection and the possibility of resubmitting the proposal elsewhere, insert it . . . " The preposition for has three nouns as objects: look, protection, and possibility. Unfortunately, you can't say the "possibility of."

Hot Tip

Here are two tips for your silver tongue:

- When speaking, you may take acceptable liberties with words and grammar, but when read, the same words may come across as improvised rather than carefully composed. But if you are blessed with a distinctive voice or style, try to make sure your prose captures it.
- One way to know if your words and sentences are as smooth as you want them to be is to read them aloud to hear how they sound.

Words to Avoid

Avoid being "writerly." Don't reach for long or unusual words when short, direct words will do.

Avoid the adverb *obviously*. Don't tell an editor what is obvious.

Avoid adverbs and adjectives. Write with nouns and verbs.

Avoid the verb to be, if you can find a stronger verb.

Avoid sentences that begin *It is* or *There is/are*.

Avoid *this* chapter or *this* book; use *the*.

Avoid weak, indefinite words: *maybe, probably, perhaps, few, some, something, anything, thing(s), many, a lot, lots of, plenty of, numerous, almost, quite, little, awhile* and *several*. Be accurate, definite and specific without using the word *specific*.

Avoid obscure, out of the ordinary words like *drollery* unless they are part of your style and you use them throughout your proposal.

Avoid the word *recent*; it won't be for long.

Avoid *three years ago* or *three years from now*; it will date your proposal. Give the year.

Avoid weak verbs. Instead, try using:

- *can* for *could*
- *will* for *would*
- *is* for *seems to be*
- *is* for *may be*

Readers want to be informed by an authority, so write like one. The more forceful your statements the better, particularly in the overview, when you're trying to sell your idea and yourself to an editor. Don't pussyfoot around. Be accurate, but be bold.

Avoid too many *and*s. Because computers make it so easy to add words, writers sometimes just string words together that are redundant or do not fit the sentence.

Avoid negative words or expressions. As *The Elements of Style* says, "Put statements in positive form."

Avoid sexist words or phrasing. Use *excel in* for *master, humanity* for *man* or *mankind*.

Avoid the he/she problem by using the plural *they*.

Avoid trendy buzz words like *mode, process* or *in process, viable, reader-* or *user-friendly, baby boomer,* or *impact* as a verb.

Avoid *utilize* for *use*.

Avoid *due to*; use *because of*.

Avoid *ongoing* for *continuing*.

Avoid *prior to* for *before*.

Avoid *different ways* or *various ways*. Enumerate the ways or tell how many ways there are. If you're discussing more than one way, they must be different or various.

Avoid jargon. You may be a psychologist or a computer hacker but not all of your readers are. Don't make your vocabulary a barrier to communication.

Avoid the prefix *inter* in *interrelated* and *interconnected*; it's redundant.

Avoid exaggerating anything. Don't let your accuracy become suspect.

Avoid superlatives unless they are warranted.

Avoid all-encompassing words like *all*, *every*, or *never*, unless they are accurate.

Avoid creating new words or bulky word combinations united by hyphens or slash marks. Don't take liberties with the language; it's a glorious instrument that already has enough keys to create all of the color, texture, vitality, variety, and emotion you need.

Avoid citing a dictionary and defining terms; it comes across as academic.

Avoid inevitable words. If you're writing a book about sex, avoid the word. It's going to show up often enough anyway when there's no alternative. Use a synonym, write around it, or just leave it out. Your title will tell readers what you're talking about.

Avoid imprecise words. Editors are word people. How well you choose your words will be important to them.

Avoid clichés like the plague. Don't use expressions you always hear or see in print; be original.

Avoid ordinary, overworked, lifeless words, phrases and images. Strive to make your writing vivid and colorful. This doesn't mean that you should never use war horses like *show, tell, make, give, get* (guilty as charged!), *do, put, good, very, interesting,* or *fascinating*, but your goal is to infuse your prose with as much feeling, resonance, vitality, and originality as your subject allows.

Avoid saying *the reader*. You will have more than one, so use the plural.

Avoid *etc.* You will slow editors down by forcing them to think about what it refers to. Either use the whole list or use part of the list, and preface it with *like, such as,* or *including*.

Avoid the word *City* in *New York City*.

Avoid the abbreviation *U.S.* Editors will assume you're talking about this country. If you need it, spell it out.

Avoid abbreviations such as *i.e.* and *e.g.* that are suitable for business memos, unless, like P.M., they are accepted in formal prose. For the same reason, avoid using *per* for *a*.

Type the subtitles of chapters in upper and lower case.

Avoid putting words in capital letters for emphasis; it looks amateurish. Let your choice of words and how you position them create emphasis.

Instead of *upon*, use *on*.

Delete *current* or *contemporary* if the context makes it clear that you are discussing the present.

Avoid the word *core* as in *core values*.

Avoid the word *targeted*; it's implied.

Avoid throat-clearing prefaces to a sentences such as "It is interesting that . . . " or "I truly believe that . . . "

Change *make sure that* to *will*.

Change *demonstrate* to *show*.

Change *over* to *more than*.

Change *critical* to *crucial* or *essential*.

Numbers

Avoid the words *replete, plethora, numerous, hundreds*, and *thousands*. Unless a precise number is needed, use a round but accurate number. If necessary, preface it with *almost, nearly*, or *more than*.

Use words for the numbers one to ninety-nine and for numbers at the beginning of sentences. Otherwise, digits are acceptable. Follow the usage in comparable books. If you're writing a how-to book in which numbers are important, use arabic numbers.

Don't mention cents or the lack of them. Stick to round dollar figures.

Your readers will get bogged down in precise numbers unless they really need to know them. Use your judgment in deciding whether to use *twenty-two* rather than *more than twenty*, or *twenty-four* instead of *almost twenty-five* or just *twenty-five* if absolute accuracy isn't necessary. Round numbers are easier to remember.

Punctuation and Italics

Avoid underlining for emphasis.

Print the names of books, periodicals, and movies in italics.

Avoid exclamation points; unless needed, they look like you're trying to force an emotion out of the reader.

Avoid parentheses in your introduction and outline. If something's worth saying, say it; if not, leave it out.

One dash mark is a hyphen for linking words or dividing them into syllables. If you wish to use a dash to set off a word or phrase, type two hyphens with no spaces between the dashes and what surrounds them.

Hyphenate two or more words used to modify a noun, when the hyphenation clarifies the meaning: black-and-white photos, fifteen-page document, and high-quality work. However, avoid hyphenating an adjective and an adverb ending in *ly*: *beautifully written*.

Use quote marks if you're quoting someone and always make it clear whom you're quoting and why. Otherwise, avoid them.

Use a single quote mark as an apostrophe or for a quote within a quote. For example: *Then he smiled and recalled, "She said: 'You don't say!' "*

It's is short for *it is*; *its* is the possessive of *it*.

Two closing suggestions:

- Resist the desire to include charts except in your sample chapter.
- Avoid mentioning Oprah, Dilbert, or 9/11, as you avoid Plato, Shakespeare, and the Bible. It's been done.

You will be doing yourself a favor if you scan these suggestions again after you write your proposal.

❖ ❖ ❖

After you make you prose sparkle, and your networks agree that your proposal is 100 percent, you have two choices: contact publishers yourself or hire an agent. If you're considering using an agent, chapter twenty-five will help you make up your mind.

22 | From Networks to Net Worth

The Golden Rule of Networks
The more people you know, the farther you'll go.

Nothing in life is more important than relationships. People give life its meaning and value. The holy trinity of becoming and remaining a successful author is writing, promoting, and networking. Make building your six international networks, online and off, a lifelong endeavor because nothing will be more crucial to achieving your goals than the people who help you build and sustain your career. If this trinity were an equilateral triangle, the pinnacle of it would be success, writing and promoting would be the two sides, and networking would be the bottom line because your networks will be the foundation of your success.

Think Link

How would you like to remove the possibility of your book failing? You can guarantee the success of your books by test-marketing them. But to do that, you need six overlapping networks:

1. Your personal network of your family, relatives, neighbors, school friends, and people in your community

2. Your writing network of people you share your work with, professionals who have gone farther down your path than you have

3. Your publishing network of writers, editors, members of writers' organizations, writing teachers, booksellers, librarians, reviewers, sales reps, organizations, publicists, and fans of your work

4. Your network of opinion-makers in the field about which you are writing, including those in the media, academia and government, members of related organizations, and professionals working in the trade

5. Your promotion network of people who can help you promote your work: publicists, sales and marketing people, sales reps, authors, media people, reviewers, booksellers, speakers, and tour escorts

6. Your speaking network of speakers, audiences, your clients, speakers' bureaus, meeting planners, and members of speakers' organizations, if your book lends itself to talks

You have two sets of networks: direct and indirect. Your direct network is everyone you know; your indirect network is everyone they know. You won't get your writing, your promotion, or your career right by yourself, but you don't have to. Your networks can:

- Give you feedback on your ideas, titles, writing, and promotion plans
- Help you find an agent and publisher
- Give you quotes for your books
- Give you leads and recommend you for speaking engagements
- Do seminars with you
- Connect you to other members of your networks
- Exchange e-mail lists with you
- Sell your book at their presentations
- Give you information about the media contacts and booksellers in their area
- Give you a place to lay your head while researching and promoting your book
- Forward your e-mails about your book and your needs to their networks

> ### O'Connor's Golden Rule of 250
> Each of us has 250 friends, family members, colleagues, associates, and critics. And each of those 250 in turn has 250 of their own, and so on.
> —Richard F.X. O'Connor, author of *How to Market You and Your Book: The Ultimate Insider's Guide to Get Your Book Published With Maximum Sales!*

Multiply 250 by 250, and that's more than 62,000 people. Multiply that by 250, and it's more than 15,000,000 people. Word of mouth is the most potent form of promotion for books, just as it is for movies. And technology has collapsed time and distance. Now word of mouse—spreading the word by e-mail—can make your books bestsellers the day they're published. Your mission is to:

- Go to literary events.
- Scour the Web for kindred spirits.
- Collect business cards.
- Build your e-mail list.
- Follow the careers of authors in your field and get to know them.

Technology makes it easier than ever to build and maintain your networks. They will remain essential and willing allies who will help you build your career. Make building your networks a lifelong endeavor. They will repay your efforts many times over.

Two More Steps to an Irresistible Proposal

An editor once said to us, "An editor is someone who can talk about anything for five minutes and nothing for ten." Experts in your network can give you advice that agents and editors can't because they're not experts. For the people who read it, however, your proposal will be a Rorschach test. They will spot only what they are able to see when they read it. So the more people who review your work, the fewer problems it will have when you submit it.

By the time you've finished your proposal, you will need a respite. Author and editor Marty Asher, who is Vintage and Anchor Books executive vice president and editor-in-chief, believes in putting finished work under the bed for three months, so you can look at it again, with fresh eyes, before submitting it. You may find yourself developing tunnel vision that impairs your ability to judge your work objectively. You may be so close to it that you can't distinguish its faults from its virtues. Now's the time to give yourself a break, and put your networks to work by asking them how you can improve it. Send your proposal to five kinds of readers:

1. Friends and family. You need and deserve encouragement. If you want a pat on the back, let your friends and family give it to you. Unless they have hidden resentments and criticize your proposal as the means to express them, they will tell you they like it because they like you. After all, what are friends and family for?

2. Potential buyers of your book. They may not know good writing, but they know what they like. Would they buy your book if they found it in a bookstore? Try to enlist booksellers to render an opinion, at least on your idea, title and promotion plan.

3. Literate, objective readers. They can tell you what's wrong with your proposal as well as what's right with it.

4. Experts in your field. Approach people who know what you are writing about, including authors of related books. If you're presenting a controversial idea, find members of the opposition to go over your proposal and try to poke holes in it. You may not convert them, but you might earn their respect and avoid embarrassing yourself later.

5. A mentor. This person is most valuable of all, the most critical critic, a devil's advocate, someone whose taste and judgment you respect and in whose knowledge you have absolute confidence. A devil's advocate can combine truth with charity, analyze the structure and development of your book, and spot every word, punctuation mark, idea, character, and incident that can be improved or removed. Devil's advocates are worth their weight in royalties.

See if you can get one or more of your angels to at least skim this book before reading your proposal so they can judge if you have provided editors with what they need. The proposal checklist, Appendix A, will help you decide if all of your pieces fit together in a salable proposal.

Three Other Ways to Find Readers

Use these three ideas if you need help finding readers:

1. Join or start a critique group. Getting together with a table full of writers that meets regularly online or in person to discuss its members' work will enable you to get feedback as you write. Working with more experienced writers than yourself will prove more productive than working with those who have less experience than you.

Giving and receiving constructive criticism is crucial. But writers saying something doesn't automatically make it right, especially if they haven't had a book published. You may have to try more than one group until you find one that gives you what you need and whose members will benefit from your advice.

2. Tell writers that you will be happy to review their proposals. This will give you experience critiquing prose and help you build a network of writers willing to return the favor. People love to see their name in print, so promise readers that you will mention them on the acknowledgments page and give them an autographed copy of your book.

Hot Tip

When you negotiate the sale of your book, ask your publisher if they will provide copies you need for people who have given you feedback on your proposal and manuscript. These copies deserve to be considered part of the promotional copies you receive at no cost because the people you acknowledge will be salespeople who will show your book to people they know and display it prominently in their living room so it will be a conversation piece.

3. Call a book doctor. If you don't have anybody nearby or online, consider hiring a freelance editor or a book doctor. Such editors should show you a list of published nonfiction books aimed at the general public that they edited, either at proposal stage or after. Also, before you hire one, ask prospective editors if you may contact their clients or the agents who represent their clients. Freelance editors charge either a flat fee or an hourly rate that ranges from $25 to more than $100 an hour.

Book doctors charge more than editors, because, if necessary, they can doctor your manuscript, that is, rewrite it, not just show you what's wrong with it. So be clear about the help you need and your budget for it.

When you find an editor you want to work with, ask for an assessment of the proposal and an estimate of what it will cost to edit it and to check the revised version of it based on the editor's recommendations.

If your networks do not lead you to any editors, check the listings in *Literary Market Place* or *Writer's Market* in your library.

The Breakfast of Champion Writers

We receive work with obvious faults every day. And it says two things about the writers who submit it, one unfortunate, the other fatal. First it means that the writer isn't ready to approach an agent. The rejection note on our Web site (www.larsen-pomada.com) is as gentle as it can be because writers may improve over time, so it's impossible to judge whether they will someday be able to write at a professional level.

However, mistakes that leap to the eye in a cover letter or on page one of a proposal also mean that the writers don't have the network of readers they need to help them ensure that their work is ready to submit. That's fatal because getting feedback is essential for writing publishable prose. No matter how successful they become, feedback will always be the breakfast of writers who are champs in their field because they know that it will enable them to have whatever they want for dinner.

Hot Tip

When you send your proposal and later your manuscript to be critiqued, include a note telling readers what you need feedback on. The more specific and thorough your request is, the better the feedback you will receive. Ask them to give you feedback on your grammar, word use, and punctuation, and to rate the parts of your proposal that you most need their responses to, such as jokes and anecdotes. Ask them to grade your proposal as a whole on a scale of one to ten both for content and pleasure. Include as nice a pen with red ink as your budget allows.

Because people's reactions are subjective, receiving them will prepare you for the range of responses your book will create. You must trust your instincts. Sift conflicting or confusing suggestions and follow only the advice that makes sense to you.

Once you have sorted out the opinions of others and feel ready to return to your proposal with a fresh eye, revise it one more time. When you're sure your proposal is ready, it's time to cut the literary umbilical cord and send your baby out into the real world.

❖ ❖ ❖

Your book will be a pebble cast into a still body of water with no shore. It will continue to make ripples as long as people, paper, and the Net help you keep it alive.

The pleasure, enlightenment, or inspiration in your book will continue to affect readers, and they will express their gratitude for the experience. That alone is a compelling reason to put yourself in the service of your readers and write your books as well as you can. After your efforts to write and promote your work, it's the effect that your books have on your readers that will determine your future.

23 | Test-Marketing Your Book

Ten Ways to Take Your Book for a Test Drive

By the time your publisher test-markets your book with its first printing, its fate will probably be sealed. You can raise your publisher's expectations for you and your book by test-marketing it first. Here are ten ways to test-market your book:

1. You can test-market the idea and title for your book, and gauge how it will fare against your competition. Use your networks.

2. You can test-market your book and build your national platform by raising your speaking volume. If your book will lend itself to being promoted with talks, readings, or seminars, start doing them as soon as you can. The parts of your presentation will become the chapters of your book. Books generate talks, but talks generate books.

You can use your talks to:

- Test-market your title and the information for your book. Try to make the title of your talk the title of your book. Use them to create synergy by selling each other. Whether you're asking people to read your work or hear about it, you're asking for their time. And your title must convince them that it will be time well spent. In addition to helping sell your talks, the right title will help sell your book, its subsidiary rights, and your spin-off books.

- Use handouts to test illustrations and material from your book. We did it with some of the information in this book at writer's conferences, and the conferences did the photocopying—an example of win-win partnering.
- Perfect the *money moments* in your book—the humor, drama, or inspiration—by trying them out on audiences until they convince you that your words have the affect you desire.
- Use an evaluation form to get feedback and do market research by asking what other information, books, and talks your audiences want.
- See if you enjoy talking about the subject enough to make it a way of life and to test the limits of how many talks you can give a year without burning out.
- Gauge the response to your book by the number of people who come to hear you.
- Receive instant feedback on how audiences respond to the subject and to you so you can fine-tune the most felicitous way to express and structure your ideas.
- Build advance publicity and the market for your book.
- Encourage your audiences to give you humor, anecdotes, and information that you can use in talks, articles, newsletters, revisions, and new books.
- Use the experiences your audiences e-mail you about how your information helps them, and collect testimonials from individuals and organizations that you can use on your Web site, in your media/speaker's kit, and your book.
- Sell cassettes or CDs of your talks along with other products and services.
- Build your networks and your e-mail list of people to whom you can market everything you sell. Ask your fans to forward your e-mail to their networks.
- Build your credibility as a speaker and an authority on your subject with book buyers, agents, editors, media people, speaking bureaus, and meeting planners.
- Develop your confidence in your ability to write your proposal and your book.
- Use an advance order form to sell books as you approach pub date.
- Sell your manuscript to get feedback on it.

Hot Tip

After your mind and your fingertips, your tongue is your body's most powerful promotional tool. I hope these tips help you get started with your speaking career:

- Invite everyone you want to know about you to hear you speak. Your talks may snare an agent or publisher. Even if they don't attend, you'll hear from them if your idea interests them. John Gray found his agent when he saw the listing for her talk at Learning Annex.

- Sooner or later, depending on your subject and your skill, people will start offering you money to speak, which in turn gives you the opportunity to market yourself and your continually growing body of products and services to their audiences.

- Look beyond talks. Your book may lend itself to seminars, consulting, training sessions, and continuing classes. Bridging technology enables you to use your Web site to give "webinars"—seminars on the Web.

- Every town has organizations that need speakers. Rotary meets every week, and there are a lifetime's worth of chapters. The bigger the town, the more opportunities there are. Read books on speaking. Join Toastmasters to polish your skills. Join the National Speakers Association to build your speaking career. Both have chapters around the country, and their contact information is in the resource directory.

Don't regard speaking as a purely self-serving activity. If your talks and books help your audiences lead better lives, you are doing them a service. If you can do well by doing good, long may you flourish.

3. You can test-market your book by writing articles. Getting one or more articles about your subject published, like writing a sample chapter, is passing an audition for being able to write your book. It also helps prove the interest in your idea. Here are the benefits you gain by writing articles:

- Your article can be the embryo from which your book evolves.
- Having an article published about the subject of your book helps to establish your credibility as a writer and an authority.
- One or more articles that are long enough and strong enough in a respected periodical may substitute for a sample chapter.
- Your article may sell your book. Agents and editors always read in hopes of discovering writers and ideas. If your article attracts an editor, you may only need to write a mini-proposal.
- Who publishes your article, how much they pay for it, and the reactions from agents, editors, and readers will help you gauge

whether your idea is a winner.

- Researching an article will enable you to prove to yourself that there's a book in the subject.
- Writing articles will give you a feeling for how well you handle the subject, how you can solve the problems involved in writing the book, how long it will take, and how much you will enjoy writing it.
- The experience will help you decide if you are a sprinter—an article writer—or a marathoner able to go the distance.
- If you need to interview hard to reach people, they may be more agreeable to talking if you're on assignment for a newspaper or magazine than if you're just doing research for an unsold book.
- Since your proposal may not sell, placing an article will help offset the cost of your time and research. If your article is popular enough, it may lead to additional articles on the subject, which will aid your research and increase the chances of selling your book.
- If your advance won't cover your expenses, selling articles based on the book or serializing it in a magazine, online or off, or in non-competing newspapers, will help make up the difference. If you can include a commitment from a major publication, it will be a powerful piece of ammunition for your promotion plan.
- Responses from readers may correct mistakes and provide new facts, sources, and lines of inquiry.
- Instead of or in addition to getting your articles published, you can put them on your Web site where they will promote your book, generate feedback, and enable editors to see more of your book.
- Writing articles after publication will continue to publicize your book. You can adapt your book or write new articles to test-market your next book.
- Articles will also generate speaking opportunities.

Hot Tip

If your talk will interest business audiences, trade magazines may be a continuing source for placing articles. You can resell the same article to non-competing trade magazines. What they lack in money, they make up for in promoting your book and generating leads for speaking gigs.

4. You can test-market your book by self-publishing it. New technologies have spurred a surge in self-publishing, a venerable tradition in American letters. When self-publishing guru Dan Poynter gives workshops, he hands out a list of famous authors who have published

Four Tradeoffs to Writing Articles

The reasons for writing articles usually outweigh the following four risks, but be aware of them:

- An article involves risk because another writer may also decide to do a book on the subject. To lessen this danger and stimulate responses from readers, agents, and editors, ask the editor of the publication to state in the bio that accompanies your article that it is from a book in progress. This suggests that you have a head start and will deter potential competitors while attracting agents and editors.

- Magazines may offer less for an article than they would for first-serial rights to excerpt your book before it is published. The best time for your articles to appear is when your books are in stores, so that readers who like the article or excerpt will rush out to buy your book.

- Sell only first-time North American serial rights and no electronic rights to articles that will become part of your book. This will limit potential sales, because print media are increasingly anxious to keep electronic rights.

- If you're writing an exposé containing newsworthy revelations, you can only let the cat out of the bag once. To learn more about writing articles, check with your networks, and writing magazines and books that cover the subject, including *Writer's Market*.

their own work, including Walt Whitman, Henry David Thoreau, Edgar Allan Poe, and Mark Twain.

The One Minute Manager, *What Color Is Your Parachute?*, *The Celestine Prophecy* and *The Christmas Box* were all best-sellers, and they were all originally self-published books. AAR member Laurie Liss sold *The Christmas Box* for $4.2 million, a record sum for a self-published book, all the more remarkable because it only included North American hardcover rights!

It used to be said that if you publish your own book, you'll have a lot of books in your garage, so you'll work hard to sell them because you want to park your car. Thanks to technology, self-publishing your book no longer requires you to sacrifice your garage. Desktop publishing and short-run printing have liberated writers from having to pay others to have their work published. The new ease of publishing books is empowering tens of thousands of writers a year to publish their books, the ultimate way to test-market a book. If you have the luxury of writing your book before you sell it, then you owe it to your book to self-publish it at least in manuscript form.

Appendix C lists nine options for getting your books published. Self-publishing your book, using one or more of the following options, is one of them:

- photocopying your manuscript
- publishing it as a book using print-on-demand (POD) or print-quantity-needed (PQN) for short-run printing, or offset printing for long runs
- publishing it online as a downloadable book
- publishing it with one of the more than four hundred e-book publishers

You can also self-publish in other media, such as:

- audiocassettes
- videocassettes
- software
- CD-ROM
- and in other forms, such as a calendar

After you integrate initial feedback into your manuscript from your beta testers, your inner circle of readers, print a *Special Limited Reader's Edition*. Photocopy just enough double-spaced, one- or two-sided copies for each event and sell them in loose-leaf binders.

Hot Tip Material in a loose-leaf binder has a greater perceived value than other forms of binding.

Even if you have sold your book to a publisher, this will enable you to test-market it. You want people taking your manuscript home and getting the benefit your title promises without your help. Then you want their responses and suggestions or, better yet, a photocopy of their marked-up copy.

The goal of this self-published edition, which you can also sell on your Web site, is to cover your costs, not necessarily to make a profit. Include a feedback page at the beginning of the book, and offer an autographed copy of the published edition and a mention in your

Myths and Realities of Self-Publishing

If you want to test-market a published version of your book before selling it to a publisher, you can make an all-out effort and create the book you've dreamed about. Thousands do. Self-publishing is a major trend because of a myth and a reality.

The myth is that it's somewhere between difficult and impossible to get an agent and attract a big publisher, that the New York publishing world is a fortress too well guarded. (The truth is that every time agents and editors pick up a submission, they hope that they will love it.)

The reality is that self-publishing has advantages that can be summed up in two words: money and control. If you self-publish, you have complete control over every aspect of your book: the title, the content, the editing, the format (hardcover, trade paperback, or mass-market), the size, the length, the cover, the design, the production, the publication date, the price, the marketing, and the selling and distribution.

You also keep control of your book's subsidiary rights, including film, foreign, and electronic rights, and you make more money on every copy.

One editor said to us, "If the author can sell two thousand copies a month for eight months, I want to see it." Other editors will not need as strong a track record. If you test-market your book and sell enough copies, a publisher will buy it.

If you decide to sell your self-published book to a publisher, you will still need the first part of the proposal (the introduction) along with sales figures and information about subsidiary-rights sales. Indicate any changes needed in the new edition, how many manuscript pages they will be, and how many months it will take you to finish them. Include reviews and articles about the book with the key passages underlined.

Note that self-published authors must do all the work to promote and sell their books. Gregory Godek drove around the country in his specially painted RV and sold more than one million copies of his self-published book *1,001 Ways to Be Romantic*. However, Gregory acknowledged that he spent 5 percent of his time writing his book and 95 percent of his time and $600,000 promoting it. One day he realized that he isn't a writer who promotes, he's a promoter who writes. The book has now sold more than two million copies.

acknowledgments in exchange for a marked-up copy. Keep adding changes before you reprint, and keep reprinting until your audiences run out of suggestions.

If you generate enough publicity and sales through your efforts, publishers will be eager to buy the rights to publish your book. If your self-published book is professionally designed and edited, the publisher may be able to just change the cover and the front matter, and print it as is.

5. You can test-market your proposal with agents. Chapter twenty-five is about agents.

6. You can test-market your Web site. Your Web site will be so important to your future that you want to make sure it's up and running before pub date. A great site can help you promote your book and make a living. Use the sites of other authors and other professionals in your field as models, and do the same things better. Hire a Web master if you're not tech-savvy enough to go it alone or can't enlist a teenager to help.

Encourage your networks to visit the site and make suggestions. Also, forge as many links as you can with other sites. The goal is for your site to have maximum impact when your book is published.

7. You can test-market your goals. For example, you can:

- Write the ideal review for your book in the ideal newspaper or magazine by the ideal reviewer. (See the ideal review of this book on page 187.)
- Design the ideal full-page ad for your book in *The New York Times Book Review* or *USA Today* with copy about the book and quotes from the ideal people.
- Write down the advance you want (not need) for your book.
- Name the ideal publisher(s) for your book.

You can test how realistic your goals are by including your goals with your proposal when you send it out for feedback. Ask your readers if they think your proposal can achieve your goals. If not, revise your goals or your proposal.

8. You can test-market your promotion plan. There are two levels at which you can test-market your promotion plan:

- Once your book is on store shelves, do a publicity campaign in your city or the nearest major market to test-market your publicity materials, see if you get publicity, and if the publicity boosts sales.
- Integrate what you learn from your first city into your promotion

Writing Your Own Dream Review

The Ideal Review of
How to Write a Book Proposal
by E.B. White, The Ideal Reviewer

Literary agent Michael Larsen makes his living by using *How to Write a Book Proposal* to sell his clients' work. His book does an excellent job of showing writers how they can make their living by following its advice. He has taken *The Elements of Style* to heart, and the book is an impeccable example of the writing he hopes to inspire.

Larsen keeps the structure of a proposal admirably simple. He divides a proposal into three parts: an introduction with information about the book and the author, an outline, and a sample chapter. Examples illustrate his points, and the book includes several annotated proposals he has sold.

The author maintains an engaging balance between a realistic, proven approach to writing and selling proposals, and a can-do inspirational tone that will keep aspiring writers turning the pages. Just the hot tips he scatters throughout the book are worth far more than the cover price.

Larsen believes that the right book will change the world. His book contributes to that noble cause by helping writers to get the best possible editor, publisher, and deal for their books. The proposal book is part of a synergistic trilogy of equally helpful and enjoyable books on agents and promotion that will help writers get the most out of this book.

A member of the Association of Author's Representatives, Larsen has been a literary agent in San Francisco for more than thirty years. During this time, he and his partner, Elizabeth Pomada, have sold books to more than one hundred publishers as well as writing or co-authoring fourteen books themselves.

How to Write a Book Proposal was the first book on the subject and remains the best. Larsen is sure enough of his approach that he includes a money-back guarantee, which only one reader in eighteen years has taken him up on. I guess you just can't please everyone. But then, 100,000 to one suggests a degree of satisfaction that justifies the risk.

His upbeat, can-do approach will leave readers inspired and eager to start on their books. The only problem I had with the book is that when I finished reading it, I couldn't resist starting one of my own!

plan and your promotion materials. Ask your networks in other cities for publicity contacts and a place to lay your head. For the cities you don't visit, do a publicity mailing using what you learn on your tour.

9. You can test-market your commitment to your book. All of these opportunities to test-market your book also test your commitment to it. If you want your book published by a big house and you want big-time sales, you have to be willing to do whatever it takes to make your book successful.

You can't wait for the time to write; you have to make the time. You have to steal it from other activities, things that may give you more immediate pleasure and allow you to stay in your comfort zone. But writing your proposal should give you a growing sense of excitement about:

- how much fun and satisfaction you will have writing the book
- how good your book will be
- how great an adventure promoting it will be
- how gratified you will be about its impact on your readers
- how you will build a career out of doing a series of books on the subject

10. You will test-market your series with the first book. If you are proposing a series of books, whether you write the second one depends on the fate of the first. The bigger series you envision, the more important it is that the first book do well enough to justify your efforts as well as those of your publisher.

❖ ❖ ❖

When you're ready, test-marketing your books will make them fail-proof, and once you do that, success is inevitable. The next part will show you how to get that proposal to market!

24 | The Mini-Proposal

If your proposal is a universe, your mini-proposal for it will be the brightest stars of that universe. Once you have a full proposal, distill the essence of it into a mini-proposal of five to ten double-spaced pages beginning with title and table-of-content pages.

The Seven Parts of a Mini-Proposal
Here are the seven parts of a mini-proposal:
1. **Your Overview.** A two-page overview of your book including:
    - your subject hook
    - your book hook
    - special features (optional)
    - a celebrity foreword (optional)
    - your back matter (optional)
    - the markets for your book
    - subsidiary-rights potential (optional)
    - your spin-off books (optional)
    - competitive books (optional) and complementary books

2. Your Mission Statement (optional). If you feel a sense of mission about writing and promoting your book, describe it in one first-person paragraph.

3. Your Platform (optional). This is a top-down list of what you have done and are doing to give your work and yourself continuing national visibility.

4. Your Promotion Plan. List the five or six most impressive things that you will do to promote your book. For books that writers want to sell to big houses, they are usually:

- a matching promotion budget (optional)
- the name of the publicist that you will hire, ideally someone known to the publisher you plan to approach (optional)
- the number of major markets you will visit during your book's one-to-three month launch window (optional)
- the number of talks you will continue to give a year (optional)
- the number of books that you will sell a year, assuming that you sell a book to one out of four listeners (optional)
- anything else of equal promotional power

5. Resources Needed to Complete Your Book. Give a list of resources you need to complete your book, or just a sentence that says, "You will receive the manuscript x months after receipt of the advance."

6. Your Bio. A half-page bio should list the most impressive info about you and your accomplishments not mentioned in your platform. Include a small head shot at the end of your bio.

7. Your Outline. On one to two pages, list your chapter titles and flush right, the number of manuscript pages each will be. Then provide one to three phrases about what's in each chapter. Start each phrase with a verb, varying the verbs as much as you can. After the title of your sample chapter, add the parenthetical phrase (*available on request*) or, if you're e-mailing your mini-proposal, provide a link, hyperlink if possible, to where you post the chapter.

For a how-to book, provide an annotated list of catchy chapter titles explained by subtitles that may start with numbers or gerunds (such as *using*, *making* and *selling*). Numbers may provide the structure of the chapter, such as "6 Ways to . . . "

If you can, create chapter titles that relate to a metaphor in the title of your book. For example, if your title was *The 10 Keys to Success in Sales: Unlocking the Doors to a Million-Dollar Income*, you could have ten chapters about the keys, and bookend chapters before and after them.

Alter the section lengths of your mini-proposal as needed to show off your book to best advantage. But as with your full proposal, the criterion for what to include is what will most excite editors about you and your book in as few words as possible.

Using Your Mini-Proposal

Here are nine ways that you can use your mini-proposal:

1. If writing your proposal or any part of it seems intimidating, write a mini-version of it first and then expand it.

2. If your idea is commercial enough, your writing credentials are strong enough, or if you've already had a story or a book published about the subject, you may be able to sell your book with just a mini-proposal.

3. If you are writing a book that only you can write, and you don't have to worry about people knowing about the information it contains, mail or e-mail your mini-proposal with your query letter. It will be short enough that agents and editors may treat it as a letter that gets immediate attention rather than a full proposal. Editors consider full proposals after they read the work of writers they've already signed, submissions from agents, and submissions that arrived before yours. Agents or their assistants screen proposals to see if any merit immediate attention.

Submit to as many agents or editors as you wish, but mention in your one-page cover letter that other agents or editors have the mini-proposal, and that you also have an *xx*-page proposal.

4. Agents and editors reject almost all of the thousands of submissions they receive a year. Because they are perpetually swamped, they may welcome the chance to read a short proposal. If you have a full and a mini-proposal, give them a choice.

5. You may be able to send agents or editors your mini-proposal as an e-mail letter, but not as an attachment. This will speed up their response time, which may be crucial if your book is about a timely topic.

Hot Tip

Not all agents and editors accept online submissions, so follow their guidelines. Regardless of how they prefer to be approached, they will still respond more quickly to 5 to 10 pages than 35 to 50.

6. Send both a mini-proposal and a full proposal, and let agents or editors decide which to read. An editor may prefer a full proposal. But editors at large houses have to gather support from other people in the house, and a mini-proposal may be all their colleagues need to see. Place the one they request first, the other one behind it, and mention both in your cover letter.

Hot Tip | In *A Writer's Guide to Book Publishing*, AAR member Rick Balkin recommends skipping the query letter and sending your full proposal. If you're not concerned about agents or editors knowing your idea or the information in your proposal, send both proposals to as many agents or editors as you want. Let recipients choose which to read, and let them know other people have it. Put your mini-proposal first. It will be faster to read, and if readers are hooked, they will turn the pages and read more.

7. You can put your full and mini-proposals on your Web site at an address that you share only with agents or editors. Then you can e-mail or snail mail editors the site URL. If your complete manuscript is ready, you can also make your manuscript available online so editors can read as much as they want.

8. You or your agent may be able to use your mini-proposal to interest foreign publishers or other subsidiary-rights buyers.

9. You can adapt a mini-proposal to approach magazine and newspaper editors about writing articles or about serializing your book.

❖ ❖ ❖

Your mini-proposal will be a win-win. Time-starved agents and editors will appreciate receiving it, and it will speed up the process of getting you the agent or publisher you want. When your networks tell you that your proposal is 100 percent and ready to sell, you have three basic choices. One of them is hiring and agent. So the next chapter will help you decide the right choice for you.

25 | How an Agent Can Help You

New writers approach agents without an understanding of agenting or publishing. So one of the fundamental services that agents perform for their clients is to transform them from writers with something to say into authors with something to sell. This literary alchemy changes writers from artists and craftspeople who can spin words into professionals who can spin words into gold.

When your proposal or manuscript is ready to sell, you have three basic options for getting your book published:

1. You can self-publish it, an option discussed in chapter twenty-three.
2. You can find a publisher yourself.
3. You can hire an agent.

How Agents Help Writers

Here's how and why an agent can help you:

- An agent is a mediator between two realities: you and the marketplace.
- An agent is a scout who knows what publishers are looking for.
- An agent is a filter who sifts thousands of submissions a year, discovers the few gems, and after helping writers polish them, offers them to editors who are grateful to agents for making their jobs easier

because agents understand what will sell and how to present books to publishers.

- An agent is a midwife who can provide editorial guidance and help you give birth to your idea.

- An agent is a matchmaker who knows which editors and publishers to submit your book to and, just as important, which to avoid. An agent continues to send out a manuscript until it is sold or until the agent has tried all likely publishers. It's taken us as few as four phone calls and as many as ten years to sell a book.

- An agent is a negotiator. There's an Arab proverb that says, "Trust in Allah, but tie your camel." In publishing, you tie your camel with a contract. When a publisher makes an offer for your book, your agent becomes a negotiator who hammers out the most favorable possible contract for your working marriage with your publisher.

Publishers will offer an advance against royalties usually based on their estimate of first year's royalties. Large houses pay between $5,000 and $25,000 for most books, but they'll pay whatever agents or competitive bidders convince them your book is worth.

The contract, which may be as long as thirty-six pages, which is between you and your publisher, and which you must understand, approve and sign, enables an agent to act on your behalf and receive income earned through the contract. The agent deducts a 15 percent commission from the advance and forwards the rest to you.

- An agent enables you to keep more subsidiary-rights income and receive it sooner than if your publisher handles the rights.

- An agent follows up on subsidiary-rights sales and may appoint co-agents for film and foreign rights.

- An agent helps you avoid haggling about rights and money with your editor, so you can work together harmoniously on making your books successful.

- An agent serves as a buffer and liaison between you and your publisher on editorial, financial, production, and promotional questions that arise throughout the publication process.

- An agent is an advocate who helps solve problems such as a late or rejected manuscript, a bad jacket design, or your editor leaving the house.

- An agent may be a rainmaker who can get you assignments from editors or come up with ideas for you.

- An agent is a mentor who is a source of knowledge about writing and publishing, and of advice about your writing and your career.

- An agent is an oasis of encouragement in what may be a desert of rejection.

Agent as Painkiller

Some writers think that people become agents for the same reason they become dentists—they like to inflict pain. And although it's true that, like publishers, agents reject more than 95 percent of the submissions they see, agents receive far more rejections than writers. Consider these additional ways an agent can help you:

- By absorbing rejections and being a focal point for your business dealings, your agent frees you to write.
- Publishers respond more quickly to submissions from agents than from writers because agented work is more likely to be publishable.
- As a continuing source of manuscripts, agents have more clout with editors than writers do.
- Writers who approach multimedia, multinational conglomerates without help are asking for trouble. The selling of your book deserves the same level of care, skill, knowledge, and experience that you lavish on writing it. An agent can't write your book as well as you can; but you can't sell it as well as an agent can.
- When editors may change jobs and publishers may change hands at any time, an agent may be the only stable element in your career.

Eleven Ways to Find the Agent You Need

Novelist Colleen McCullough's sister was on a diet when her birthday arrived, so Colleen made her a tuna fish casserole as a birthday cake. Colleen was looking for an agent at the time. As she was looking at the listings in *Literary Market Place*, she saw the name Frieda Fishbein. And that's how Frieda got the chance to sell *The Thorn Birds*.

If you want your book published by a big house, and you don't have a track record, you may find it hard to get an agent. But this list of eleven ways to find an agent proves that it is easier than ever to find one:

1. Your networks. Chapter twenty-two discusses networks. Your networks can help you is by recommending agents. You will receive better treatment if writers recommend you to their agents. This is a big step up because agents know that their clients won't waste their time, so if one of their authors recommends a writer, they will pay serious attention to the writer's work.

Agents give referrals special treatment because agents know that a writer sent by a professional is more likely to be legitimate than one coming, for example, through a directory. At the same time, agents will also gauge the enthusiasm with which the recommendation is made. A note to the agent from an author, teacher, or editor is more effective than their just telling the writer to mention their name. And the more passionate a recommendation is, the more eager agents will be to see the writer's work.

Hot Tip

Start a mastermind group, a handful of professionals who meet regularly by phone or e-mail and act as a board of directors for each other. Including professionals you can learn from in other fields will provide you with fresh perspectives. In some groups, members give themselves goals to accomplish by the next meeting, one member makes a note of them, and members are held accountable for meeting their goals. One of our authors quadrupled his earnings after the first meeting with his mastermind group.

2. The Association of Authors' Representatives (AAR). The 350 agents in AAR are the best source of experienced, reputable agents. Members are obligated to follow the AAR's code of ethics. The directories below indicate when an agent is a member of AAR. The group's Web site is www.aar-online.org.

3. Writers' organizations. Members of writing organizations will tell you about their agents.

4. The Web. Many online directories include agents' e-mail addresses and Web sites. You can try:

- www.writersmarket.com
- www.authorlink.com
- www.publisherslunch.com
- www.publishersweekly.com
- www.publishersmarketplace.com

5. Directories. Each directory listed in the Resource Directory varies in the kind and amount of information it provides. For the best results, check what several of them list about the same agency.

6. A newsletter. *Talking Agents: The AR&E Newsletter* is a bimonthly newsletter about agents and their sales. It's available by subscription in print or online. E-mail info@agentresearch.com or visit www.agentresearch.com.

7. Literary events. Writing classes, readings, lectures, seminars, book signings, conferences, and book festivals present opportunities to meet and learn about agents and publishers. Some conferences feature one-on-one meetings with agents.

8. Magazines. If you don't want to splurge on a subscription to *Publishers Weekly*, read it at the library. The Hot Deals column is a roundup of agent sales. You can also track publishers who are doing books on your subject. The spring, summer, and fall announcement issues are particularly helpful. *Writer's Digest* does annual publisher roundups, and most writing magazines have articles by and about agents.

9. Publishers' catalogs. Hardcover and trade paperback publishers produce catalogs that are sent to booksellers and are used by their sales reps to sell books. You can request catalogs free from publishers; they will enable you to learn about what's being published.

If you think the editor of a book you see in a catalog might be receptive to yours, call the editorial department and ask who the editor is. Also, big publishers' catalogs often contain the names of the agents who control subsidiary rights on their clients' books.

10. Books. The research you have done on competing and complementary books will come in handy now. Check the dedication and acknowledgment pages books related to yours. Grateful authors thank their editors and agents.

11. Media attention. Let agents or publishers find you: Get published and get yourself media exposure.

Doing It for Love and Money

Like publishers, agents are motivated by love and money. They need big books to make big bucks. They also love to get excited about their books and authors. And, they must do a good job on the first book if they expect to work on an author's next one. One of the hardest parts of their job, though, is finding books and authors.

Look at the challenge of finding and keeping an agent as creating and sustaining a working marriage that has personal and professional aspects to it. That's why you should meet with potential agents to test the chemistry for your working marriage.

Four Ways Agents Can Help You That You Can't Help Yourself

If you have a salable book, you can sell it. Writers do it all the time. But there are four ways that an agent can help you that you can't help yourself:

The Golden Rules for Getting an Agent

- Find a salable idea.
- Write a salable proposal or manuscript.
- Research potential agents.
- Follow their submission guidelines.
- Do a multiple submission, letting agents know that other agents have it.
- Meet interested agents.
- Choose the best one for you.

1. Agents understand editors' expectations, so when they submit a proposal, it is closer to 100 percent than you can make it without help. Editors, instead of editing, have become in-house agents who sign up books and sing their praises all along the road to publication and after it. As mentioned earlier, this has forced agents to become editors. Agents must make sure a proposal is 100 percent before they submit it because editors aren't interested in books that will require a lot of editing.

2. An agent can get you the best possible editor, publisher, and deal for your book. There's a world of difference between a *yes* and the best possible *yes*. And as mentioned earlier, how publishers buy a book usually determines how they publish it.

3. An agent can negotiate the best contract terms. If you do receive an offer for your book, you can probably find an agent to negotiate the deal for you. If you prefer, an agent or intellectual property attorney can help you negotiate the contract on an hourly basis. Not getting help will cost more than the cost of professional advice. Writers' organizations like the Author's Guild and the National Writer's Union counsel their members for free.

4. An agent can respond to the questions and problems that arise during the long publication process that you won't be able to answer for yourself. You can use your networks for advice, but whether you'll receive the same level of guidance is questionable. And it's unlikely that you will be able to speak on your behalf as well as an agent will.

❖ ❖ ❖

Elizabeth and I are trapped in the publishing pyramid, but not, we hope, in the burial chamber. At the apex of the pyramid are the 6 percent of writers that *Writer's Digest* estimates earn a living as writers. If they want an agent, they have one. Writers do change agents, but agents can't earn a livelihood waiting for it to happen. At the bottom of the pyramid are the more than 80 percent of writers who aren't yet ready to sell their work to big houses, so agents can't make a living selling their work. Sandwiched between them are the less than ten percent of writers who are ready for the big time.

But more than eight hundred agents are searching for this same small group of writers. You think you've got problems! And the tougher business gets, the more urgently agents need writers whose work they can sell to New York houses. If you have a book that will interest large publishers, you should feel like a kid in a candy store with an unlimited allowance. After all, you are the most important person in the publishing business because you make it go.

26 | How and Where to Submit Your Query Letter and Proposal

The Fourth Part of Your Proposal: The Query Letter

It's been said that a query letter should be like a skirt: long enough to cover the subject but short enough to keep it interesting. Limit your letter to one single-spaced page with indented paragraphs and a space between paragraphs. In three or four paragraphs, give agents and editors the following information in this order:

- The reason you are contacting them: a recommendation from one of their authors, an acknowledgment or dedication in a book they've done, or because they have done books on the subject. Knowing what they've done will make you look more professional.
- A short subject hook that justifies your book.
- The essence of your book: the full title and selling handle.
- The largest markets for it if they aren't obvious.
- The four or five strongest parts of your promotion plan, if author promotion is important for your book.
- What you have ready to submit: an x-page mini-proposal, an xx-page proposal or an xxx-page manuscript. If you have completed the manuscript, mention it.
- Why you are the best person to write the book.

- That the book will be the first in a series on the subject.
- Anything else that will convince them to ask for your proposal.

Just as a mini-proposal is a shorter version of your full proposal, your query letter will be a mini-mini-proposal that boils down five to ten pages into one. Use the information from the first part of your proposal, but change the wording so you won't diminish the impact of your proposal.

Author Leon Fletcher believes that a query letter is the fourth part of a proposal. He's right. Like the other three parts, each line must convince editors to read the next line. Poor prose dooms more query letters and proposals than anything else.

Your query letter doesn't have to be funny or imaginative, but it creates the first and perhaps only impression agents or editors will have of you, so it must be impeccable. If your letter is poorly written, you've saved editors the trouble of looking at it.

Agents and editors prefer that writers query them by mail or e-mail. You can simultaneously query as many of them as you wish, letting them know that that's what you're doing. Although they also prefer queries by mail or e-mail, small agencies and publishers are open to phone queries, but they may not return long-distance calls from strangers.

Consider sending queries to only the more desirable half of the people you want to approach. Even if you don't get any positive responses, you may get feedback that you can use to revise the letter you send to the rest of your list. The simplest way to do it right: Follow submission guidelines in directories.

Agents vary in how they work. We prefer to receive a No. 10 business-size envelope with queries so we can reply with our free sixteen-page booklet, "How to Make Yourself Irresistible to Any Agent or Publisher," and a list of recent sales. Agents expect to receive an SASE with a proposal so they can return the submission, if necessary, with a rejection slip. Most agents will reply only if they're interested in a book or if the writer includes an SASE.

Two no-nos in query letters:

1. Don't send anything to more than one person at the same agency or publisher. We receive enough submissions that are sent to both of us to convince me that some knave out there is suggesting that writers do it. Duplication makes a bad impression. It's a waste of money for writers and a waste of time for them and us.

2. Don't send just anything to a publishing house. Big houses will

return it unopened. Find the name of the right editor for your book and verify that the editor is still at the house. This is less important with agents, although you will create a more professional impression if you check to see which agent handles the kind of book you're writing and use the agent's name. Elizabeth handles fiction at our agency, but we receive fiction queries addressed to me.

To the front of the letter, clip a postage-paid self-addressed postcard with the agent's or editor's name and your return address on it. On the back of the card, write three lines of copy:

> Please send the proposal ____
> Sorry, we can't help ____
> [And for your benefit, include the name of
> the person and the house or agency]

No matter how busy they are, agents and editors interested in finding new writers, will take the time to read a one-page letter, and put a checkmark on a postcard. Although they may have their assistants do it.

Once editors express interest in seeing your proposal, it is no longer unsolicited. You can do a multiple submission of your proposal, and it will not wind up in the dreaded slush pile. Indicate as you did in your query letter that it is a multiple submission. Start your cover letter with, "Many thanks for giving me the opportunity to send you my proposal for . . ."

Find out how long it takes agents or editors to respond, make a note of the date by which you should have a response, and follow up by e-mail or phone if you don't receive a reply. Another benefit of having an agent: Their submissions are reviewed faster than those from writers.

Submitting Your Proposal

Someone once defined a manuscript as "something submitted in haste and returned at leisure." For the best treatment on the receiving end, submit your proposal properly. Agents and publishers do not assume responsibility for lost or damaged manuscripts, so it behooves you to package your proposal carefully. Place the proposal in a manila envelope or, for greater protection, a No. 5 mailing bag.

In *How to Write Short Stories*, Ring Lardner observed, "A good many young writers make the mistake of enclosing a stamped, self-addressed envelope, big enough for the manuscript to come back in. This is too much of a temptation to the editor."

Always enclose a stamped, self-addressed mailer if you want the material returned. Or enclose a prepaid return label from United Parcel Service or Federal Express.

If you don't need the material back, say so, but include a stamped, self-addressed No. 10 business-size envelope or postcard for a response. It can be cheaper to reprint your material than to pay for the return postage. Most agents won't take the time to give you feedback on your work, but you are more likely to get it if you include an envelope. They have no obligation to respond or return submissions unless writers provide them with the means to do so.

Hot Tip | If you don't need to have your work back, and you're willing to settle for hearing back from agents or editors only if they are interested in your book, don't enclose a SASE. My guess is that only the government recycles more paper than publishing people.

Five staples will seal a mailing bag effectively; avoid string or tape. The post office recommends that you tape the side of the staples with the points. Naturally, you want to be sure your proposal arrives, but don't call! Most agents don't keep a log of submissions, and like editors, they hate wasting their time with "did-you-get-it?" calls. Use United Parcel Service, spring for a return receipt at the post office, or clip a postcard to the front of your letter with your address filled in as explained earlier.

If you don't use a postcard, find out in advance by phone or by mail, or from their Web site or directory listing, how long the reading will take. A six- to eight-week turnaround is typical for established agents. Publishers also vary in how quickly they process submissions, but they usually take longer than agents.

❖ ❖ ❖

If you receive an offer from an editor or agent, give the others a week to respond. Better still, thank the publisher for the offer but don't discuss it. Tell them you'll get back to them and seek help from an agent or an intellectual property attorney who can respond on your behalf or at least help you with the contract. Once your proposal is accepted by a large house, allow two months for the contract to arrive and another two months for the advance.

The publication of your first book will open new possibilities for you. It will give you the opportunity to become an authorpreneur®. The last chapter will tell you how.

27 | An Ending Prologue

This book can change your life. I hope that reading it will mark the beginning of your career as a successful author. If you have a salable idea, prepare a proposal, sell it, write it, and hold your book in your hands, you will no longer be just a writer with an idea. Once your book is published, you will be an author with a book to your credit.

You will have increased your writing skills, your understanding of publishing, and the size and value of your networks. All of these strengths will make you more valuable to your publisher because you will be a better writer and more able to help make your future books successful.

Once you or your agent starts submitting your proposal, take one of three steps:

- If you need to, take a break to recharge your batteries.
- If you have enough faith that your proposal will sell, continue to research and write your book.
- Start your next proposal. Aim to have the proposal for your next book arrive on the first day your editor is willing to look at it.

Don't waste any time waiting for your proposal to sell. You are also less likely to suffer postpartum depression after your baby leaves the nursery if you have another bun in the oven. A fantastic idea may hit you at any time, so be ready to take advantage of it.

Eighteen Keys to Becoming a Successful Author

This chapter is a prologue because I hope that the end of this book will be the beginning of a writing career that will fulfill your dreams. Your life is a solution. The challenge for you is to find the problem. An agent or publisher can help you get where you want to go, but only you can decide where that is.

The following eighteen keys will help you unlock the door to your future:

1. Your ideas. Your ideas create opportunities for talks, articles, publicity, networking, all of the books you want to write, and all of the ways you can profit from them.

2. Your ability to write. Nothing can save a bad book, and if a book is good enough, nothing can stop it.

3. Your ability to talk. Communicating effectively is essential for writing, researching, selling, and promoting your work.

4. Your goals. Your short- and long-term literary and financial goals must keep you motivated. Inventor Charles Franklin Kettering said of the Wright brothers that they "flew right through the smoke screen of impossibility."

Take the advice of the Chicken Soup mavens: Have giant goals. Writers who don't write as well as you do and aren't as articulate or as good-looking as you are successful authors. If they can do it, you can. But if you are not passionate about writing and promoting your book, don't do it. Only if you are, will you succeed.

5. Your commitment to your career. Make whatever you want as important as becoming a successful author; make nothing more important. Everything you do must be an expression of your commitment.

6. Your daily life. In *Harry Potter and the Chamber of Secrets*, J.K. Rowling wrote, "It's not your abilities that show who you are. It's your choices." The goals that inspire you and are worthy of devoting your life to can only be reached by paying attention to what you do every day to achieve them. What you do is who you are. No matter what you say or believe about yourself, how well you embody the strengths on this list is who you are as a writer.

The world needs the information, inspiration, entertainment, and enlightenment that only you can provide. Since you can't know how many days you have left to share what is best within you with what is best in your readers, you don't have a moment to lose. Make every day, like very word, count.

7. Your passion. Oscar Wilde once wrote, "In this world there are only two tragedies. One is not getting what one wants, and the other is getting it." Having more than you need to write your best work won't help you or your readers. What you do need is to wake up every day and rekindle your passion to write. You must be passionate about writing and promoting your books so you can pass on your passion to everyone you know so they can pass it to everyone they know.

8. Your creativity. It separates you from everyone else on the planet. It's what you alone can bring to everything you do. The more you use your creativity, the more creative you will become.

9. Your ability to promote your work. For most nonfiction, the proven ability of authors to promote their books is far more important than their content in determining the editor, publisher, and deal they receive for them.

10. Your networks. You are in three businesses: the book business, the marketing business, and the people business. You need people, and if Babs is right, then that makes you one of the luckiest people in the world. May you thrive on this formula: Networks + Net Speed = Net Profits.

11. Your ability to practice nichecraft. You either have to keep coming up with new ideas or be a nichecrafter: Choose a subject that lends itself to becoming a series of books that you will enjoy writing and promoting, and that you can carve a career out of. Nichecraft will enable you to build your brand and your identity. Make everything you do create synergy.

12. Your dedication to being an authorpreneur®. Author and speaker Sam Horn, who counsels authors on titles, thought up the word authorpreneur®, which you must embody to be a successful author. Authorpreneurs® make their living by continuing to come up with new ideas so they go from idea to idea, book to book, city to city, talk to talk, and advance to advance. And they don't just rely on their publishers to make their books successful. They take responsibility for the fate of their books.

13. Your thoroughness at test-marketing your books. Test-marketing your books every step of the way, from idea through promotion, will guarantee their success.

14. Your models. The great Carthaginian General Hannibal said of crossing the Alps, "We will either find a way or we will make one."

Writers have to do both. Fortunately, there are more models than ever—both books and authors—for you to emulate. You don't have to reinvent the wheel. You can adapt the best ideas in the books you admire. And you can track the careers of successful authors to learn how they achieved success and adapt their techniques to help you build your career.

Although you stand on the shoulders of all of the authors before you, you can only follow the path laid down by other books and writers so far. Then you have to find the path that only you were born to tread, the path that inspires you to create and promote your books as only you can. Don't be the next anybody, be the one and only you. That's your mission. It's what you were born to do.

15. Your computer. Technology is the greatest tool writers have ever had for networking and for researching, writing and promoting their books. Do what your competitors are doing: Continue to integrate new technology into the way you work.

16. Your obstacles. The greater your goals and the greater the obstacles in your path, the sweeter your success will be. You can't have achievements without challenges any more than you can have courage without fear. But as Henry David Thoreau wrote, "It is the greatest of advantages to have no advantage at all."

17. Your knowledge. Jazz great Dizzy Gillespie was right when he said "It ain't all technique, baby!" But you can't improvise until you can play. Make learning about writing, publishing, and your field a lifelong endeavor so you can continue to grow as a writer and an author.

18. Your readers. Authors and publishers don't keep books alive; readers do. After you, they are the most important people in publishing. So do whatever you can to maintain lifelong relationships with your fans.

What you want is what your readers want. Your role as an author is to do what authors have always done: Help your readers get what they want out of life. English writer Wilfred Grenfell wrote, "The service we render to others is really the rent we pay for our room on earth." Technology makes it easier than ever for the right book to change the world.

Envisioning Your Future

Make a wish list of everything that you want to make you happy. The answers to the following questions will help determine the kind of books you write, how many you write, and what you will do to promote them:

- What do you want your annual income to be?
- How much of that income do you want to come from books?
- Where do you want to live?
- Do you want a family?
- How large do you want it to be?
- What do you want to achieve to live to the life you want?
- What kind of a house do you want?
- What kind of car do you want?
- What possessions do you want most?
- How many vacations do you want a year?
- How do you want to spend your vacations?
- How much income do you want when you retire?

Start each answer with the word *I*, and put your answers on the wall where you write. Revise it as often as you must to motivate yourself to do your best.

Heartwork Is Where You Find It

You have to find heartwork, the calling that sustains and inspires you. Heartwork may be hard but it will never be too hard because it's sustained by love. I hope that writing is your heartwork, because the world will never have too many writers who are devoted to putting their lives in the service of their ideas, their books, and their readers.

Every book is a book, yet every book is different, a unique combination of content, author, agent, editor, publisher, design, format, size, length, price, and timing. Once you set out on the journey to reach your literary goals, you must trust your instincts and rely on your common sense.

Life is indeed a journey, and you are both the traveler and the destination. As you approach the horizon of your possibilities, you will grow into them and become a more capable you. May your journey be filled with goals that you reach and horizons that continue to recede as you advance. Happy trails.

Many thanks in advance for any suggestions you have to make the book better. Please call me at (415) 673-0939 or e-mail me at larsenpoma@aol.com if you have questions. Good luck!

Checklist for Your Proposal

Once you have finished writing your proposal, and before you seek feedback on it, go through this list to make sure your proposal is ready to send out. After each question are the page numbers on which you can find the information you need to answer the question. You can also download the list at www.larsen-pomada.com, so you can print it out and check your work.

Overview

Have you started your proposal with the strongest subject hook that you have? Pp. 8-13

Does your title sell your book effectively? Pp. 14-24

Does your selling handle make your book sound compelling? Pp. 25-29

Does your book hook include the length of your manuscript, including the number of pages of back matter and illustrations? Pp. 31-32

Did you mention your book's special features? Pp. 33-40

Have you convinced a well-known person in your field to agree to write a foreword for your book, and have you named the person on your title page and in your proposal with the person's business, institution, or credentials? Pp. 41-45

If you had your proposal reviewed by a specialist in your field or by a literary attorney, have you mentioned it? Pp. 41-45

Did you list all of the back matter your book will have and include how long each part, except for the index, will be? Pp. 38-40

Have you listed all of the markets for your book, both the groups of people who will buy it and the channels that can sell it? Pp. 46-53

Did you list your book's subsidiary rights potential starting with the most commercial one? Pp. 54-57

Have you listed the spin-off books you will write in the order of their commercial appeal? Pp. 57-59

Did you write a mission statement about your commitment to writing and promoting your book? Pp. 60-64

Have you included your platform, a list of what you have done and are doing to give your work and yourself visibility around the country? Pp. 64-68

Does your promotion plan list what you will do to promote your book in descending order of importance? Pp. 69-83

Have you listed competitive books with the information needed about them? Pp. 98-101

Did you also list complementary books? Pp. 102

Resources Needed to Complete the Book

Did you list expenses, other than office expenses, of more than $500? Pp. 103-109

Have you mentioned when you will deliver the manuscript? Pp. 106-108

About the Author

Have you included everything editors need to know about you, except what you already included in your platform, in descending order of its importance and relevance? Pp. 110-116

The Outline

Is the first page of your outline a list of chapters with page numbers that indicate on which page each outline begins? Pp. 117-119

Have you come up with the best titles for your chapters? Pp. 117-119

Did you include the length of each chapter flush right on the line with your title or subtitle? Pp. 123-124

Did you follow the page count with the number of illustrations, artwork, or other visual elements, such as lists, sidebars, and charts? Pp. 124-125

Have you given your outlines a structure? Pp. 128-130

Do your outlines use outline verbs and have you varied them? Pp. 130-132

Have you done about one line of outline for every page of manuscript that you intend to write? Pp. 122-123

Did you start each outline with the strongest anecdote or piece of copy from each chapter? Pp. 127-128

The Sample Chapter

Are you including twenty to thirty pages of sample material? Pp. 228-274

Have you chosen the most exciting, representative chapter? Pp. 148

Are you submitting photocopies of any photos or artwork scanned into the text, or photocopied on a following blank page with captions? Pp. 154-156

Craft

Have you looked at the sample proposals in Appendix E to see how other writers have done them? Pp. 228-274

Have you checked your proposal to make sure it avoids common writing problems? Pp. 161-165

Have you used the book's suggestions about variety, repetition, words to avoid, numbers, and punctuation? Pp. 166-172

Did you share your proposal with enough readers? Pp. 173-178

Have you test-marketed your proposal? Pp. 179-188

Selling Your Proposal

Have you included impressive sample clips? Pp. 156

Did you create cover art? Pp. 156-157

Did you follow the recommendations for formatting your proposal? Pp. 157-159

If you are planning to use an agent, did you consult the list of eleven ways to find one? Pp. 195-197

Have you made a list of potential agents or editors and publishers? Pp. 195-197

Are you heeding the advice about contacting agents and editors? Pp. 193-199

Are you letting them know if you are querying more than one at a time? Pp. 198

Did you use the suggestions for writing query letters? Pp. 200-202

Are you using the advice about mailing your proposal? Pp. 202-203

Have you written the ideal review of your book and included it with your proposal? Pp. 186-187

The more professional you are at preparing, sharing, and submitting your proposal, the better reception it will receive. The author Dorothy Parker once said, "The two most beautiful words in the English language are 'Check enclosed.' " Using this list is one way to make sure that you see them often.

Resource Directory

Writing

Editorial Services

Literary Market Place (LMP) has a list of editorial services. Rates vary greatly depending on the editor's experience and the help you need. Seek an editor with publishing experience whose books have been sold to the kind of publishers you want to sell your book to. Check with writers they've helped. Start by asking your networks about editors.

Bay Area Editor's Forum
PMB 120
1474 University Ave.
Berkeley, CA 94702
Tel.: (415) 979-3035
E-mail: Forum@editorsforum.org
Web site: www.editorsforum.org

Editorial Freelancers Association (EFA)
71 W. Twenty-third St., Suite 1910
New York, NY 10010
Tel.: (212) 929-5400
E-mail: info@the-efa.org
Web site: the-efa.org

Writer's Digest 2d Draft Professional
   Writing Reviews
4700 E. Galbraith Rd.
Cincinnati, OH 45236
E-mail: wds@fwpubs.com
Web site: www.writersdigest.com/seco
   nd_draft

Independent Editors Group
% Jerry Gross
63 Grand St.
Croton-on-Hudson, NY 10530

Writer's Organizations

For the most part, these are national organizations. LMP lists

A Disclaimer: If you google the titles of four sections of these listings, you will find at least a six-figure quantity of links. So the grab bag that follows is a jumping off point. If you explore these listings, they, along with your networks, will lead you to the resources you need.

many others that are statewide or regional, so please check the latest annual edition if the information below doesn't connect you.

American Medical Writers Association
40 W. Gude Dr., Suite 101
Rockville, MD 20850-1192
Tel.: (302) 294-5303
Web site: www.amwa.org

American Society of Journalists & Authors (ASJA)
1501 Broadway, Suite 302
New York, NY 10036
Tel.: (212) 997-0947
E-mail: info@asja.org
Web site: www.asja.org

Authors Guild
31 E. Twenty-eighth St., 10th Fl.
New York, NY 10016
Tel.: (212) 563-5904
E-mail: staff@authorsguild.org
Web site: www.authorsguild.org

Christian Writers Guild
P.O. Box 88196
Black Forest, CO 80908
Tel.: (886) 495-5177
E-mail: contactus@christianwriters
  guild.com
Web site: www.christianwritersguild
  .com

Education Writers Association
2122 P St., NW #201
Washington, DC 20037
Tel.: (202) 452-9330
E-mail: ewa@ewa.org
Web site: www.ewa.org

International Association of Crime Writers, North America Branch
P.O. Box 8674
New York, NY 10116-8674
Tel./Fax: (212) 243-8966
E-mail: mfrisque@igc.org

International Food, Wine, & Travel Writers Association
P.O. Box 8429
Calabasas, CA 91372-8249
Tel.: (562) 433-5969

The International Women's Writing Guild (IWWG)
P.O. Box 810, Gracie Sta.
New York, NY 10028
Tel.: (212) 737-7536
Web site: www.iwwg.com

National Writers Association
3140 S. Peoria, Suite 295 PMB
Aurora, CO 80014
Tel.: (303) 841-0246
Web site: www.nationalwriters.com

National Writers Union (NWU)
113 University Pl., 6th Fl.
New York, NY 10003
Tel.: (212) 254-0279
E-mail: nwu@nwu.org
Web site: www.nwu.org

PEN American Center
568 Broadway, Suite 401
New York, NY 10012
Tel.: (212) 334-1660
E-mail: pen@pen.org
Web site: www.pen.org

Society of American Travel Writers
1500 Sunday Dr., Suite 102
Raleigh, NC 27607
Tel.: (919) 787-5181

E-mail: satw@satw.org

Web site: www.satw.org

Society of Children's Book Writers & Il-
lustrators (SCBWI)
8271 Beverly Blvd.
Los Angeles, CA 90048
Tel.: (323) 782-1010
E-mail: scbwi@scbwi.org
Web site: www.scbwi.org

Western Writers of America
1012 Fair St.
Franklin, TN 37064
E-mail: tncrutch@aol.com
Web site: www.westernwriters.org

Other Organizations of Interest to Writers

Association of Authors'
Representatives
P.O. Box 237201, Ansonia Station
New York, NY 10003
Web site: www.aar-online.org

American Booksellers Association
828 S. Broadway, Suite 625
Tarrytown, NY 10591
E-mail: info@bookweb.org
Web site: www.bookweb.org

The Center for the Book in the Library
of Congress
The Library of Congress
101 Independence Ave. Southeast
Washington, DC 20540
Tel.: (202) 707-5221
E-mail: cfbook@loc.gov
Web site: www.loc.gov/loc/cfbook

Friends of Libraries USA
1420 Walnut St., Suite 450
Philadelphia, PA 19102-4017

E-mail: folusa@libertynet.org

Web site: www.folusa.com

Books on Writing

The ASJA Guide to Freelance Writing: A Professional Guide to the Business, editor Timothy Harper. St. Martin's Press. A collection of state-of-the-art pieces about writing and publishing.

Bird by Bird: Some Instructions on Writing and Life, Anne Lamott. Pantheon Books. Inspiration and advice about all areas of writing from the writer's life to publication.

The Elements of Style, William Strunk Jr., and E.B. White. Macmillan Publishing Co. A concise, easy-to-use guide on writing fundamentals, grammar, and style.

How to Write With a Collaborator, Hal Bennett with Michael Larsen. Writer's Digest Books. Though out of print (check your local library for a copy), it's still the only comprehensive book on writing with a collaborator.

Nonfiction Proposals Anybody Can Write: How to Get a Contract and an Advance Before Writing a Book, Elizabeth Lyon. Perigee Books. Another approach to writing proposals that includes a wealth of valuable information.

On Writing Well, William Zinsser. HarperPerennial. Instruction on how to make your nonfiction work.

The Shortest Distance Between You and a Published Book, Susan Page.

Broadway Books. Twenty essential steps to make your book a success.

Online Resources

Artslynx: International Writing Resources
Web site: www.artslynx.org
Lists organizations for writers and has links to other sites.

Associated Writing Programs
Web site: www.awpwriter.org
Includes lists of college writing programs and writer's conferences.

HTML Writers Guild
Web site: www.hwg.org
Hosts a network of Web authors and offers help on writing and marketing for the Web.

Writer's Digest
Web site: www.writersdigest.com
From the editors of *Writer's Digest* magazine, includes daily publishing news, information about promotion, articles from the magazine, and information on writer's conferences.

Publishing
Intellectual Property Attorneys
Large cities have intellectual property attorneys who can help negotiate a contract and resolve problems. You can find them through the local chapters of the American Bar Association. ASJA, the Authors Guild, and the National Writer's Union (all listed above) also have attorneys who may be able to help you.

One such organization that provide writers with legal assistance includes:

California Lawyers for the Arts
Fort Mason Center, C-255
San Francisco, CA 94123
Tel.: (415) 775-7200
E-mail: cal@calawyersforthearts.org
Web site: www.calawyersforthearts
.org

Volunteer Lawyers for the Arts
1 E. Fifty-third St.
New York, NY 10022
Tel.: (212) 319-2787
E-mail: info@vlany.org
Web site: www.vlany.org

Lawyers for the Creative Arts (LCA)
213 W. Institute Pl.
Chicago, IL 60610
Tel.: (312) 649-4111, (312) 944-2787
E-mail: info@law-arts.org
Web site: www.law-arts.org

Books on Publishing

Be Your Own Literary Agent: The Ultimate Insider's Guide to Getting Published, Martin Levin. Ten Speed Press. Helpful information about agenting and the industry.

Book Publishing: The Basic Introduction, John. P. Dessauer. Continuum. A comprehensive look at what happens in publishing.

How to Be Your Own Literary Agent, Richard Curtis. Houghton Mifflin. A guide to contracts and the business.

Editors on Editing: What Writers Need to Know About What Editors Do, edited by Gerald Gross. Grove Press. Top experts provide information on skills and demands of editors.

Kirsch's Handbook of Publishing Law, Jonathan Kirsch. Acrobat. An intellectual property attorney's perspective on contracts.

Literary Agents: What They Do, How They Do It, and How to Find and Work With the Right One for You, revised and expanded, by Michael Larsen. John Wiley & Sons. Insider tips on what agents do and how to determine which one is right for you.

Literary Market Place. The Directory of American Book Publishing, by R.R. Bowker. Lists publicists, publishers, agents, speakers bureaus, organizations, contests, and media and writer's conferences.

Max Perkins: Editor of Genius, A. Scott Berg. Dutton. A wonderful, inspiring biography of the editor who discovered F. Scott Fitzgerald, Thomas Wolfe, and Ernest Hemingway.

The Portable Writers' Conference: Your Guide to Getting and Staying Published, edited by Stephen Blake Mettee. Quill Driver Books. Forty-five authors, editors, and agents bring a writers conference right to your door.

Writer's Market, edited by Katie Struckel Brogan. Writer's Digest Books. Annual publication listing publishers and their submission guidelines, conference information, contest guidelines, etc. *Writer's Market On-*

line, an online edition, also is available.

Online Resources

Booktalk
Web site: www.booktalk.com
Has an archive of articles about publishing and links to other sites.

BookWire
Web site: www.bookwire.com
Provides links to other helpful sites including dozens of online marketing companies.

Holt Uncensored
Web site: www.holtuncensored.com
Provides access to archived articles, book reviews, links, etc. Also offers a free newsletter from Pat Holt, a former book review editor of the *San Francisco Chronicle*.

ProfNet
888 Veterans Hwy., Suite 200
Hauppauge, NY 11788
Tel.: (800) PRO-FNET
E-mail: info@profnet.com
Web site: www3.profnet.com

Self-Publishing
Organizations for Self-Publishers

Although the primary goal of the organizations below is to help self-publishers and small presses, they are valuable to all authors. They provide information, online and off, about publishing and promotion, and present workshops. LMP also includes listings of printers, editors, designers, wholesalers, and other resources for self-publishing.

Bay Area Independent Publishers Association (BAIPA)
P.O. Box E
Corte Madera, CA 94976
Tel.: (415) 257-8275

The Jenkins Group
Jerrold Jenkins
400 W. Front St., Suite 4A
Traverse City, MI 49684
Tel.: (800) 706-4636
E-mail: info@bookpublishing.com
Web site: www.bookpublishing.com

Open Horizons
John Kremer
Box 205
Fairfield, IA 52556
Tel.: (614) 472-6130, (800) 796-6130
E-mail: info@bookmarket.com
Web site: www.bookmarket.com

Para Publishing
Dan Poynter
P.O. Box 8206-146
Santa Barbara, CA 94118-8206
Tel.: (805) 968-7277
E-mail: info@parapublishing.com
Web site: www.parapublishing.com

Publishers Marketing Association
Jan and Terry Nathan
627 Aviation Way
Manhattan Beach, CA 90266
Tel.: (310) 372-2732
E-mail: info@pma-online.org
Web site: www.pma-online.org

Small Publishers Association of North America (SPAN)

Tom and Marilyn Ross
P.O. Box 1306
425 Cedar St.
Buena Vista, CO 81211
Tel.: (719) 395-4790
E-mail: span@spannet.org
Web site: www.spannet.org

Books on Self-Publishing

The Complete Guide to Self-Publishing, fourth edition, by Tom & Marilyn Ross. Writer's Digest Books. Provides information on publishing your own book, including everything from how to find a reliable printer to how to generate working capital.

How to Publish a Book & Sell a Million Copies, by Ted Nicholas. Dearborn Trade Publishing. Uses real-life examples of successful self-published books to provide tips on self-publishing.

The Self-Publishing Manual, by Dan Poynter. Para Publishing. Provides information on the publishing industry and offers tips on how to successfully self-publish.

Events

BookExpo America (BEA)
383 Main Ave.
Norwalk, CT 06851
Tel.: (203) 840-2840
E-mail: inquiry@bookexpo.reedexpo.com
Web site: http://bookexpo.reedexpo.com

PMA Publishing University

Publishers Marketing Association
627 Aviation Way
Manhattan Beach, CA 90266
Tel.: (310) 372-2732
E-mail: info@pma-online.org
Web site: www.pma-online.org

Speakers' Organizations

National Speakers Association
1500 S. Priest Dr.
Tempe, AZ 85281
Tel.: (480) 968-2552
Web site: www.nsaspeaker.com

Toastmasters International
P.O. Box 9052
Mission Viejo, CA 92690
Tel.: (949) 858-8255
E-mail: tminfo@toastmasters.org
Web site: www.toastmasters.org

Marketing and Publicity

Books on Marketing

Guerrilla Marketing for Writers: 100 Weapons to Help You Sell Your Work, by Jay Conrad Levinson, Rick Frishman, and Michael Larsen. Writer's Digest Books. Tips on everything from creating a media kit and promotional calendar to appearing at fundraisers.

1001 Ways to Market Your Books, by John Kremer. Open Horizons. Includes hundreds of marketing success stories from authors and publishers, as well as marketing advice.

The Writer's Workbook: A Full and Friendly Guide to Boosting Your Book's Sales, by Judith Appelbaum and Florence Janovic. Pushcart Press. Provides tips on how to take an active role in marketing your book.

Media Directories

Bacon's Media Alerts
Bacon's Information, Inc.
332 S. Michigan Ave.
Chicago, IL 60604
E-mail: directories@bacons.com
Web site: www.bacons.com

Burrelle's Media Information Systems
75 E. Northfield Rd.
Livingston, NJ 07039
Web site: www.burrelles.com

Yearbook of Experts, Authorities & Spokespersons
Broadcast Interview Source, Inc.
2233 Wisconsin Ave., Northwest
Washington, DC 20007
Tel.: (202) 333-4904
E-mail: editors@yearbook.com
Web site: www.yearbook.com

Publicity Services

Media Distribution Services
307 W. Thirty-sixth St.
New York, NY 10018
Tel.: (800) MDS-3282
E-mail: services@mdsconnect.com
Web site: www.mdsconnect.com

MediaPro
5900 Hollis St., Suite L
Emeryville, CA 94608
Tel.: (510) 596-9300
E-mail: info@infocomgroup.com
Web site: www.infocomgroup.com

Organizations of Publicists

Book Publicists of Southern California
6464 Sunset Blvd., Rm. 580
Hollywoood, CA 90028
Tel.: (323) 461-3921

Public Relations Society of America
33 Irving Pl.
New York, NY 10003
Tel.: (212) 995-2230

Publishers Publicity Association (PPA)
1745 Broadway
New York, NY 10019
Tel.: (212) 782-8626
E-mail: ihaut@randomhouse.com
Web site: www.publisherspublicity
   .org

A Final Note

This directory also is available on my personal Web site at www.larsen-pomada.com. Please send suggestions for changes and/or additions to larsenpoma@aol.com or to 1029 Jones Street, San Francisco, California 94109. Many thanks!

Getting Your Book Published

At my agency, we only represent books that we believe we can sell to large and major medium-sized publishers. Since most new writers won't be able to sell their books to a big publisher, I have tried to make the book equally valuable for writers in approaching any publisher.

If you want to write a book aimed at a small or specialized audience, or if you do not yet have the credentials and promotional muscle that big publishers want, you have more options than ever to choose from. If you will be satisfied with a small or university press, then you don't need to be as concerned with your promotion.

New York publishers want their nonfiction books to have first-year sales of fifteen thousand copies or more. Small and university presses, because of their smaller advances and lower overheads, don't need to sell as many copies as large houses. Their openness to new writers is one reason they're essential to the future of publishing. Set financial as well as literary goals for your books, then write proposals that enable you to reach those goals.

The View From Sixth Avenue

It's been estimated that agents supply 90 percent of the books put out by the major houses. That means publishers buy 10 percent of their books directly from writers. That's more than three thousand books a year.

An editor toiling at a Big Apple conglomerate once confessed to us: "Big authors are boring. The joy is in working with new authors." Editors at large houses, while just as eager as those at small houses to discover promising new writers, face higher stakes.

House-Hunting for an Independent Press

The economics of publishing hinder big publishers in continuing the tradition of nursing writers along through losing efforts until they build an audience, write their break-out book, and hit the best-seller list.

This has created an opportunity for university and small independent presses. University presses were established as nonprofits to publish books by scholars for scholars. However, they are under growing financial pressure, so they take on more new writers and publish books that are not commercial enough for the big houses. They acquire most of their books directly from writers. Small and university presses are also looking for crossover books to sell in both the trade and academic markets.

The founder of a small house in San Francisco spoke for all publishers when he proclaimed his philosophy of publishing: "I see it, I love it, I publish it." Your book's subject and market may determine the number of publishers who respond that way to your book:

- If it's a guidebook to Seattle, look for a publisher like Sasquatch in Seattle who does regional books as well as books for a national readership.
- If it's an instruction book about karate, find a mainstream publisher who does martial arts books or a press that specializes in them.
- If it's a biography of a lesser-known writer with a small market, it will more likely be right for a small literary or university press.

Small houses can profit by selling as few as three thousand copies of a book, so they are eager to find new writers and will succumb to their passion for a book, regardless of how commercial it may be. Small publishers have advantages over their large competitors:

- Smaller overheads liberate small publishers; they can be more open minded and adventurous about the projects they take on.
- They encourage writers to become more involved with the publishing process.
- They publish far fewer books so every book is important.
- Fewer people are involved, and writers may work with the house's owners, who are committed to what they're doing.
- They offer less money up front, and a writer may make less money in the long run, but the writer's personal satisfaction may be greater.
- The number of small publishers grows every year, so there are always more potential homes for writers' books.

Large houses have high overheads and need books that maintain them, so their passion for a book has to be tempered by their concern for the bottom line. If your book will have a large national audience and you can give it continuing national impact through your promotional efforts, major houses will be glad to hear from you. They have the resources to provide bigger advances and better promotion and distribution than small houses, and their books receive more attention from booksellers, reviewers, and subrights buyers.

Communication within large houses may not be good, and unless yours is one of the company's lead or midrange books, you will probably be disappointed with the attention you and your book receive. You may be better off as the author of a big book at a small house than a small book at a big house.

Size is not the only factor to consider in choosing a publisher. Editors have their own tastes; publishers, their own character.

Over time, they develop widely varying standards for how literary, commercial, serious, practical, and well illustrated they want their books to be. Changing ownership and market conditions can shift buying criteria as houses respond to what sells. For example, gift books.

Publishers may be reluctant to publish in a field in which they've had no experience and will probably avoid a book if they've had a bad experience with a similar book. The opposite effect is called *cluster publishing*. Publishers develop a knack for doing certain kinds of books and are open to more of them.

The trade-off is that although books on a subject may do well if the house is successful at publishing them, such books will compete with the publisher's past, present, and future books on the subject. That's why gauging the passion an editor and a house have for your book is important. In the long run, passion may yield more profit than a larger advance from a house that is less committed to your book.

Since you can't really tell whether a publisher will be right for you and your book by its size, location, or books, and you are after the best possible editor, publisher, and deal for your book, you may want to find a literary agent (a subject discussed in chapter twenty-five).

Nonetheless, whether you approach agents or publishers, big houses or small, expect rejections, at least at first. Console yourself with the words of one Penguin senior editor: "Editors don't judge books, they choose them," and there will be times when "the plug doesn't fit the socket." So you have to keep plugging until you find the right socket.

Whether you try to sell your book yourself or hire an agent, your goal is to get your proposal into the hands of the right editor at the right house at the right time. If you want to or have to sell your book yourself, find out by phone, mail, e-mail, or through a directory who the right editors are for your book. Then send your proposal to as many editors, by name, as you wish, and let them know other editors have it. Depending on your subject and the market for your book, that number may be five or fifty.

Big houses publish a wide range of books, and their editors have specialties such as business books, sports or health books, cookbooks, or gardening books. Editors talk to colleagues with the same specialty at other houses, so your proposal may become a topic of conversation.

If no publisher is smart enough to buy your book, try writing articles about the subject or go on to your next project. As Jane Adams advises in *How to Sell What You Write*, don't regard unsold work as a loss; look at it as inventory that some day will sell.

If your book is good enough, anybody can sell it because any likely publisher will buy it. Many first-time authors are so excited about having their first book published that the publisher or the terms of the deal are less important. You have to decide whether any yes or only the best possible yes will do.

Hot Tip

The track record of your first book will affect the sales of your next book. When it comes time to sell your second book, booksellers will check their computers to see how many copies your previous book sold and, especially if it's on the same subject, will order accordingly. Be sure to choose the publishing option that will generate the biggest sales your first time out. If you want to change publishers for your second book, the sales of your first book will also help determine which publisher buys the second one and for how much.

Nine Options for Getting Your Book Published

A *New Yorker* cartoon shows Charles Dickens sitting across a desk from an editor with a manuscript between them, and the editor is saying, "Make up your mind, Mr. Dickens. Was it either the best of times or the worst of times? It could scarcely have been both."

If you are a new writer who wants to be published by a big house, it is both the best and the most challenging of times. New writers confront a paradox: Publishers, like agents, must find new writers in order to survive, but the large houses are less willing than smaller houses to develop new writers. As a result, breaking into the business with a big publisher (or agent) is difficult.

However, if your book takes off, it's the best of times because, as editors say, the *upside potential* is far greater than ever.

You have at least nine options for getting your books published:

1. You can collaborate with other writers in a co-op venture in which you share the production and marketing costs to create an anthology including your work.
2. You can pay for all of the costs to publish your book, but vanity publishing has no credibility in the industry.
3. You can use subsidy publishing, which means that you pay part of the publishing costs, another option with no credibility.
4. You can partner with a foundation that will support the writing and promotion of your book because it will further their cause.
5. As I mention in the chapter on test-marketing, you can self-publish your book using one or more of the following options:
   - Photocopying your manuscript
   - Publishing one copy at a time using print on demand (POD)
   - Using print-quantity-needed (PQN) for short runs
   - Using offset printing for long runs
   - Publishing it online so it can be downloaded onto a computer or personal digital assistant (PDA) with one of the more than four hundred e-book publishers, some of whom will do it for free
6. Publishing it in media such as audiocassettes, videocassettes, software, CD-ROMs, and in other forms such as a calendar.
7. You can sell the rights to:
   - An on or offline trade or consumer periodical that will serialize it
   - A publisher for a flat fee, as a work for hire
   - A small press, niche, specialty, or regional publisher
   - An academic or university press
   - A medium-sized house
   - A large publisher
8. You can work with a packager who provides publishers with a copy edited manuscript, a disk ready for the printer, or finished books.
9. You can use an agent to sell your books.

Align your literary and financial goals with the publishing options you need to achieve them. Choose the right options for you and your books now but take the long view. Your options will change as your writing and promotional skills grow and your career develops.

How to Find and Research Competing Books

Editors will expect you to know about your field well enough that you can size up the strengths and weaknesses of competitive books. These nine sources will help provide the information you need:

- **Ingram.** If you call (615) 213-6803 with the ISBN (the International Standard Book Number on a book's copyright page and in its bar code), you can find out how a book is selling at the industry's largest wholesaler. You can learn about Ingram online at www.ingram bookgroup.com.

- **The copyright pages of competitive and complementary books.** They include an ascending line of numbers with the highest to the left. The lowest number to the right is the number of the latest printing—the higher the number, the greater the sales. There may also be a line of numbers for the year of the printing that will tell you when the latest printing was.

- **Booksellers.** Before trying out your title and idea on editors, first try them out on the customers for your book: booksellers. Two of the joys of the literary life are browsing in bookstores and buying (tax-deductible!) books. Become friends with local booksellers who love books. Support the people you want to support you. Buying books and discussing your favorites is all you have to do. Booksellers thrive on their passion for books, and they light up when they find a kindred spirit with whom they can share their latest discovery. Someday, they will stock your book and have a book-signing party for you.

- **Online Booksellers.** Amazon has become a handy alternative to *Books in Print*, so you can let your fingertips do the browsing. The ultimate online list of books is ABEBooks.com, which at this writing lists fifty million books from 12,000 booksellers.

Hot Tip

Ask your local or online bookseller to notify you about new books in your field. Online booksellers take advance orders as soon as they receive publishers' catalogs, which are months ahead of publication. Advance orders can be a hot tip for publishers on how many copies to print. One independent bookseller I asked had more than three hundred advance orders for the fourth Harry Potter book. Amazon had more than 500,000.

- *Books in Print* (BIP). An annual that lists all books in print three ways: by title, author, and subject. The subject guide in BIP will tell you what's available on the subject you're writing about. For children's books, check *Children's Books in Print*. Online bookstores have up-to-date listings. Search the BIP database online at www.booksinprint.com.
- *Publishers Weekly*. The industry's weekly trade journal reviews upcoming books and publishes spring, summer, and fall announcement issues in which publishers list their new titles. For more information, visit www.publishersweekly.com.
- *Forthcoming Books*. Issued bimonthly, *Forthcoming Books* lists the books announced since the latest edition of BIP.
- *Publisher's Trade List Annual* (PTLA). The PTLA lists books by publisher so you can see which publishers are most interested in your subject. Reading the catalogs of those publishers will enable you to get a feel for the lists of different publishers.
- **Bibliographies of competitive books.** These can be a valuable source of information, providing details as to what competing titles cover and what sources they use.

Sample Proposals

Here are four excellent, annotated proposals. At the start of each proposal, you'll find an explanation of why we were able to sell it.

Because of space limitations, the proposals are not double-spaced and don't have page breaks; your proposal must. Look for Double Space and Page Break icons on each page to remind you. Also, your proposal will begin with two unnumbered pages: the title page and the table of contents page. Make the first page of your overview page one. You'll also see Editor's Note icons where I've added my thoughts.

Here are the proposals you'll find in this section:

Proposal 1: *It's More Than Money, It's Your Life*, a personal finance book by Ginita Wall and Candace Bahr. The book was purchased by John Wiley & Sons and was published in 2004. The proposal begins on page 229.

Proposal 2: *How High Can You Bounce?*, a self-help proposal by Roger Crawford. Bantam published it in 1998. The proposal begins on page 244.

Proposal 3: *Reading Water*, a memoir by Rebecca Lawton. Capital Books published it in 2002. The proposal begins on page 258.

Proposal 4: *Playing It Smart*, a parenting book by Susan M. Kettmann. Sourcebooks published it in 2004. The proposal begins on page 267.

It's More Than Money— It's Your Life!

Why This Book Sold

Ginita Wall and Candace Bahr had a lot going for them that attracted John Wiley & Sons to *The Money Club: Fiscal Fitness for Women*:

- They could double their promotional impact by giving talks and doing publicity separately.
- They had an impressive list of firsts for their book that justified publishing it.
- Ginita had already written or co-authored six books.
- Women manage the finances in 80 percent of the nation's households, and almost half of them find investing "scary."
- They already have a partner with one of the most recognizable brands in the world: Visa. And Visa was already touring them as spokespeople.
- Almost six hundred Web sites linked to their site.
- Their site was getting forty thousand visitors a month.
- Suze Orman was a competitor, but she also helped build the market for personal-finance books.
- Candace and Ginita had speaking and media experience.
- The media came to Ginita twice a month for help with stories.
- The authors had more than fifty years of combined professional experience.
- The book was the first in a series.

The book was published in 2004 under the title of *It's More Than Money, It's Your Life—The New Money Club for Women*.

A Proposal for
A MAN IS NOT A PLAN:
5 STEPS TO LIFETIME SECURITY, NO MATTER WHAT

by Candace Bahr and Ginita Wall, CPA, CFP
Founders of the Women's Institute for Financial Education (WIFE.org)

First in a Series of Ten Books

Candace Bahr
Street
City, State, Zip Code
Phone Number
E-mail
Web Site

Ginita Wall
Street
City, State, Zip Code
Phone Number
E-mail
Web Site

Agents:
Michael Larsen and Elizabeth Pomada
1029 Jones St.
San Francisco, CA 94109
(415) 673-0939
larsenpoma@aol.com

Page Break

Table of Contents

Page Break

Introduction
The Overview

Every woman needs a wife.

—Gloria Steinem

Dear WIFE,

Last year I married a wonderful man with two young children. I think I'm happily married, but lately I've been having little anxiety attacks. Life is so much more complicated than when I was single. My husband says that marrying me was the best thing he ever did, and I agree—he's got me to take care of the kids, to shop and cook, and to comfort him when he's had a bad day. Meanwhile, I'm working full time, trying to keep up with household chores. I don't have anyone to lean on: Everyone is leaning on me. Help!

Frazzled in St. Louis

Dear Frazzled,

You aren't alone, WIFE understands your dilemma. When a man takes a wife, he marries someone to help him climb the ladder toward success. When a woman marries, she's taking on that much more responsibility. You've discovered the dirty little secret of women's lives: Behind every successful woman is a basket of dirty laundry waiting to be done and a family waiting to be fed. You need a clone, and fast! Sit your husband down for a little talk about how you feel. Then the two of you can review your finances to figure out where you can save money. (The budgeting tools at the WIFE.org Web site can help.) Use the funds you save to hire someone to take up the slack. You'll have more quality time to spend with your husband and the kids, and save your sanity to boot. Life today is much more complicated for women than it was in grandma's day. You can't do it all, so don't even try.

Women's relationships with men and money are more complex than ever before. The WWII generation revered breadwinner dads and stay-at-home moms who looked forward to company pensions that would support them in their "golden years." The baby boomers are caught in the middle: Costly corporate pensions have been axed, expensive homes require two incomes to support, and easy access to credit cards is far too tempting. As divorce has become acceptable, boomer marriages have unraveled and their finances have suffered.

Now their daughters are wondering how to cope in a world where a good man is hard to find, marriages fall apart, women still earn less than men, and studies say that children thrive when raised by stay-at-home moms. Today's women must find new perspectives on men and money, discarding their mothers' view that a man *is* a plan, because that model no longer works.

Books tell women how to change their relationships with men, but only a few of them help them change their relationships with money. Many books have been written about finances for women, but none provide the tools women need to manage complicated issues with men and money.

Based on the authors' combined 58 years of professional experience, *A Man Is Not a Plan: Five Steps to Lifetime Security, No Matter What* will be the first book to:

- focus on the seven myths about money and relationships that are roadblocks to financial security for women, as well as giving practical, easy-to-digest advice on topics such as budgeting, slashing expenses, buying a home, retirement planning, investing and raising money-savvy kids
- use women's preferred style of circular information, linking finances with peripheral information such as relationships and sharing, rather than the linear presentations in most financial books
- suggest alternatives to traditional approaches for managing money in marriage, putting both partners on a firm financial footing
- provide information about women's concerns: going from two incomes to one, keeping a career edge, starting a business, coping with divorce and widowhood, giving time and money to charity, and managing investment advisors
- challenge readers to maintain responsibility throughout their lives no matter what their circumstances or marital state, rather than becoming dependent on others for their well-being,
- offer a new perspective on finances in relationships and tools to communicate with mates about money

The finished manuscript will be 278 pages, including anecdotes, quizzes, and sidebar information. It will include eighteen worksheets, plus questionnaires, charts, and checklists, and each chapter will end with an action list. Back matter will consist of a nine-page resource guide, including a four-page bibliography of books, periodicals and software, a three-page guide to Internet resources, a two-page listing of agencies and organizations, and an index.

The authors will update the book continuously on their Web site and, each time the book goes to press, will create new information for the resource directory and other sections that can be revised without changing pagination. They will revise the book every four years.

The first part of the book will help women identify their issues and money styles, teach them strategies for confronting the financial issues that surface at each of the five stages of relationships.

The next part of the book will explore the five steps women must take to ensure themselves lifetime security. It will provide financial tools and strengthen the skills for helping women take charge of their financial destinies.

The third part of the book will provide strategies to cope with life's changes and money troubles, such as unemployment, debt, divorce and widowhood. The last part of the book will focus on the joy of money, providing women a template for managing wealth, including giving to charity and teaching children about money.

Editor's Note

The five numbers below are a lot to throw at editors in one paragraph, but they make a solid case for the book. Numbers from one to a hundred are usually written out, but for a book like this, they fit.

Women in America spend $4.8 trillion a year. Although women manage the finances in 80 percent of the nation's households and account for more than half of investment decisions, only 53 percent of women have confidence in their investing abilities (vs. 82 percent of men), and 48 percent of women in a recent survey said that investing was scary (about double that of men).

A poll by AARP revealed that 40 percent of women claim they do not want to become wealthy. Why? They fear that wealth will turn them into greedy, insensitive people who consider themselves superior to others. It's time for women to scrap what they've been told since childhood about the corrupting power of money. Over the next twenty years, $15 trillion will be transferred through settled estates and trusts, and the bulk of that money will go to women. Instead of fighting the power of wealth, women must learn to manage it, channel it, and use it to change the world.

Markets for the Book

The book will appeal to women between the ages of 25 and 55 who need simple, practical financial information, seek ways to transform their own relationships with men and money, and want to empower their daughters. It will appeal to women looking for information on personal finance and relationships and can be displayed in both sections of bookstores.

Women are hungry for financial information. In the past ten years, the percentage of women in investment clubs has grown from 20 percent to 70 percent. Women start businesses at twice the rate of men, and women-owned businesses employ more people than all the Fortune 500 companies combined. Faith Popcorn estimates there are 9 million women business owners with 27 million workers, producing $3.6 trillion in revenue.

Editor's Note

Another stat: Women buy 78 percent of books, and, as the next line shows, the book is aimed at the women who buy most of them.

Financial professionals who are ravenous to tap the women's market need to educate women investors, but there are few books out there that they can recommend. Most of the traditional financial books for women bash financial advisors, portraying them as evil, money-grubbing charlatans who want to take advantage of women. This book will be one financial professionals can give or recommend to clients, because it educates their clients while teaching women the benefits of working with financial professionals, showing them the way to establish an investment relationship based on communication, trust, and shared goals. This will generate special sales to brokerage houses, mutual fund companies, and banks.

Subsidiary rights

The book has potential as a book club selection, for both financial book clubs and general book clubs.

The book will have potential for audio and videocassettes as well as a workbook. The authors will produce and market these if the publisher does not.

Page Break

Spin-offs

Editor's Note

These spin-offs are an example of how a first book can be an overview of a series.

The authors will write the following ten books to create a series: [List of books.]

There will be no more than a 10 percent overlap in each book.

Editor's Note

The list was an excellent example of "nichecraft": using a book as the basis for a series. This is one of the things that drew Wiley Editor Deborah Englander to the project. The final sentence assuaged her fears about how much overlap the books will have. The series will only continue as long as sales justify it, but if the first book works as well as we hope, Candace and Ginita will have laid the foundation for a lifetime's work in the field, because other ideas will emerge as they go along.

Page Break

Promotion
Mission Statement

Our mission is to empower women to succeed and prosper. This book is the next step. We have pursued our mission through our award-winning Web site, speaking engagements, media appearances and private practices. We have a solid base we can leverage to promote the book and expand our impact.

The Authors' Platform

In 1988, Ginita and Candace founded the Women's Institute for Financial Education (WIFE.org), the only non-profit organization dedicated to providing unbiased financial information to women. The WIFE.org Web site, with 40,000 hits a month, will serve as a promotional vehicle for *A Man Is Not a Plan.*

The site has gained national prominence, and last year was named one of the top 500 financial sites by Online Investor. WIFE.org is visited by women searching for financial advice, financial professionals looking for information about the women's market, and members of the press seeking insights about women and money. Although it is impossible to determine how many reporters visit the site, about twelve reporters a month telephone or e-mail for additional information.

The authors have extensive media experience and are well-known lecturers, writers, and experts in their field.

Ginita speaks twenty times a year to conventions, women's groups, and professional meetings. She talks to an average of three reporters a week and is quoted in *Business Week*, *The Wall Street Journal*, *Forbes*, *USA Today*, *Money*, *Redbook*, and other print and internet publications. She averages two media appearances a month, appearing on such programs as *NBC Nightly News*, *CBS This Morning*, the Discovery Channel's *Home Matters*, National Public Radio, PBS, and about 150 other radio and television broadcasts a year.

Candace addresses corporate and philanthropic organizations fifteen times a year, and she is interviewed for newspaper articles, radio and TV programs, and special documentaries on women and money about twenty-five times a year.

As a prominent adviser to wealthy women, Candace has entrée to executives at forty-five mutual fund, annuity, and insurance companies through their representatives who regularly call her.

The authors worked with television producers at Third Wave Productions in creating a PBS special on women and money narrated by CNBC's Maria Bartiromo.

Promotion Plan

On signing the contract, the authors will match the publisher's consumer, out-of-pocket promotion budget up to $x0,000.

The authors will undertake a three-part promotional effort for this book with the following components:

1. Media campaign
    a. The authors will develop with the publisher a media campaign that will include the 185 media contacts with whom the authors have established relationships. The authors will use the resources of Peppercom, a New York public relations firm with whom Ginita has worked for the past three years promoting the General Electric Center for Financial Learning and WIFE.org.

b. The authors will go on a media tour to twenty-five cities to be sponsored by GE, VISA USA, or another financial services firm with whom they have contacts. The cities will include San Diego, Los Angeles, San Francisco, San Jose, Oakland, Sacramento, Portland, Seattle, New York, Washington, DC, Baltimore, Philadelphia, Boston, Las Vegas, Phoenix, Tucson, Albuquerque, El Paso, Denver, Atlanta, Memphis, Orlando, Tampa, Chicago, and Milwaukee. They will continue to give at least thirty-five presentations a year. In the cities in which they appear, Candace and Ginita will give interviews.

c. Third Wave Productions has expressed an interest in working with the authors on future television specials on women and money.

d. Leslie Rosenberg, collaborator on the book, has contacts at major trade and consumer magazines, such as *Ticker*, *Registered Rep*, Multexinvestor.com, *Smart Money*, and *Bottom Line/Personal*, and through those contacts, the authors can get the book reviewed in trade and consumer publications and in corporate newsletters and magazines.

e. The authors will attract media attention through a survey to be released on publication. GE, VISA USA, or another financial-industry contact will sponsor the survey on women's attitudes about men and money.

f. The authors will (e-) mail bimonthly press releases to publicize the book. The focus of the releases will be the results of online surveys that dovetail with the contents of the book. WIFE.org will create two new online surveys a month.

2. Seminars

a. In conjunction with a financial-services company, the authors will create a seminar called "Lifetime Security, No Matter What" based on the book. The company will acquire the rights to distribute it to financial advisers throughout the country for presentations beginning on publication.

There are more than 75,000 independent representatives (excluding major Wall Street firms) that view women as a prime market. The seminar sponsor will purchase 5,000 to 10,000 books a year to distribute to financial professionals and their audiences.

b. The authors have presented seminars for TD Waterhouse, Schwab, Wells Fargo, Independent Bank of Memphis, WCI Communities, AICPA, American Association of School Administrators, Nordstrom, Union-Tribune, Putnam, Sharp Hospital, GE Financial, the Post Office, UC Berkeley Women's Leadership Conference, AARP, AAUW, First Pacific Bank, Linsco Private Ledger Annual Conference, and Hewlett Packard. Leslie Rosenberg has contacts in the marketing and corporate communications divisions of four major brokerage houses. The authors will ask these and other organizations to sponsor seminars. In addition to the national media tour, they will present thirty-five seminars a year and sell x,000 books.

3. Internet
   a. The authors will integrate the book with the WIFE.org site content that builds on the book. WIFE.org's loyal audience as well as new visitors to the site will want to read the book. Readers who have purchased the book will find many opportunities at the site to advance their knowledge. First, ten-minute online quizzes will encourage readers to test their knowledge as they progress through the book. After finishing the quizzes, they will be able to print a completion certificate.

      They can answer semi-monthly online surveys on topics taken from the book, and visitors to the site can ask questions and offer feedback on the book. Women visiting the site will learn how to form Focus-on-Finances discussion groups that use the book as a study guide. Paid members of WIFE will receive a complimentary copy of the book, and the book will be featured and promoted by WIFE.org in monthly electronic newsletters that will be sent to 12,000 registrants. The site already offers free bumper stickers featuring the name of the book.
   b. According to Google, 590 sites are linked to WIFE.org. The authors will contact 100 of those sites to offer them content in exchange for promoting the book.
   c. The authors will encourage other sites with which they have relationships to promote the book with Web-site content. Those sites include iVillage, the GE Center for Financial Learning, *Divorce Magazine*, and *Dollar Stretcher*.

The authors will send *x00* promotional copies to:
- *X00* to existing and new media contacts
- *X00* to mutual fund companies, banks and insurance companies, professional organizations

- *X00* to influential people in the field
- *X00* to potential sponsors of seminars

The authors will seek quotes about the book from people with whom they have connections, including:

Gloria Steinem, Barbara Stanny (*Prince Charming Isn't Coming*), Joyce Brothers, Barbara DeAngelis, Ivana Trump, Iyanla, Suze Orman, David Bach (*Smart Women Finish Rich*), Bo Derek, Jennifer Openshaw (*What's Your Net Worth*), John Gray, Amy Domini, Ellen McGirt (*Cassandra's Revenge* and *Kaching*), iVillage executives and Laurie Beth Jones (*Jesus CEO*).

Page Break

Competing Books

The most successful competitive books are:

The Road to Wealth by Suze Orman (Putnam Publishing Group, 2001, $29.95), the most recent of Suze Orman's best-selling books. Makes broadly sweeping statements, and slams brokers and certain financial products. Not aimed at women, but Suze is a favorite of many women for her noncomplicated style.

Smart Women Finish Rich: 9 Steps to Achieving Financial Security and Funding Your Dreams by David Bach (Broadway Books, rev. 2002, $14.95). Analyzes values and money. Written in a linear and somewhat patronizing style. Doesn't explore the emotional underpinnings of women's financial lives, and breaks no new ground.

What's Your Net Worth? by Jennifer Openshaw (Perseus Publishing, 2002, $16.00) Discusses online resources, including WIFE.org, that women can access to help them manage their financial resources. Doesn't deal with the relationships that women have with men and money.

Fund Your Future by Julie Stav and Lisa Rojany-Buccieri (Berkley Publishing Group, 2001, $20.95). Very narrow in scope deals primarily with mutual funds and 401(k)s. Doesn't explain how to handle personal finances.

The competing books on money management don't help women identify and handle specific money issues, or give women the tools they need to manage complicated issues involving men and money.

Page Break

Resources Needed to Complete the Book

Completion of the book will require the following expenses:

Permissions	$x,xxx
Graphic art	x,xxx

The authors will deliver the manuscript six months after receipt of the advance.

Page Break

About the Authors

Ginita Wall, CPA, CFP is a sought-after expert on women and money. *Worth* magazine named her one of the top 250 financial planners in the country for the most recent seven years. She has written or co-authored six books on personal finance:

Your Next Fifty Years: A Completely New Way to Look at How, When and If You Should Retire (Holt & Co., 1997, 270 pages, $14.95, trade paper).

Cover Your Assets (Crown Books, 1995, 243 pages, $14.00, trade paper).

Smart Ways to Save Money During and After Divorce (Nolo Press, 1994, 170 pages, $14.95, trade paper).

The Way to Invest: A Five-Step Blueprint for Investing in Mutual Funds With As Little As $50 a Month (Holt & Co., 1995, 164 pages, $10.95, trade paper).

The Way to Save: A Ten-Step Blueprint for Lifetime Security (Holt & Co., 1994, 196 pages, $8.95, trade paper).

Our Money, Our Selves: Money Management for Each Stage of a Woman's Life (Consumer Reports Books, 1992, 233 pages, $16.95, trade paper).

Editor's Note

Ginita's impeccable credentials are what all editors hope for but rarely get.

Although the subjects of the author's previous books overlaps with the book, all the information in the book will be new and updated.

She also wrote two manuals for continuing education courses for CPAs and the financial section of the manual "Focus on Forever" for the American Academy of Matrimonial Lawyers. Her self-published booklets on divorce, taxes, love, and money have sold five thousand copies. Ginita writes for iVillage.com, CNBC.com and Cox Interactive Media, and she is on the advisory boards of *Divorce Magazine* and the General Electric Center for Financial Learning, which also feature her work. She is also listed in *Who's Who in Finance*.

In her private practice, she specializes in helping people through life transitions, including divorce and widowhood.

Candace Bahr is a successful entrepreneur and wealth manager with twenty-two years of experience. As a managing partner of Bahr Investment Group, she specializes in portfolio design and implementation for high net worth individuals with one million dollars to invest. She is listed in *Who's Who in Business*.

During the past eight years, she has produced and hosted more than four hundred installments of her signature television feature "The Bottom Line" on KDCI/CNN Headline News. She is a monthly personal financial columnist for *Décor & Style Magazine*. Candace began her career with six years in radio, producing and co-hosting the top-rated talk show in Milwaukee.

Candace has lived in the San Diego area for the past twenty-three years with her husband John and teenage daughter Carrie.

Leslie Rosenberg will be a collaborator and ghostwriter on the book. In her more than ten years of experience as a financial marketing writer and journalist, she has contributed to consumer and trade publications, including *Success, Registered Rep, Newsday,* and *Internet World*. From 1997 to 2001, she wrote a monthly column for *Ticker* magazine. She writes about personal finance for Multexinvestor.com. Leslie has extensive experience in marketing. Her previous employers and clients include AIG, Prudential Securities, Salomon Smith Barney, Morgan Stanley Dean Witter, US Trust Co. of NY, and Chase Insurance Group. Leslie lives and works in New York.

Page Break

The Outline
List of Chapters

PART I: WOMEN, MEN AND MONEY
Chapter 1: Why a Man Is Not a Plan and Why He Never Was
Chapter 2: Winning at Money Without Losing at Love
PART II: BUILDING LIFETIME SECURITY, STARTING NOW
Chapter 3: My Brilliant Career
Chapter 4: Saving for a Sunny Day
Chapter 5: Taking Shelter: Housing and Real Estate Investing
Chapter 6: Insuring Your Future
Chapter 7: Investing Made Simple
Chapter 8: Reaching Your Goals: Investing for Education and Retirement
PART III: COPING WITH LIFE'S CHANGES
Chapter 9: Hope Is Not a Strategy: Dealing With Money Troubles
Chapter 10: When The Vows Break: Getting Through Divorce
Chapter 11: Suddenly Single: Getting Through Widowhood
Chapter 12: Taking a Chance on Love Again: Remarriage
PART IV: THE JOY OF MONEY
Chapter 13: Wealthy Women and the Men Who Love Them
Chapter 14: Giving to Charity: Doing Well by Doing Good
Chapter 15: Teaching Your Children About Money

Page Break

Chapter 2

Winning at Money Without Losing at Love   22 pages

Dear WIFE:

My fiancé and I are getting married next spring, and I couldn't be happier. I'm a little nervous, though, because we have really different attitudes about money. Richard loves to spend—to put it his way, "Five bucks in the bank is a six-pack waiting to happen." I'm more careful with my money and like to have something saved for a rainy day. We've never talked about our finances. In my family, money wasn't the subject of polite conversation. But I'm afraid our finances will be a mess after we get married. What should I do?

Aiming for the Aisle, Cleveland, OH

Dear AFTA:

Money is a touchy subject, so WIFE understands why couples veer away from it while dating. But get everything out in the air before you sign that marriage certificate, or you could both be in for a rude awakening after the honeymoon. There's nothing to do but be brave and talk to your fiancé about your future as husband and wife. Decide together how you'll handle the finances in your household, and the lifestyle you both envision for your family. Once you are clear on your goals, you can work toward achieving them together. A household budget and a savings plan to fund future needs, such as buying a house or retirement, are important steps in building your life together and ensuring you will live happily ever after, no matter what.

This chapter provides readers with solid information they can use to deal with finances with their partner. It begins by focusing on the five ways in which men and women think differently about money. Next come tips on how readers can cope with the financial issues that surface at every stage of a relationship, whether dating, living together, or married, including steps to help them join their financial lives with the relationship skills that they can use to achieve financial success.

A quiz lets readers scrutinize areas in which they face the greatest challenges in handling with money with their partner and provides strategies for coping with those issues.

How High Can You Bounce?

Why This Book Sold

Roger Crawford's book was published by Bantam in 1998. His proposal shows:

- How he has been able to transform the misfortunes of his birth into a life of achievement to which people born without the benefit of his disadvantages can only aspire
- That his speaking schedule, which was included with his proposal, guarantees that he will sell more than enough books to justify publishing it.
- That the book will crossover potential. The need for resilience is universal. It's as important to corporations as it is to the nonprofits Roger speaks to. It's also as important in people's personal lives as it is at work.

Editor's Note

Roger wrote this proposal before I recommended including a mission statement and the platform, but his proposal is all the ammunition it needs.

A Proposal for
How High Can You Bounce?
The 9 Keys to Personal Resilience

By Roger Crawford

Roger Crawford
Street
City, State, Zip Code
Phone Number
E-mail
Web Site

Page Break

Table of Contents

Introduction
   Overview
     Promotion
   About the Author
The Outline
   List of Chapters
Sample Chapter

Enclosed separately in the folder:
- The author's brochure
- His speaking schedule for the year [which was four pages long]
- A partial list of the author's clients, speaking and media appearances, and articles about the author
- A jacket of the author's previous book
- Reprints of two stories about the author
- A photograph

Editor's Note

Another major plus Roger brings to the project is a fun, upbeat, visual title that is perfect in how it captures the feeling for a book on resilience. The subtitle for the book was changed to Turning Setbacks into Comebacks.

Page Break

Introduction
Overview

Some people are born survivors. Nothing can get them. They bound through life, gaining energy and momentum from the same pressures that slow everybody else down. This is because they have resilience. People don't have to be born with this power. It can be learned. *How High Can You Bounce? The 9 Keys to Personal Resilience* will show readers how to strengthen their own personal resilience so they can:

- regain stability more quickly in difficult situations
- stay physically and emotionally healthy during periods of stress and uncertainty
- remain hopeful and optimistic when others have given up
- rebound from adversity even stronger than before
- make life richer, more productive, happier, and more successful

Roger Crawford is unique, and the book will have a unique message. *How High* will be the first book to describe the nine characteristics of highly resilient people and show readers how to acquire them by building on skills and attitudes they already have to achieve optimum resiliency. Each chapter will include extraordinary personal anecdotes in which Roger shows how to exercise attitudinal muscles the same way one exercises physical muscles. As a physically challenged champion athlete, he has had plenty of experience doing both.

Editor's Note | The following paragraph captures the essence of Roger's appeal and promotability.

    As an internationally acclaimed motivational speaker, Roger knows how to touch minds and hearts while providing practical, easy-to-follow instructions that can improve productivity, increase pleasure, and change people's lives. *How High Can You Bounce?* will be 253 pages and will include an introduction, three sections containing three chapters each about the nine keys, a conclusion, a two-page bibliography, and an index.

    Each of the three sections will have a two-page introduction and explore a different theme. Each of the nine chapters will include:

- a strong, humorous opening story about one of Roger's personal experiences
- an inspirational profile of someone who symbolizes each key
- a Skill-Builder section, with exercises and quizzes to demonstrate and strengthen the reader's current abilities
- a summary of key points in the chapter and a humorous closing anecdote

Markets for the Book

At least fifty million Americans a year purchase business, inspirational, and self-help books. A practical, mainstream, no-nonsense guide to strengthen personal and professional resilience will appeal to a broad range of book buyers.

Editor's Note

Roger's idea is so universal that he didn't have to say much about markets.

Spin-Offs

The author will write two follow-up books:
- *The Resilient Leader.* Roger is already gathering material for this sequel. In his dozen years of speaking around the United States, Roger has seen resilient leadership in action. These enlightening and inspiring stories will make a strong business book.
- *The Resilient Salesperson.* Few careers require more resilience than selling. Fifteen percent of the American workforce is involved in sales. That makes nineteen million potential buyers.

Promotion

The author will help the publisher promote the book in the following twelve ways:

1. PR Budget. Roger will match the publisher's consumer promotion budget up to $xx,xxx.

2. Tour. Roger will contact local newspapers and TV and radio stations in the more than one hundred cities he visits annually to set up interviews about his book.

3. Book Sales. Roger will sell x,xxx books a year for four years and will continue to sell them after that.

4. Mailing List. Roger has a database with more than 13,000 of

the people who purchased his first book, *Playing From the Heart*. He will pre-sell autographed copies of *How High Can You Bounce?* prior to its release.

Editor's Note

The list of quotes that Roger will obtain proves that he has a solid professional network.

5. Endorsements. Here are four early quotes:

"*How High Can You Bounce?* is chicken soup for the resilient soul. If you desire to rise above your current level of performance, buy and read this book. Prepare to be inspired and empowered by someone who understands the incredible power of resilience, because he has lived it."
—Jack Canfield, coauthor of *Chicken Soup for the Soul*

Editor's Note

You'll see in the bio below why Roger got a quote from Jack.

"Roger Crawford is a great model of the resilient quality needed to excel in today's high-stress world. Read this book and you'll learn how to perform with grace under pressure."
—Dr. Robert Kreigel, author of *If It Ain't Broke . . . Break It* and *Sacred Cows Make the Best Burgers*

"Roger Crawford is an inspiration to me. Inspiration means 'in-spirit.' His work, indeed his life, is in-spirit. Read carefully and be inspired."
—Dr. Wayne Dyer, author of *Your Erroneous Zones, Pulling Your Own Strings,* and *Real Magic*

"Roger has captured the essence of that most elusive and essential quality for life, resilience. Even more remarkably, he proves that resilience can be learned."
—Alan Loy McGinnis, author of *The Friendship Factor*

Roger will obtain cover quotes from ESPN Anchor Robin Roberts and the following motivational speakers and authors:

- Zig Ziglar, author of *See You at the Top*
- Og Mandino, author of *The Greatest Salesman in the World*
- former New York Knicks basketball coach Pat Riley
- Dr. Robert Schuller, author of *Possibility Thinking*
- Nancy Austin, co-author with Tom Peters of *A Passion for Excellence*
- Denis Waitley, author of *Seeds of Greatness*
- Olympic Gold Medalist Mary Lou Retton

National Media Experience

Good Morning America, NBC, *USA Today*, CNBC, *Real People*, and *Dr. Schuller's Hour of Power* are among the two dozen national and local TV shows that publicized Roger's first book, and he has maintained his contacts with them. He has also done more than fifty radio interviews.

Spin-Off Articles in Corporate and Association Magazines

Of the many organizations and associations that Roger has addressed, at least 150 publish a magazine or newsletter. Roger will customize excerpts from the book and offer them to these publications. Each article will end with an 800-number that readers can use to order copies of the book. These publications will be receptive to the articles, because many of their readers have heard Roger speak.

Six examples of organizations with publications that have featured the author's work are:

1. National Association of Credit Unions, with 250,000 subscribers.
2. National Association of Life Underwriters, with 200,000 readers.
3. The United States Professional Tennis Association, a magazine that goes to 6,500 people. Roger is very well known in tennis circles, so an article should generate great interest in the book.
4. General Motors, which Roger has spoken to twelve times in the past two years, published an article in the company magazine (circulation 25,000), and it was well received. A follow-up book excerpt should do well.
5. National Association of Accountants, circulation 10,000.
6. The National Parents and Teachers Association, circulation 27,000.

Spin-Off Articles in Magazines

Many of the topics and anecdotes in the book will make effective articles for magazines like *Parade*, *Reader's Digest*, and *People*. Roger has already been featured in and will approach the following three magazines: *Success*, *Personal Selling Power*, and *Tennis*.

A Tie-in to a TV or Feature Film

Several producers are considering a script of Roger's first book, *Playing From the Heart*.

A PBS Special in Conjunction With the Book

PBS in Los Angeles taped Roger's speech before the Los Angeles County Teachers' Association and aired it as an inspirational program like those of Leo Buscaglia. Roger received more than sixty phone calls and booked ten speaking engagements as a result. Deanne Hamilton, former producer of the long-running People are Talking for KGO-TV (San Francisco's ABC affiliate) and now a producer for KQED-TV (PBS-San Francisco), is eager to see the finished book and will assist Roger in contacting other PBS stations.

Corporate Sponsorship

Roger will send autographed copies of *How High Can You Bounce?* to organizations that are mentioned in the book, such as Prudential Insurance, Wilson Sporting Goods, and AT&T. This will encourage them to block-buy books for their employees and others. Roger used this technique with his first book, *Playing From the Heart*.

An 800 Telephone Number

Roger will set up an 800-number for ordering the book and will mention it in all publicity connected with the book.

Editor's Note

Like Elise, Roger was lucky to have no competitive books when we were selling his proposal. Two did come out afterward, however. Roger was also lucky to be able to tie his book into a new trend in business books.

Complementary Books

This book is part of the new "kinder, gentler" school of crossover business books, focusing on how to acquire a permanent source of personal energy, a positive attitude, that is crucial to business success. Recent books appealing to the same audience include:

- *The Seven Habits of Highly Effective People*, by Stephen R. Covey, Fireside Books, 340 pages. Describes the characteristics of highly effective people and offers step-by-step how-to information.
- *Zapp: The Lightning of Empowerment*, by William Byham and Jeff Cox, Fawcett Columbine, 200 pages. How to give unmotivated employees a "Zapp" of excitement and positive thinking.
- *The Goal*, by Eliyahu M. Goldratt, North River Press, 333 pages. A best-seller about discarding old solutions and applying positive new thinking to new problems.
- *The Pursuit of Wow: Every Person's Guide to Topsy-Turvy Times*, by Tom Peters, Vintage Original, 330 pages. Survival skills for difficult times.
- *Making a Difference: Twelve Qualities That Make You a Leader*, by Sheila Murray Bethel, G.P. Putnam and Berkley, 273 pages. On several best-seller lists and still selling briskly.

Roger's story is part of a best-seller:

- *Chicken Soup for the Soul: 101 Stories to Open the Heart and Rekindle the Spirit* by Jack Canfield and Mark Victor Hansen. Roger Crawford was a contributing writer. The book has sold almost four million copies. Those readers should respond positively to reminders of Roger's chapter in this book.

The author will deliver the manuscript six months after receipt of the advance.

About the Author

Roger is the author of *Playing From the Heart* (Prima Publishing, 1989, with Michael Bowker). This inspirational story of how he overcame his own challenges has been especially popular with younger audiences.

Roger addresses 120 organizations and more than 100,000 people a year. His enthusiastic clients include Adidas, Aetna, Allstate, American Airlines, Amway, AT&T, Blue Cross/Blue Shield, Chevrolet, Citibank, Coldwell Banker, Hewlett-Packard, IBM, Kraft General Foods, Metropolitan Life, NCR, Pacific Bell, State Farm, Travelers Insurance, Union Carbide, and Xerox.

Roger has made speaking appearances in all fifty states and thirteen foreign countries, including Germany, Spain, Canada, Brazil, Jamaica, Bermuda, Portugal, Mexico, and New Zealand. He contributed to the 1991 G.O.A.L.S. Program, still used by the state of California to motivate welfare recipients.

Despite his physical limitations, Roger holds certification from the United States Professional Tennis Association as a tennis professional. In high school, he was a four-year letterman in tennis with a 47 win/ 6 loss record. At Loyola Marymount University in Los Angeles, he earned a Bachelor of Arts degree in communications while becoming the first athlete with a severe disability to compete in an NCAA Division I college sport. Roger stars in tennis exhibitions and has teamed up with celebrities such as Joe Montana. In 1984, Roger carried the Olympic torch for one-and-a-half miles through downtown San Francisco.

More than a million people have come into contact with Roger Crawford in person, on video, or on the printed page. Roger has tried to change the way they feel about their lives. His sensible, positive philosophy is highly contagious.

About Eleanor Dugan

Although Eleanor Dugan will not be credited on the cover, she will co-author this book, converting Roger's presentation material into written form and supporting it with research on resilience. Eleanor is the author of more than a dozen books on communications and business subjects, including:

Editor's Note An impressive list of eleven books followed.

Why the Author Believes the Book Will Be a Success

Here are eight reasons why *How High* will succeed:

Editor's Note The following list is a creative idea: an effective summary of the strengths Roger brings to the project.

1. Roger Crawford is highly credible.

2. He has the promoting and marketing experience needed to make the book a tremendous success.

3. Roger's heavy calendar of speaking engagements—at least 120—a year proves that his message is timely and salable, and guarantees continuing national exposure for the book.

He is represented by forty of the top speaking bureaus in the country, including the prestigious Washington Speakers' Bureau, the exclusive agent for George Bush, Margaret Thatcher, Tom Peters, Dan Quayle, Colin Powell, Lee Iacocca and Olympic Gold Medalist Mary Lou Retton (the only speaker on their roster younger than Roger).

4. In 1994, 75 percent of Roger's clients were corporations or business associations, up from 30 percent in 1990. The remainder were educational, medical, civic and fraternal organizations.

5. His first book, *Playing From the Heart*, received a unanimously positive response and is about to come out in paperback.

6. The diverse audiences that the author addresses prove that the book will have wide appeal. In the first six months of 1995, Roger spoke to a total of 35,000 people in sixty different groups, including:

thirty-five corporate clients (14,000 people)

twelve business and civic associations (7,200 people)

eight educational groups: students/teachers/principals/counselors (6,500 people)

touring medical groups (5,000 people)

one general public (1,500 people)

7. Having spoken in thirteen foreign countries, Roger already has a level of international exposure.

8. Roger is thirty-four years old and plans a long speaking career, so the book will have strong backlist potential.

Page Break

The Outline

Editor's Note

Another of the proposal's virtues that will appeal to editors is the book's harmonious structure: The book has three parts and each of the parts has three chapters. Roger chose to start the outline with the text of his introduction, which we couldn't include here, to give editors the flavor of the book.

List of Chapters

Introduction: Your 9 Keys to Personal Resilience (included in proposal)
PART I: "Where Have You Been?" Your Attitudes
    Chapter 1: Believe Success is Possible
    Chapter 2: Use Humor (included in proposal)
    Chapter 3: Anticipate Life's Difficulties
PART II: "How Long Have You Been There?": Your Self-Image
    Chapter 4: Build on Your Achievements
    Chapter 5: Use All Your Resources
    Chapter 6: Take Responsibility
PART III: "Where Are You Going?" Your Motivations
    Chapter 7: Have Clear Personal and Professional Goals
    Chapter 8: Develop Your Innate Leadership Abilities
    Chapter 9: Embrace Challenges

Page Break

Chapter Two: Use Humor

Editor's Note

> Roger's use of anecdotes at the beginning and end of each chapter gave editors a feeling for what the chapter would be like and made the outlines more enjoyable to read. Roger didn't have one line of outline for the thirty-two pages he projected for the length of the chapter, but his anecdotes helped assure that editors wouldn't think his outline was "thin."

Fifteen thousand people still remember a charming, unintentional slip of the tongue by my wife Donna. I was the closing speaker at the National Amway Free Enterprise Day in Ogden, Utah, sharing the platform with Les Brown, Dr. Joyce Brothers, and Oliver North. (I was the only person on that platform that I'd never heard of.)

After my presentation, the master of ceremonies saw Donna in the audience and urged her to come up and say a few words. She was totally unprepared, but thanked everyone for their tremendous hospitality and then spoke briefly and eloquently about how important it is to see difficulties as challenges. She described how we had met and fallen in love, and how she had learned to look past my physical challenge to the real person.

She concluded, "Even though Roger is missing seven fingers and one leg, he's still the most fully equipped man I've ever met." The audience laughed for five minutes. To this day, when we run into anyone who attended that convention, the first thing they mention is Donna's impromptu remark.

The core of Roger Crawford's message is humor—cultivating the ability to put a positive spin on negative situations. Flexibility is essential for resilience, and a sense of humor is essential for flexibility. This chapter includes anecdotes about developing flexibility through the use of humor. The chapter's practical skills include:

- reframing and redefining negative situations with humor
- using humor to handle change and to help others handle change
- getting people on your side through the skillful use of humor

Profile: Harry Golden, essayist and editor of the *Carolina Israelite* during the stormiest days of the civil rights movement in the 1960s. As a Northerner, a Jew, and a liberal where any one of those qualifications could bring a midnight visit from men in hoods, Golden was in the middle of it and showed remarkable resilience. His incisive humor clarified the issues for both Northerners and Southerners, and helped bridge the ideological differences and encourage his readers to seek peaceful solutions.

The chapter concludes with a Skill Builder exercise, a humorous anecdote and a summary of the key points in the chapter. Here is the closing anecdote:

> Airports are great places for people watching. Whenever I'm between planes, I try to find time to observe my fellow humans. One summer day, I approached the only empty seat in the waiting area and found that someone had left a newspaper on it. My hands were full of luggage so I sat down right on top of it. Since it was a hot day, I was wearing shorts and a short-sleeved shirt.
>
> A man was sitting about ten feet away from me. He immediately noticed my artificial leg and, a few moments later, my hands. He looked like he was desperately trying to conceal his curiosity. I could tell he was staring at me, because whenever our eyes would meet he would quickly glance at the floor or up to the ceiling. After a few minutes, he walked over to me. I anticipated he was going to ask me one of the questions that I've heard many times in the past: "Sir, were you born this

way?" or "Were you in an accident?" But I was wrong, and I had to laugh at my own preconception.

"Excuse me, sir," he said. "I'm sorry to bother you, but are you still reading that newspaper?" And I thought to myself, what kind of physical challenge does he think I have?

Chapter Eight: Develop Your Inborn Leadership Abilities

In 1993, my family and I were flying back to San Francisco from Albuquerque. This was a rare occasion when Donna and my daughter, Alexa, accompanied me on a speaking trip.

We had had a wonderful time, but when we got to the airport, we were really ready to get back home. As I approached the counter, I noticed something was going on. People were standing around looking upset, while a boarding clerk explained that the plane was delayed because of mechanical problems.

We were all pretty tired, but we understood. As I have always said, I've never had a bad flight because I've lived through every landing. Therefore, I always appreciate it when an airline takes the time to fix mechanical problems.

But the delay stretched on and on. We were finally allowed to board four hours later. We stowed our bags and buckled our seatbelts. The plane backed up about ten feet and stopped. Then the pilot returned the plane to the gate and apologized for the inconvenience: "Ladies and gentlemen, I'm terribly sorry, but I must cancel this flight." People around us were ranting and raving about the meetings they would miss and the urgency of reaching their destinations.

Back inside the terminal, people were shouting furiously at the boarding clerk: "I'm never going to fly this airline again." One man said, "Why can't you fly even though the brakes are bad?" He didn't care about the landing as long as he got there.

It wasn't the clerk's fault, and I calmly arranged another flight the next day with the clerk. As I turned from the counter, a man approached me. "I heard you speak this morning," he said, "and I've been watching you for the last four hours. You told us about responding positively to negative situations, and I just wanted to see if you lived what you preach. Thanks for not disappointing me."

We lead by example. Leaders are always being scrutinized. As the saying goes, "I'd rather watch a good leader than hear one any day."

Resilience must be shared. People who are not served well internally do not serve well externally. This chapter shows readers how to use the language of resilience to communicate optimism and resilience to others. Resilient people feel they have control. Therefore, it is usually possible to grow resilient people by giving them a sense of control. Every leader sells two fundamental things: solutions and a positive attitude. The first is useless without the second.

Anecdotes will include how the Atlanta Downtown Marriott won back the baseball team that had switched to a less expensive hotel; how a remarkable school bus driver, Mrs. Torchianna, kept seventy-five energetic kids in their seats; and a poignant story about the time Roger met the man who had ridiculed and tormented him when they were children.

Profile: Ten years ago, on a bitter winter day, Flo Wheatly of Hop Bottom, Pennsylvania, made an emergency sleeping bag for a homeless person. Now she heads "My Brother's Keeper Quilt Project," a nationwide movement of thousands of volunteers in dozens of cities that has produced and distributed more than 10,000 sleeping bags.

Skill Builder: a multiple-choice quiz for rating leadership behaviors and skills.

Editor's Note

P.S. Roger met with three editors in New York who all made offers. Once again, the winner was Toni Burbank at Bantam.

Reading Water

Why This Book Sold

Kathleen Hill, at Capital Books, accepted Rebecca Lawton's memoir because she:

- Was, like us, seduced by the beauty of the writing
- Saw that the book was paradoxically a fish-out-of-water memoir about a woman who led river rafting trips, which was mostly a calling for men
- Felt that the book's overlapping but significant combination of markets—women, nature lovers, armchair travelers and readers of memoirs, all of which are timeless interests—would help ensure the book's frontlist and backlist sales
- Was impressed with Rebecca's track record and her professional approach to promotion

Editor's Note | People value nature, but environmental books don't do well. However, *Reading Water* is a beautiful blend of nature and a woman's memoir which together portend a healthy, continuing readership for the book.

A Proposal for
Reading Water
Lessons from the River

By Rebecca Lawton

Rebecca Lawton
Street
City, State, Zip Code
Phone Number
E-mail
Web Site

Page Break

Table of Contents

Page Break

Introduction
Overview

The study of rivers is not a matter of rivers, but of the human heart.

—Tanaka Shozo

Editor's Note

Rebecca draws editors into the book immediately with an exciting excerpt in quotes. When she does it at the beginning of each chapter, editors won't be surprised.

"Despite my best efforts to stay out of Teepee Hole, we're being sucked toward it like logs to a timber chute. My raft with its sole passenger is lined up perfectly for the brown, crashing current that's fast approaching less than a hundred yards downstream. We're going to have to run the frothing mess, a reversal of flow that collapses back on itself in the middle of the rapid's main wave train.

"Accepting our fate, I'm pushing on the oars to move us into Tee-pee, building momentum. In fact, a spectator happening on the scene at this instant might guess that I'd intended to run the hole all along. Forget that it's a brisk morning when no one wants to get wet, half an hour before the sun will light the water and warm the canyon. Forget that a Volkswagen-sized boulder lurks just beneath the hole. And never mind that for as awake as I feel, I should still be in my sleeping bag. We're committed.

"From experience, I know that Teepee is a keeper, a watery trap to be avoided anytime. The river dances in it like droplets in a hot pan, shaken and imprisoned. Boats that enter the hole share the fate of the water, becoming one with it. How will my passenger react when we drop into it? Will his head spin and eyes pop? Will he register anger, joy, surprise? He has the bulk of two men—can his weight carry us through if we land dead center in it? What if we flip and he has to swim?

"We charge over the brink of the hole and bump down with a jolt. For a moment we continue to track and it seems we'll continue down river with no problem. Praying we won't be stopped, I keep working the oars to move us forward, dipping the blades frantically fast. A brief time passes in which I seem to be effective, until the boat gives a telltale shudder and abruptly halts. For one awful moment, we hover as if undecided, then we're drawn backward toward the heart of the hole. There's where the nasty business can occur—we may get sucked down, engage in endless spins, or overturn in a sudden, breathless flip.

"My passenger remains relaxed and facing downstream, as motionless as a mannequin. He seems to be unaware of our upstream creep, or he may consider it just part of the show, or he's too petrified to move. I figure he'll be alarmed, though, when I climb over the gear and walk past him to the nose of the boat. But no—when I do, he doesn't react, as he doesn't seem to react when I grab the front D-ring and step off the bow into the water.

"Quickly I lower myself into the cauldron of churning current. Submerged except for my head and forearms, I hold tight to the D-ring with both hands. No way I'm letting go of it. My body and legs catch a tendril of current headed down river, and the boat with passenger intact follows me out of the hole. I climb back into the raft, wet but feeling heroic and finally awake.

"That evening in camp, my fellow guides congratulate me for the neat trick in Teepee. They say, 'Throwing out a human sea-anchor! Where'd you learn to do that?'

"I don't credit a rowing teacher or river sensei or any other mentor. Instead I recite a litany of killer holes that have claimed me or others before me: 'Skull, Crystal, Phil's Folly, Clavey, Warm Springs, Lava Falls, Satan's Gut, Widowmaker—'

" 'Right,' someone says, familiar with these famous watermarks of the boating world. 'But you know? You looked asleep when you jumped off the front.'

" 'Maybe I was asleep.' My move to the bow may have been instinctive, an unplanned response contained within my cells, more destiny than decision. How else to explain a move smooth as a dream, slow as a waltz?

"The river engaged me in numberless journeys to the source, year after year, every day for more than a decade. I 'earned my oars' on the beautiful, doomed Stanislaus River, and became embroiled in years of environmental battle to save it."

Editor's Note

The following two paragraphs give Rebecca credibility by showing both that she is familiar with the books on the subject and that she sets her literary sights admirably high. Her list of complementary books is earlier in a proposal than the book recommends but for Rebecca, it's effective.

As I connected with the river, I also dove into its growing body of literature. I discovered modern river writing that has become well loved and celebrated, such as Norman Maclean's *A River Runs Through It,* Barry Lopez's *River Notes: The Dance of Herons*, and David James Duncan's *The River Why*. I used as guideposts the classics of river explorers, researchers, and conservationists, such as John Wesley Powell's *Exploration of the Colorado River and Its Canyons* and Marc Reisner's *Cadillac Desert*.

Still, there was a book about rivers that remained unavailable, and after leaving commercial rafting, I set out to research and write it. *Reading Water: Lessons from the River* will be that book, an exploration of rivers as they change lives and influence the heart. In the tradition of natural histories such as Gretel Ehrlich's *The Solace of Open Spaces* (Viking Penguin, 1985), Terry Tempest Williams' *Refuge: An Unnatural History of Family and Place* (Pantheon, 1991), and Kathleen Dean Moore's *Riverwalking: Reflections on Moving Water* (Harcourt Brace,

1995), *Reading Water* will relate the readers' daily experiences to the whim and wildness of nature.

The book will blend river know-how with riverine lessons about charting a life course. *Reading Water* will also record a time never to be recaptured—when navigable North American rivers first caught national attention, and when river guides were the pioneers of a new nomadic culture. As they view river life through the lenses of science, spirituality and personal experience, even armchair river runners will enjoy the book's affection, adventure, wisdom, and sense of place.

Editor's Note

Articles are an effective way to test-market an idea and can serve as sample chapters as they did for Rebecca.

Reading Water will be 40,000 words and is more than one-third completed. Travelers' Tales and Santa Barbara Review Publications published the sample chapters. The author will deliver the manuscript six months after receipt of the advance.

Editor's Note

I usually suggest that writers put the completion date at the end of the Overview, but it's fine here.

Page Break

Promotion Plan

Editor's Note

No big numbers here, but Rebecca's plan does show that she knows how to reach the audience for her book, and that she will be as professional about promoting the book as she is in writing it.

To promote *Reading Water*, the author will get more chapters of the book published with a bio that mentions the book. She will approach the following markets, many of which have featured or reviewed her work:

- International Rivers Network, Northland Press, Travelers' Tales, and other outdoor, travel, and river book/anthology publishers
- Environmental and adventure periodicals such as *Sierra, Orion Afield, Outside, Backpacker, The Boatman's Quarterly Review, Canoe, Wild Duck Review, Northern Lights,* and *Earth*
- Local newspapers such as the *Sonoma Index-Tribune, Santa Rosa Press-Democrat, Marin Independent Journal,* and *Northern California Bohemian,* which publishes editorials by the author in its "Open Mic" series

The author will solicit reviews at:
- Bookseller Web sites, such as B&N and Amazon.com.
- Local and national radio and television programs
- Literary and outdoor trade publications, such as *San Francisco Chronicle Book Review, The New York Times Book Review, Los Angeles Times Book Review, Chicago Tribune Books, The Washington Post Book World, Booklist, Publishers Weekly,* and *Outdoors Unlimited.*

The author will promote *Reading Water* through her Web site, www.becca.lawton.net. The Web site will be a source of information about *Reading Water* with reviews, a bulletin board, links to vendors, environmental and writing news, and anecdotes about rivers and the outdoors. The author will call attention to *Reading Water* and create promotional opportunities through related projects:
- *River Spirit,* an anthology of river stories, to be co-edited with Kathryn Wilder, editor of the *Walking the Twilight* anthologies by Northland Press
- *Leaving Felliniville,* a work of fiction that takes place in the river and ranching communities of the Green River basin
- *Only Water,* a collection of short stories about rivers and other bodies of water
- *Seasons of Water: A Book of River Days,* to be co-edited by Kathryn Wilder

The author teaches outdoor and river writing workshops that will offer *Reading Water* as reference material. The workshops, advertised through direct marketing, the Internet, and trade publications such as *Poets and Writers* magazine, take place at wilderness and outdoor retreats throughout North America, and also in Hawaii and Fiji.

The author will promote *Reading Water* through readings and signings in the following venues:

- Bookstores in major California cities: San Francisco, Los Angeles, San Diego, and San Jose
- Cities in other states with large literary and nature markets: New York City, Philadelphia, Chicago, Washington, Phoenix, Portland, Seattle, Salt Lake City
- Regional bookstores that have featured her work previously such as Readers Books, Bookends, Book Passage, Borders, and Copperfield's
- Small cities and towns such as Durango, Colorado; Flagstaff, Arizona; Salmon, Idaho; Ashland, Oregon that promise strong word-of-mouth potential through their river communities: Book fairs, river festivals, and environmental events organized through groups such as Friends of the River, American Rivers, International Rivers Network, and Sierra Club

---

Page Break

About the Author

Editor's Note

By this point, editors understand that the book is a labor of love born out of Rebecca's love of her labors. To this, her bio adds the weight of Rebecca's academic background in nature and writing, and her track record.

Rebecca Lawton was among the first women river guides in California, Idaho, Utah, and Arizona. Breaking into river running in the early 1990s, she worked her way on rivers throughout the West. Among her experiences was to become the first commercially licensed oars woman on the technically difficult Selway River in Idaho. She also spent ten of her seasons as one of a handful of original boat women rowing Grand Canyon. With a BS in earth sciences from the University of California at Santa Cruz and an MFA in creative writing from Mills College, she remains devoted to moving water through her travels, writing, and research as a geologist for the nonprofit Sonoma Valley Watershed Station.

Rebecca's life on rivers has been chronicled in publications including *Womensports, Phoenix Sun Times,* and *Boise Statesman* and in the books *Women and Wilderness* (Sierra Club, 1980) and *Breaking into the Current* (University of Arizona, 1994). Her written work has also appeared in anthologies and journals. She has received awards for her prose and poetry, as well as a nomination for the Pushcart Prize.

Rebecca co-authored *Discover Nature in the Rocks,* a book on geology for Stackpole Books in 1997. Her recent work includes "Headwaters," an essay in *The Gift of Rivers,* and "On the Colorado River" in *365 Travel* (Travelers' Tales, 2000 and 2001).

Page Break

The Outline
List of Chapters

Page Break

Chapter 6

Two Lovers   8 pages

"When I was seventeen and just learning about rivers, I fell for the blue-eyed assistant boatman on my first raft trip. We ran the river in the late spring when wildflowers still blanketed the hillsides and lined the white sand beaches.

Being the only teenagers on the trip, McGav and I gravitated toward each other. It was a good match. We had just a two-day trip together, more attracted to the river initially than to each other. First we were captivated by the canyon wren's song, the cliffs with maidenhair fern dripping spring water, the cold clear snowmelt river barely warm enough to be called liquid. Next we noticed that we both yearned for these things and someone to share them.

"After the trip our paths diverged. I went off to college while he devoted himself to river life. He moved to a small silver trailer on the banks of the Stanislaus—our river—near a deep green eddy upstream from Parrotts Ferry Bridge. In all seasons, all weather, he rafted and kayaked. When he wasn't boating, he hiked throughout the watershed, finding the bones of animals, the remnants of old placer mines, the grinding stones of the departed Miwoks. I envied his time with the river as if they were two lovers and I wanted them both."

Editor's Note This outline is an example of a way to do outlines for short chapters by using phrases instead of sentences, and starting each phrase with a verb, as below.

Introduces the braided stream, in which the flow divides and rejoins, only to divide again like the separate cords in a plait of hair. Explains how braided patterns are neither predictable nor repeatable—nor is romance, as the author learns from her boatman boyfriend, who is bound for the Colorado River just as she is headed for the Green.

Playing It Smart

Why This Book Sold

Here are nine reasons Hillel Black at Sourcebooks snapped up the book for publication in 2004:

- Offering 2,000 fun, free things to transform playtime into quality time that will improve children is a powerful promise. But then 2,000 fun, free anythings is eye-catching.
- Susan has the credentials and professional experience to write it.
- It's a crossover book that will interest teachers as well as parents.
- The two principal markets for the book are large and self-renewing, giving the book backlist potential.
- Sourcebooks does gift books well, and the book lends itself to a design that can be a gift for showers, the birth of the baby, the mother's birthday, Mother's Day, or graduation for an education major.
- Mother's Day provides an annual opportunity to promote the book.
- The book's markets also include grandparents, and childcare professionals.
- The book has potential for partnering with a company that produces products and services that mothers need.
- The book is a natural for school, college, and public libraries.

A Proposal for
Playing It Smart
2000+ Fun, Free Ways to Teach Children Seven Essential Life Skills

By Susan M. Kettmann, M.S.Ed.

Susan M. Kettmann
Street
City, State, Zip Code
Phone Number
E-mail
Web Site

Page Break

Table of Contents

Page Break

Introduction
Overview

Editor's Note

What? No subject hook? For a consumer reference book like this, it works. Editors already know that there are far more than parents and teachers to justify doing the book, and because it's a reference book, it's not important how well the author can tell a story. The first paragraph, even the first sentence captures the essence of the book and its appeal. And structuring the book around seven life skills that children will learn from the book is a powerful feature.

Playing It Smart will be a collection of more than 2,000 fun, free ways to give children a head start on life. It will be the perfect book for anyone who suspects that quality time can't be bought at a toy store and that spending time with children pays off. The activities are designed for children's first eight years, require only common household items, and are easy to do. Suggestions for optional low-cost play supplies are included, but every activity can be done without them.

Playing It Smart will be more than a recipe book for dazzling children or filling their time. It will be a planning guide for parents, foster parents, parents-to-be, grandparents, aunts, uncles, teachers, friends and anyone who spends time with children and wants to provide worthwhile learning and memorable fun.

Children acquire basic skills during the first eight years of life, building a foundation for everything that follows. The result is a wide range of skill levels, mainly because of the presence or absence of adults. *Playing It Smart* will focus on seven life skills that are essential to children's academic and social success: communication, curiosity, decision-making, kindness, playfulness, self-control, and self-esteem.

Editor's Note

The third sentence in the next paragraph deftly weaves Susan's credentials into her discussion about the book.

Children love to try new things and when they succeed, particularly at something new or difficult, powerful changes take place. *Playing It Smart* will capitalize on that drive by building success into each activity. The activities were collected and kid-tested during the author's twenty years working in educational and preschool settings, and training preschool teachers and parents in community college child development classes. Children do get left behind, even children who have expensive resources at their fingertips. Well-planned play with caring adults is the crucial ingredient for optimal early development, and *Playing It Smart* will give adults tools to build essential skills.

Page Break

The Book's Structure

The activities in *Playing It Smart* will work in any sequence or combination. But the book suggests that readers begin with one that is personally appealing in some way. The activities for each skill are arranged by age so it is easy to quickly scan across ages and skills. The book has an introductory chapter to get readers hooked, a chapter outlining development milestones, seven chapters devoted to the skills and activities, and an appendix with further resources, Web sites, and lists of play materials parents can buy.

Each activity includes:
- a descriptive title
- the expected time of play
- materials needed
- directions for starting
- ideas for extending the activity when interest wanes

This easy-to-follow format allows adults an easy way to plan a sequence of play activities that is customized to a particular time, setting, and child.

Playing It Smart will offer two additional features to help adults build on their play success:
- Nearly every activity has extensions, which are slight variations that add interest and increase the attention span.
- There are suggestions for optional materials that can be purchased to add to an activity. All are low cost, basic materials that are time-tested and worth the modest investment. These materials are also included in a complete list, by age, in the appendix.

Editor's Note

Susan has the credentials she needs to write the book, but parents and teachers will feel more comfortable buying a book by a stranger if they see an M.D. name on the cover of the book.

The book will have drawings by Jan Adkins and a foreword by Arthur Kornhaber, M.D., a child and adolescent psychiatrist and frequent guest on NBC and CBS morning talk shows.

Page Break

Competitive Books

Recent titles (2000–2002) focus primarily on creating art and craft products, or meeting the challenge of keeping children busy. Although these are worthwhile goals, *Playing It Smart* goes beyond them and offers adults a process for planning play experiences that develop essential life skills. Best of all, the skill and activity selections will be different every time, creating play that is custom-tailored to the adult-child team.

The author could find nothing with a breadth of 2,000 + activities and only one book that spans the age range of birth to eight years.

- *The Playful Preschooler: 130+ Quick Brain-Boosting Activities for 3- and 4-Year-Olds*, Becky Daniel, 2000, paperback, $14.99.
- *Kids Around the World Play: The Best Fun & Games From Many Lands*, Arlette Braman, 2002, paperback, $12.95, 116 pages.
- *Winter Day Play: Activities, Crafts and Games for Indoors and Out*, Nancy Castaldo, 2001, paperback, $13.95, 176 pages.
- *Let's Play: Traditional Games of Childhood*, Camilla Gryski, 2000, paperback, $6.95, 48 pages
- *Play Together, Share Together: Fun Activities for Parents and Children*, Cynthia Holtzschuler, 2000, paperback, $14.95, 160 pages.
- *Play and Learn: More than 300 Kid-Pleasing, Skill-Building, Entertaining Activities for Children from Birth to Age 8*, Karen White, 2000 (covers the full early childhood age range), paperback, $14.95, 167 pages.
- *Everybody Play: Group Games and Activities for Young People*, A. Loscher, 2000, paperback, $14.95, 95 pages.
- *365 Days of Creative Play for Children 2 Years and Up*, Judith Grey, 2001, paperback, $9.99.

Page Break

Markets for the Book

Playing It Smart will have a wide range of readers parents, foster parents, parents-to-be, grandparents, aunts and uncles, preschool, after-school and K-3 teachers, camp leaders, babysitters, older siblings—anyone with children in their personal or professional lives. It is useful for primary caregivers and parents or for play when visiting family or friends. The book will also have potential as a text in adult-education and community-college parenting and preschool education classes.

Promotion

Editor's Note

This is a good plan but not a powerhouse promotion plan, but then it doesn't have to be. Reviews, bookstore distribution, and word of mouth have to drive sales.

Top help promote the book, the author will:
- Feature the book on her Web site
- Make presentations at professional conferences for parents and teachers with back-of-the-room sales; state child development and teacher education conferences, PTA, Parents Without Partners, and AARP conventions/conferences
- Use AARP connections in Washington, DC to publicize book to grandparents
- Hold bookstore promotions with hands-on play activities
  *Design and present adult-education parenting classes, using the book as the text
- Develop press releases on the importance of adult participation in children's play
- Use a network of parenting experts to publicize the book nationally in journals and syndicated columns
- Submit feature articles to national magazines including *Parent Magazine, Baby Talk, Working Mother*, and *Parents Without Partners*
- Use in fundraisers for children's organizations, such as child advocacy groups

Page Break

About the Author

Susan Kettmann has an MS in child development and has twenty years of experience teaching, directing and coordinating curriculum in childcare and educational settings, doing regional childcare planning for local governments, and teaching preschool teachers and parents at local community colleges. The author chaired a regional task force for the Governor's Child Development Advisory Committee and was instrumental in the passage of key childcare legislation in California.

The author accepted AARP's invitition to work in Washington,

DC with seven national experts to recommend a grandparent platform. She has written feature articles and regular columns for *Baby Talk* and *Your Grandchild* magazines, and contributes to the nationally syndicated column, *Parent to Parent*.

Ms. Kettmann is the author of two family/parenting titles:

- *Family-Friendly Childcare: Every Question to Ask Before You Choose*, Paperback, $12.95, 156 pages, WRS Publishing, Waco, TX, 1994.

- *The 12 Rules of Grandparenting: A New Look at Traditional Roles and How to Break Them*, paperback, $14.95, and hardcover, $24.95, 198 pages, Facts On File (Checkmark Books), 2000. Barnes & Noble: " . . . highly recommended for the parents in these children's lives . . . an educational experience for all. This book could have been titled, *Guilt-free Grandparenting!*"

Book promotion for the books included television appearances on local cable, prime-time local network, a local morning talk show, and on *ABC World News Now*. The author gave interviews on local and national radio shows and for the *Chicago Tribune*, and she arranged book-signings throughout Northern California.

Page Break

The Outline

Editor's Note

The book consists of identically structured chapters, and because the outline is so short, what follows is the entire outline for the book. There was no need for a list of chapters. A sample chapter proved the value of the book and Susan's ability to write it.

Chapter One: The Gift of a Lifetime
- How play builds essential skills in the first eight years
- Three components of successful play
- Seven skills that boost academic and social success
- How to use this book

Chapter Two: The Ages and Stages of Play
- An overview of play goals
- Baby Play
- Toddler Play
- Preschool Play

- School-Age Play

Chapters Three Through Nine
- An Overview of Each Skill
- Activities broken into age groupings: year one, year two, year three, year four, years five, six and beyond

Appendixes
Appendix 1: Resources and Web sites
Appendix 2: Materials to Buy for Young Children

Acknowledgments

I would also like to thank the composers and musicians foremost among them being Bach, Mozart, George Gershwin, Dave Brubeck, Pablo Casals, Miles Davis, Bill Evans, Stan Getz, Glenn Gould, Fred Hersch, Gerry Mulligan, Art Pepper, Oscar Peterson, Andre Previn, Marcus Roberts, Shorty Rogers, and the other composers and musicians who helped sustain my efforts.

Thanks also to editor Sheila Curry Oakes for sending timely help.

Thanks again to Barnaby and Mary Conrad of the Santa Barbara Writer's Conference, and to John and Shannon Tullius of the Maui Writers Conference for giving us opportunities to learn as well as teach.

To our agent friends for their support and advice, Elizabeth and I both greatly appreciate it.

I also want to thank Jeff Herman and Elizabeth Lyon for their books on proposals. They help prove that there is no one way to write a proposal. They also provide different but helpful information. You will benefit by reading their books as well.

Huge thanks to ace editor Hal Bennett whose fearless editing challenged me to prove I was right. Kudos also to my other readers: our assistants Antonia Anderson and Adele Horwitz; our intern Candace Finn, Orvel Ray Wilson, and AAR member Ted Weinstein.

At Writer's Digest, my heartfelt thanks to everyone involved with the book for their skill, creativity and patience including Kelly Nickell, Jane Friedman, Rachel Vater, Melanie Rigney, Donya Dickerson, Jack Heffron, Michelle Ruberg, and Angela Philpot.

To our clients who remain our teachers, especially those writers who were kind enough to allow me to quote their work: Candace Bahr, Susan Kettmann, Rebecca Lawton, Jay Conrad Levinson, Dan Pilla, and Ginita Wall.

To Denny and Diana Nolan go our thanks for their friendship, help, and hospitality.

To Elizabeth's mother, Rita, for her continuing help and for urging me on, Elizabeth and I are both very grateful. Thanks also to Don and Carol Kosterka for their support.

To my brother, Ray, and his wife, Maryanne, for their continuing support and their generosity in helping us put a permanent roof over the agency's head, huge thanks from Elizabeth and me.

And last but most, my profound gratitude goes to Elizabeth, my better half, for all she did to make this edition possible, who does more than I can thank her for, and deserves more than I can give.

Index